Deadline

Deadline

THE BEHIND-THE-SCENES STORY OF THE LAST DECADE IN FRANCE

by

Pierre Lazareff

Translated from the French by

David Partridge

RANDOM HOUSE · NEW YORK

FIRST PRINTING

PUBLISHED SIMULTANEOUSLY IN CANADA BY
THE MACMILLAN COMPANY OF CANADA LIMITED

MANUFACTURED IN THE UNITED STATES OF AMERICA
BY THE HADDON CRAFTSMEN, INC., CAMDEN, N. J.

To

Reine *and* Raoul de Roussy de Sales

Contents

Deadline

Chapter One

The Beginning of the End

THE GOVERNMENT had left for Tours two days ago.

Jean Prouvost, director and owner of *Paris-Soir,* had entered the Cabinet as Minister of Information four days previously. Late in the afternoon of June 10th, he received the American correspondents. "Regardless of what may happen," he said, "the Government will not leave Paris. I suggest that you stay here, too, gentlemen."

The Ministry of Information was located in the Hotel Continental. I ran into a number of American newspapermen in the lobby. The situation looked somewhat better now, they told me.

Jean Prouvost was alone in the vast salon which served as his private office. In the harsh electric light, he looked very pale.

"Boss," I said, "tell me—is the Government leaving or not? I've just seen the American correspondents . . ."

"*They* made me do something stupid," he said. "*They* told me to announce that we were staying, when we knew perfectly well that we were about to leave. Yes, we're leaving. We're not really leaving, either; we're fleeing. We're running away. Oh, why did I ever agree to enter the Cabinet?"

"Where are you going? To Tours?"

"Yes."

"What's the press to do?"

"Stay on here as long as possible. But don't keep more than a skeleton crew at *Paris-Soir*."

"Where are the Germans?"

"They've reached the upper Oise. The Seine has been crossed at three points. They took Rouen yesterday. Totally destroyed."

"But the French Army?"

"The retreat is over. The Army is making a stand all along the line."

"In 1914 the Germans advanced as far as Lagny. From the tops of those hills, they got a glimpse of the Eiffel Tower. But that was all they ever did get to see of Paris."

Jean Prouvost seemed slightly irritated. "Your optimism, Lazareff . . ."

The door opened and Jean Fayard came in, resplendent in his captain's uniform. He had returned from the front in Flanders, and was now *chef de cabinet* in the Ministry of Information. From his father, he had inherited the position of editor and director of *Candide,* the reactionary weekly. He spent a good part of his time in salons and fashionable bars.

"Bonjour, mon cher," he said to me, smiling most agreeably, as though we had met for a cup of tea. Then he turned to Jean Prouvost. "Something quite annoying is going on," he said. "Despite all our denials and assurances, the directors of the newspapers refuse to continue publishing in Paris. They feel it to be their duty, they said, to follow the Government."

"Do they know that we're leaving?"

"Of course they do. And they also say that they won't be able to get any information here. In short, they're clearing out."

"All of them?"

"All of them."

"With your permission," I said, "we'll stay. The Germans haven't reached the gates of Paris yet . . ."

"Don't be too reckless. Don't let yourself be stupidly caught by the Nazis. You, especially, Lazareff."

"Don't worry," I said. "I'll get away if I'm notified in time."

Jean Prouvost picked up his telephone. "Hello. The *Gouverneur Militaire* of Paris"—he was speaking over a direct wire—"General Hering, please. The Minister of Information speaking . . . Is that you, *mon Général? Paris-Soir* intends to continue publishing in Paris, up to the last moment . . . I understand the others are all leaving . . . Yes, panic must be avoided. And Paris without any news at all . . . Will you be good enough to give instructions to have the staff notified, in the event that . . . Yes, so that they can get away in time. Thank you, *mon Général*. And, oh, by the way, where are they? . . . No news at all? I haven't heard anything, either. Not a word. Well, thank you. Good-bye, *mon Général*."

"If he doesn't know, Chief, who would?" I asked. "And to think that two days ago the munitions plants were forbidden to evacuate equipment and . . ."

"The order stands."

"But if the Germans . . . ?"

"We must hope that the Germans won't come. In 1914 there was the Marne. And, besides, as Reynaud has said: Paris will be defended, from street to street and from house to house."

"You said something about my being optimistic, Boss."

The door opened again. A number of the Minister's collaborators came in. One of them was my good friend, Hervé Mille, editor-in-chief of *Match*, the big weekly, belonging to Jean Prouvost's chain of publications. And there was Robert de Saint-Jean, an excellent journalist, serving as *chef de cabinet* in charge of relations with the foreign press.

"Chief," he said, "we'll have to inform the British and American press."

"They'll think we're mad . . . Oh, all right. Try to get in touch with some of them. But, remember, within two hours everybody is to be out of here."

This had taken place on the evening of June 10th.

And it was on the 12th, at about seven in the morning,

that Maurice Baker d'Isy, one of the last remaining editors of *Paris-Soir,* hung up the receiver after another futile call to the *Gouvernement Militaire.*

"They don't know a thing," he said. "They even asked whether we could give them some information. They were especially anxious to find out the meaning of the sky."

The sky. The sun hadn't risen that morning, and a heavy ceiling of what looked like dense, gray-black clouds hung low over the city. There wasn't so much as a patch of sky to be seen. It was oppressive.

And down in the street the tragic, endless parade went on. During the past twenty-four hours, the immense caravan had been streaming through the streets, without a moment's interruption—automobiles, crowded, overloaded with women and children, and with an amazing variety of things they had chosen to rescue. And almost every car carried a broad mattress, carefully tied and fastened to the roof. These vast crowds hurrying toward the southern gates were made up not only of millions of Parisians, but also of the countless refugees who had flowed into Paris from Normandy and Brittany, believing that they would be safe in the city. You had a feeling of choking, of suffocation, of being surrounded and enclosed, of being helpless before an impending disaster.

Suddenly, in the midst of all those trucks and taxis and private cars and bicycles and people on foot with their packs and bundles, I saw two heavy carts, the market-gardeners' carts going in the other direction, against the current, going into the heart of the city, to the Halles—as usual—with their appetizing cargoes of red and green and yellow vegetables.

"We'll always have something to eat, anyway," one of the secretaries said, sighing with relief.

I felt better. The familiar sight of those gardeners' carts—this was normal, clean, wholesome—in violent contrast to everything else on that hellish day. For the moment, at least, the nightmare had been dispelled.

Immediately after Jean Prouvost's departure for Tours, Hervé Mille and I began organizing the evacuation of some 800 people. One *Paris-Soir* crew had been working in Nantes, in Brittany, for the past three weeks. We were now faced with the problem of moving all the others—the staffs of the dailies, *Paris-Midi* and *Paris-Soir Courses*; of the weeklies, *Marie Claire, Match, Pour Vous;* and of the radio station, Radio 37. We wanted to send them away as quickly and as far as possible.

We had decided on Clermont-Ferrand, where Pierre Laval, the former Premier, always on the lookout for business, had promised to find accommodations for our people—provided, of course, that we used the facilities of his own newspaper, *Le Moniteur.* We knew that, with truly admirable broad-mindedness, he had made the same sort of offer to almost all the other newspapers, ranging from the Socialist *Populaire* to the Royalist *L'Action Française.* We had been the first, however, definitely to reserve rooms and the use of his printing establishment. But there were only 150 beds available; and we had to take care of 800—editors, writers, clerks, printers, and so on. And everyone, naturally, insisted on bringing his family along.

From 10 P.M. on the 10th of June to midnight of the 12th, we had worked unceasingly at this task of effecting an "orderly evacuation." Transportation by railroad was entirely out of the question. We finally managed to assemble a fleet of trucks and cars. We provided our people with money and food and supplies for the trip. We sent along a number of extra printing machines and as many of the documents and archives as we could find room for.

From then on, one of the three greatest newspapers in the world was to be gotten out—and for as long as possible—by a skeleton crew, consisting of a mere handful of volunteers: a dozen or so linotypists, who slept in the plant, alongside of their machines, and about the same number of printers and stereotypers, who slept unconcernedly in the deserted executive offices.

Since we lived almost next door—overlooking the gardens of the Palais-Royal—my wife and collaborator, Helene Gordon, invited the remaining members of the editorial staff to rest and to eat at our home.

We took turns keeping watch. That is to say, one of us was always trying to find out from the *Gouvernement*

Militaire where the German Army might be, for we were ready to leave at a moment's notice, in the event that the enemy advance seemed actually to threaten the city. Our bags were packed, our automobiles were at the door, and the chauffeurs had been ordered not to leave their seats.

We were standing at the window of my living room—Maurice Baker d'Isy and I.

"That's where Colette lives," I said, pointing across the way, "the great novelist, Colette. She hated to tear herself away from the flower beds and the pigeons, but she went down to the Corrèze, where her daughter lives. Over there, those are Jean Cocteau's windows. He went to Angoulême. Before leaving he said: 'The value of a poet in this war is precisely zero' . . ."

The panicky ones, of course, had left long ago. Some of them, away on their vacations when the war broke out, had never even returned to Paris. Others, who had thought they would be safe in Normandy, were now most probably in German hands. Many others had fled to the South and to the Basque coast, when the Blitzkrieg commenced in earnest; and a particularly great number had hastily left after the first and only bombing of Paris (June 3rd). All these people somehow found excellent excuses for their hurried departures, such as the safety of their families or the necessity of settling some distant business. Sacha Guitry, the celebrated playwright and actor, had also chosen this moment to leave Paris for the Pyrenees. Having listened to a complete assortment of hypocritical excuses and pretexts, he had said, quite simply: "I'm not leaving for the reasons that the others are. I'm leaving because, personally, I'm scared."

The news tickers were dead. The offices were strangely silent.

The censors—all Army officers—had made themselves at home at *Paris-Soir*, since all the other newspapers had suspended publication. Their cots had been moved in and the *bistro* at the corner sent up their meals.

Their chief, Major Paleirac, had won the nickname of

Trompe-la-Mort by his bravery in the last war. His lean, smooth-shaven, scarred face was alive with humor. He said to me, in his inimitable Midi accent: "You know, some of these young lieutenants thought that a job with the Censorship in Paris would be pretty soft. Now that they've seen their comrades move on to Tours, they're quite annoyed at having to stay here just because of *Paris-Soir*. They have an idea the Germans are likely to be here at any moment. Personally, I think it's slightly funny."

These censors, in fact, now seemed most anxious to collaborate with us. They were most particularly interested in our telephone calls to the *Gouvernement Militaire* and seemed to be eagerly awaiting the order to leave Paris. They spent most of their time trying to persuade us that it would be wiser not to persist, not to publish under existing conditions—on a volcano, as they put it.

These gentlemen would help us in wording the "dispatches," so-called. There weren't any real ones, of course. The wires were all dead. The only news coming in was over our little radio, on which we got short-wave broadcasts from the United States.

Georges Kessel would translate the news as it came in from New York. Based exclusively on this material, we were able to publish at least the semblance of a newspaper. Georges Kessel had been our war correspondent at the front in Finland, where he had scooped the report of the Russo-Finnish peace negotiations. He had subsequently been sent by us to the Far East, and had just recently returned to Paris.

Thanks to the American broadcasts, we were able to publish the news of Italy's entrance into the war and the full details of Mr. Roosevelt's welcome "stab-in-the-back" speech.

"It would be a funny thing, after all," Hervé Mille said, "if we suddenly heard, via New York, that the Germans were 100 meters away from *Paris-Soir*."

"Very funny indeed, but by no means impossible," Major Paleirac said.

At about half-past seven, that morning, all sorts of

rumors began coming in concerning those strange black clouds that were darkening the city. Readers called up and gave us a variety of explanations.

"They've set fire to the gasoline stores in Saint-Denis."

"The gas tanks at Saint-Cloud have been shelled."

"It's a smoke screen laid by German planes to cover the advance of their columns." (I believe that this proved to be correct.)

Still others informed us that the French had created this artificial darkness to cover their retreat.

Finally, a lady announced, in funereal tones, that this was the beginning of the end of the world, and that God was showing His displeasure at the folly of mankind by shutting off the light of the sun.

At eight o'clock our war correspondent arrived—unshaven, in khaki—directly from the front. He was Joseph Kessel, the writer—Georges Kessel's brother.

"It looks better," he said. "Paris isn't lost. Not by any means. The Army is fighting back fiercely. But, I tell you, what's going on down there is absolutely unbelievable. . . . The artillery fire. Every gun is in action."

"Is there really a definite line of defense?"

"Yes. I don't know how good it is, but there's a line . . . Pillboxes and fortified trenches and barbed wire, all prepared long ago. And barricades have been thrown across all the roads. . . . At any rate, they aren't retreating. They're holding naturally strong positions now, along the deep ditches of the Oise and the swamps of the Nonette."

"What's the Nonette?"

"The river of Chantilly."

"Are they as close as that?" one of the censors asked.

And Joseph Kessel went on: "They may be able to hold that line until reinforcements arrive. They're hoping to bring up those tanks that have been kept in reserve—for some reason or other—in Brittany and in the Center. But one thing is sure—they aren't retreating any more. . . . Oh, that retreat, I tell you, that was a nightmare."

Georges Kessel, who had been sitting close to the radio all the time, suddenly announced: "According to New

York, Paul Reynaud is at the front with Weygand, and says he's satisfied with the morale."

"Let's give that a big headline," Hervé Mille suggested. "The public could stand a bit of good news."

I was in favor of waiting. And as I saw that Maurice d'Isy was on the telephone again at the other end of the room, I called to him: "What does the *Gouvernement Militaire* have to say now?"

He put his hand over the mouthpiece. "I'm not speaking to the *Gouvernement Militaire*," he said. "It's a refugee who has just arrived. She saw some German cavalry twenty kilometers from Paris. They were calmly watering their horses in the Seine, she says."

At two in the afternoon copies of *Paris-Soir* came off the presses. At about three, an officer from the *Gouvernement Militaire* bluntly announced:

"I think you had better leave."

There was a moment of silence.

Major Paleirac finally said: "Our goose is cooked. Is that it?"

"How about the defense of Paris within Paris?" I asked.

The officer did not even reply, but he made a very eloquent gesture with his hand.

All of us knew what he meant. As soon as I could find my voice, I said: "We'll leave. Will you notify General Hering?"

I turned over the keys of the building to two office boys, neutrals who had refused to be evacuated. On my way out I encountered one of our elevator operators, Joseph Schliesse. I was under the impression that he had left two days earlier for Clermont-Ferrand.

"What are you doing here?" I asked. "Hurry! We'll find room for you in one of the cars."

"Thank you, Monsieur Lazareff, but some friends are taking good care of me."

"It won't go well with you, an Alsatian, if you fall into the Boche's hands . . ."

Schliesse smiled enigmatically. "Don't worry about me. I'll be all right."

Chapter Two

The Surrender

Paris n'est pas la France.

On the morning of June 13th, this startling slogan was launched by PTT, the official radio station, broadcasting from Tours. I first heard it in the courtyard of a school in a small town, where we had stopped for a few hours' rest. Exhausted, we had been lucky to find wooden benches to sleep on. The radio had awakened us.

The old watchman, who had been dialing the radio, repeated the words: " 'Paris is not France' . . . When they say that, it means that Paris is lost."

Paris n'est pas la France.

The people of Paris—those who had been unable or unwilling to leave—were in for a series of surprises now. They had expected enemy planes over the city, an air attack under cover of that blanket of clouds. No bombs came. No artillery bombardment. At times they heard the distant rumbling of the barrage. That was all. Nor were there any troop movements. Nor did the people see that any measures were being taken by the authorities. Nor was any proclamation issued, officially establishing a state of siege.

The only so-called news came in sporadically over the radio, and consisted of a re-hash of yesterday's reports. The most amazing stories were spread, however, from mouth to mouth. These rumors traveled along the roads, from group to group and from car to car along the endless lines of refugees; and the farther these wild stories got from their source, the more fantastic they became—and, somehow, the more credible, the more convincing.

A number of rumors caught up with us in the little town where we had spent the night.

"Russia has declared war on Germany!"

"General Weygand has launched a smashing counter-offensive and the Germans have been routed. They're falling back across the Seine in disorder."

"Two thousand English bombers are raining death and destruction on the Nazi rear."

Obviously, these stories were not only improbable; they were actually impossible. The English did not have 2,000 bombing planes; the Russians had no good reason for suddenly declaring war on their Axis friends; and as for Weygand's brilliant counter-attack, it was difficult to see just where and with what forces such a move might have been undertaken.

From time to time the caravan of cars would be held up by lines of French Army trucks, crowded with fresh troops, young fellows who were cheerfully, hopefully, moving up toward the front. But was there a front?

An officer called to us: "Hey, *Paris-Soir,* have you heard? They're taking an awful beating, those Germans."

As we drove on, we saw that more and more of the villages had been fortified—that is to say, hastily improvised and often pathetically childish defenses had been thrown up. All the bridges were well guarded, however. Men of the Engineer Corps were on hand to blow them up, if necessary. And there were the roving patrols—peasants with rifles slung over their shoulders—who would stop the refugees and subject their papers and passports to strict scrutiny. These men belonged to groups of civilian volunteers, organized to combat parachutists and Fifth Columnists.

As we got farther and farther away from Paris, we saw

more and more troops and guns and equipment—all, it seemed, on their way to meet the enemy.

And, in the meantime, what was the situation at the front, before Paris?

The night of the 12th to the 13th had been relatively quiet. At dawn the Germans launched strong, local attacks along the Oise. Bridgeheads were established. Finally, the river was crossed at numerous points. The enemy also advanced across the swampy grounds along the Nonette. But that was all. Their early drive was checked by a relentless artillery barrage and by the strong resistance offered by the French infantry. The important bridge at Creil was dominated by our batteries. The bridge at Saint-Maxence had been rendered unserviceable in a brilliant, but costly, attack by our planes.

But it was hopeless. Our men were exhausted. And the German tanks kept coming on; their planes kept raining bombs from the sky.

At 1 P.M. the *Gouvernement Militaire* of Paris received the following radiogram:

> German parlementaires will present themselves, between 6 and 8 o'clock this evening, north of Saint-Denis, at the crossroads of the Paris-Dunkirk and Paris-Calais National Highways. Send your delegates.
>
> Signed: German General Headquarters

General Hering forwarded this invitation to the Government at Tours and to the French General Headquarters which had withdrawn to Briare (between Saint-Etienne and Vichy).

In the meantime, the French forces had been ordered to retreat. Under cover of strong rear-guard and artillery action, the main body of the armies defending Paris commenced to retire in good order. The soldiers were streaming back through the countryside of suburban Paris. According to the timetable—as frequently announced by the traitors broadcasting in French from a station at Stuttgart

—Hitler is due to take Paris on June 14th. And tomorrow is June 14th. . . .

A small French outpost is stationed at the crossroads of the Paris-Calais and Paris-Dunkirk Highways. A barricade of paving-stones has been thrown across the roads. Armed with two anti-tank guns, a machine gun and several submachine guns, these men are prepared to defend the position. They are smoking their pipes and waiting. They have received their orders. And they will stand and defend every foot of this terrain, which to them means Paris.

A violent thunderstorm has just broken.

Suddenly, at 6:30 P.M., two automobiles are seen coming up the road—Germans. The men take their positions. On the running board of the first car a German soldier lifts his bugle to his lips. The call is heard, loud and clear: "Cease Firing!" In reply, a strong burst from the machine guns. The two cars stop immediately. Officers get out of the first car; they wave their arms and shout something that cannot be understood. Another burst of fire. The second car has already turned and is retreating at full speed. But the first car, within 200 meters of the stone barricade has not moved; and the officers are running now, taking cover along the walls of the villas, ducking from tree to tree, trying to escape into the fields. The road is swept by another heavy volley. The Germans are still running. Finally, they reach the outskirts of the little village of Saint-Brice, where they find a strong patrol of their own men. The delegates are safe. But their mission—to demand the surrender of Paris—has failed.

In the meantime, the lieutenant in command of the French outpost has received a message by motorcycle courier: Paris has just been declared an "open city." Nevertheless, the order to defend the position to the last man still stood.

Paris—an open city.

At Tours, the Government has decided that the situation is hopeless. The only thing to do is to ask for the terms under which Paris is to capitulate.

On June 14th, at dawn, in the delightful village of Ecouen artificial clouds are still darkening the sky.

The streets are crowded with the light scouting tanks of an East Prussian unit; camouflaged and covered with leafy branches, they add to the nightmare quality of the scene. And there is silence. The thunder of cannonading has ceased.

Here, in this typical village of the Ile de France, Paris is to be surrendered to the enemy.

An automobile arrives—French—showing a white flag. Two French officers step out of the car: a Staff Major and a lieutenant, the interpreter. Shoulders squared and chins up, they march through the garden and into the building. The German plenipotentiaries are waiting. The room is gloomy in the wavering candlelight.

The German in command reads aloud the terms and conditions on which the Supreme Command is willing to consider Paris as an open city. There will be no negotiations. The answer is to be Yes or No. . . . At the end of each paragraph, the German pauses and the interpreter translates the text.

The French Major has been listening intently, looking straight across the table. When the last paragraph has been translated, he says: "There is one point in the German conditions which we cannot accept. You constantly speak of 'Paris and the suburbs.' I must inform you that the suburbs are not under the jurisdiction of the *Gouvernement Militaire* of Paris. We can discuss terms only with regard to the city itself."

"The city *and* the suburbs. Yes or No."

"But listen . . ."

"I cannot listen to you, Major. I regret. The answer must be Yes or No. If it is to be No, German bombers will darken the sky over Paris—commencing at nine sharp—and our artillery will open fire, with heavy and light guns. Paris will be destroyed."

The French Major repeats that he has been authorized to discuss terms for the city only. He cannot undertake any broader responsibility. Orders are orders.

But the German Major, clearly, appreciates the gravity

of his own responsibility. Quite suddenly, he interrupts the discussion, gets up from his chair, and announces: "I am going to the nearest telephone within our lines to consult my superior officers. If I do not return within the hour, the negotiations are to be considered broken off." He puts on his cap, and leaves.

It is 6:30 A.M. If the German Major does not return by 7:30, the city of Paris is doomed.

In that dreary, candle-lit salon, the others are to wait—the two French officers and the two Germans—together.

Every minute or so, one of them looks at his watch. Outside, in front of the building, the sentinels are pacing up and down. Their regular footsteps can clearly be heard.

An hour is a long time. . . . Thirty-five minutes have passed. Forty minutes. Forty-five minutes.

Hope is beginning to fade. The four men are holding their breath.

And now the tanks are to be heard—starting, moving. And the roar of planes flying low above the town.

The big clock in the corner points to 7:25.

The door opens, and the Major comes in.

"I am authorized," he says, "to give consideration to your objections, and to modify the agreement accordingly."

He sits down at the table. He picks up a pen, crosses out words here and there in the document, and signs it. Then the other Germans sign. Then the French Major. The duplicate is similarly amended and signed.

They shake hands, hastily. Then the French plenipotentiaries leave.

Outside, a guard of honor stands at attention.

On the way back to Paris, the automobile bearing the white flag passes long lines of German light tanks and columns of German infantry. Coming from the north and the west, streaming through the Porte de la Chapelle and along the Seine and through the Porte de Saint-Cloud, the advance guard has already penetrated deep into the city.

Chapter Three

The Swastika on the Eiffel Tower

ON THE night of June 13-14, the police on duty at the Porte de Saint-Cloud and the Porte des Flandres heard the voices of many women, screaming and singing and shouting obscenities in atrocious French. They seemed to be in a kind of frenzy, excited, hysterical. The mob of women streamed through the city gates.

This was the manner in which the German invasion of Paris commenced. These prostitutes—girls from Poland and Czechoslovakia, and picked up here and there along the roads in Belgium, Holland and France—were part of the Hitler propaganda machine.

This invasion by painted women was a fitting ending to a day that had been crowded with surprises and paradoxes.

All in all, Paris on that day was less informed about her own predicament and probable fate than was the rest of the world. There were no newspapers, except the European edition of the *New York Herald*, which had appeared that morning, thanks to a miracle performed by one of the editors, Eric Hawkins. Entirely unaided, he had managed to get out one sheet of so-called news. The back page was filled with advertisements taken at random among the stereotypes. Hawkins had printed only a few hundred copies. They were immediately snapped up.

The radio had virtually ceased to exist. The sporadic, fumbling, and often contradictory broadcasts over the official PTT from Tours only added to the general confusion.

On the whole, the people remaining in Paris were now resigned, apathetic. The railroads had stopped running; the workers were gone; but many thousands still kept crowding into the stations, hoping against hope.

The city seemed empty.

The corridors of the Chamber of Deputies and of the Senate were deserted.

At the Hôtel de Ville (City Hall), some six or seven members of the Municipal Council—the last elected representatives of the people remaining in Paris—met and conferred the powers of President of the City Council on Jean Chiappe, the former Prefect of Police.

That afternoon, policemen and gendarmes went around to all the pharmacies and food shops that were still open and earnestly requested the owners and managers not to leave the city. Individual citizens were stopped on the streets and urged to remain calm.

The people did not quite understand. The signature to the Proclamation, announcing that Paris had been declared an open city, told them that General Dentz had replaced General Hering as *Gouverneur Militaire* of Paris. But the people did not quite know what the term "open city" meant. At any moment now, they expected a hail of bombs, the rumbling of tanks through the streets. They wandered about aimlessly.

At a street corner, a man was still peddling tickets for the *Loterie Nationale*. A few of the restaurants were still open—the *patron* and the *patronne*, in many cases, attending to the cooking and the service. Over the city, the sky was still dark and heavy. And now, in addition, acrid clouds of smoke came drifting in from the suburbs, foul, soot-laden waves of smoke from the great stores of oil and gasoline that had been set on fire.

Most of the people went to bed early that evening, after having heard the news broadcast from PARIS PTT: ". . . a great battle is raging, twenty kilometers from the city . . . The result of the battle as yet undecided . . ."

So the Germans were here! Yes, it was true. The advance-guard was making all necessary arrangements for the formal occupation. The Propaganda Section of the Army was the first to arrive at the Place de la Concorde. Four small gray cars drove up, loaded with newspapers from North Germany. These papers, just received by air, were to be distributed to the troops as they moved in.

Everything had been thought of, planned in advance. The prostitutes—the mob that had come streaming into Paris during the night—now appeared and reported for orders. They had an official role to play now. They were to appear in photographs over the caption: "Parisiennes acclaim their liberation by the Führer's troops . . . and march gaily along with them, arm in arm."

Gradually, more and more Germans were to be seen in the city. They went unhesitatingly to points designated in advance. At 9 o'clock sharp—the hour that had been set by the representatives of the German Supreme Command and the French plenipotentiaries in their conference at Ecouen—the parade commenced.

Two hours later, the red banner with the swastika had replaced the tricolor at the top of the Eiffel Tower. And, under the Arc de Triomphe, men of Hitler's Elite Corps were standing guard at the tomb of the Unknown Soldier.

On the very first day—June 14th—the Hotel Crillon was requisitioned for the German General Staff. The Hotel Scribe was completely taken over for the Propaganda and Press Sections of the Army.

During twenty-four hours, Paris had no newspapers and no radio. (The Germans jammed PARIS PTT.) Then, only the German radio, broadcasting in French, could be heard.

On June 18th, the Parisians found the newspaper *Le Matin* in the kiosks. And on June 19th, the newsboys in the streets were again crying *Paris-Soir*. Readers hungrily bought up every copy. Outwardly, the papers looked like the same old *Matin* and *Paris-Soir*. But as soon as the people commenced reading, they understood.

Le Matin was once one of the great newspapers of France. During the past years, however, by order of its owner, Maurice Bunau-Varilla (the brother of the Bunau-Varilla of Panama Canal fame), the paper had secretly been in close contact with leading Nazis. *Le Matin* was the only Parisian newspaper that did not evacuate its personnel to the provinces—although it did suspend publication on June 11th. The entire staff had been kept in readiness. Monsieur Marcel Knecht, Bunau-Varilla's right-hand man, had frequently visited Germany before the war, and had had several mysterious meetings on neutral soil during the war. On June 14th, this Monsieur Knecht went to the *Kommandatur* in Paris and arranged for the immediate resumption of publication by *Le Matin*.

As to *Paris-Soir*, what happened there is perhaps even more typical of the German procedure.

On the first day of the Occupation—on June 14th, in the afternoon—two small automobiles, carrying the swastika banner, stopped in front of the *Paris-Soir* building. Several officers stepped out of the car. One of them led the way. This German officer was none other than Joseph Schliesse, the former elevator boy, the one who had said to me, two days previously: "Don't worry about me, Monsieur Lazareff. I'll be all right."

He had, in fact, managed quite nicely. Now he was guiding Lieutenant Weber, Captain Maier and their associates, showing them around the place.

Lieutenant Weber and Captain Maier had already been appointed heads of the Propaganda and Press Departments for the region of Paris. These men knew Paris well. Lieutenant Weber had been employed there by an insurance company. And Maier was known in every newspaper office in town. He had been running around, trying to sell photographs, news pictures of Central Europe. Everyone had thought he was a poor Jewish refugee. Weber, on the other hand, was related to the big Leipzig publishers by that name. Like Schliesse, he had given the impression that he was an Alsatian patriot.

After the plant had been duly inspected, arrangements were made on the following day (June 15th) to resume publication of *Paris-Soir*. Schliesse had provided himself with the names and addresses of printers, linotypers, office personnel, etc., who had remained in Paris. He, himself, was appointed Personnel Director of the Nazi version of *Paris-Soir*. It is said that he seemed particularly hard to please when it came to selecting elevator boys. At any rate, he settled down comfortably in the office of the Business Manager.

Jean Prouvost's vast office was taken over by a dark, thick-set man—Roger Capgras—whom the *Kommandatur* had chosen to be the master of the biggest newspaper in France. This gentleman, hitherto, had been an agent at the Halles, a dealer in choice fruits and vegetables. During the Spanish Civil War he had put through some very profitable deals—exchanging Catalonian oranges for ships and munitions. Paris first heard of Roger Capgras when he organized a sort of trust of the theaters and playwrights, and then sponsored Alice Cocea's return to the stage—the blonde, frail, Rumano-Parisian star. Where—the question arose—did Roger Capgras get all his money? Just before the war broke out, Henri Bernstein, the playwright, denounced this man, calling attention to his shady record. And here he was enjoying the complete confidence of the Germans!

But this wasn't all. He brought with him—to serve as editor-in-chief of the new *Paris-Soir*—Henri Jeanson, the author of numerous controversial articles, revues and a number of successful film scenarios (*Pepe le Moko,* for one). He had long been known as a militant of the extreme Left, with leanings toward anarchism. Just before the war he wrote a number of anti-militarist articles. After war had been declared—on September 3rd—he signed his name to a seditious pamphlet which demanded immediate peace negotiations. He was sentenced to five years in prison. After having served nine months of his sentence, Jeanson was released. He was then sent to a regiment stationed at Meaux, forty kilometers from Paris.

And here he was now, transplanted—miraculously—from the French Army to the very elite of the Fifth Column, and chosen to perform the glorious task of getting out the first big Nazi newspaper in France.

He found that he was to be assisted by a really select crew—a group of disappointed writers and journalists who had been dismissed from *Paris-Soir*.

My own office was taken over by Paul Ferdonnet, the French "Lord Haw Haw," the traitor who had been broadcasting in French from Stuttgart, preaching defeatism, assuring his compatriots of Germany's excellent intentions, and dispensing the usual drivel about "perfidious Albion."

Many Parisians had felt that all this talk about a Fifth Column was nothing more than a figment of the imagination—especially of the journalist's fertile imagination.

While the first German motorized divisions rumbled through the city, a house on the Rue de Lille was awakening, as though from a long sleep—the German Embassy.

Throughout the war, and in accordance with a diplomatic agreement, two members of the staff had been permitted to remain there for the purpose of keeping the premises in good order. (Similarly, two of our officials had remained in the French Embassy in Berlin.) The comings and goings of these men were, of course, closely watched by the police.

On the morning of June 17th, a man showed himself at one of the windows of the German Embassy, facing the Seine. This man was not one of the Germans who had remained in the Embassy throughout the war. In July, 1939, he had been abruptly deported by order of the Daladier Government, after the newspapers had denounced him as the real organizer of the Fifth Column. This man, youngish, heavy-set, fair, with a somewhat bloated, sensual face and with blue eyes that looked at you a bit too squarely, was Otto Abetz. He had just arrived from Berlin. On June 16th, the Führer had named him German Ambassador to France.

Chapter Four

Youth Movement for Franco-German Rapprochement

I FIRST met Otto Abetz in 1930. The democratic Franco-German rapprochement movement was then in full swing.

To quote from *Notre Temps*, a small-circulation publication intended for youthful readers: "This rapprochement should be the handiwork of the post-war generations on both sides of the Rhine." The director of this review was Jean Luchaire, the son of Julien Luchaire, President of the Institute for Intellectual Co-operation of the League of Nations. Aristide Briand supported this movement with money from the secret funds[1] of the Ministry of Foreign Affairs.

Jean Luchaire introduced Otto Abetz to his friends. And one evening at dinner in a little *bistro* on the Left Bank, Otto Abetz told us his story, in halting, but grammatically perfect, French.

His father, overseer on a big estate in the Province of Hanover, had been killed in the last war. Otto was then eleven years old.

Ever since his childhood he had devoted himself to the task of working toward a genuine reconciliation between

[1] A special account, to be drawn on at the Minister's discretion.

France and Germany. *By himself, while the war was still raging, he had commenced to learn the French language.*

Now (1930) he was twenty-six. He said that he and his old mother depended entirely on his meager salary as drawing instructor in the public schools of Karlsruhe.

He managed to buy newspapers and periodicals, both German and French. And then he commenced writing long, violently outspoken articles which appeared in local and more or less "confidential" publications. In all these writings, he said, and in all talks with his friends, he constantly stressed the importance of achieving a real entente, a sincere understanding between France and Germany so that there could never be another war.

Those were the hopeful and happy days of Aristide Briand and of the devoutly Catholic Bruening. And Monsieur Pierre Laval was soon to make his appearance on a balcony of the Chancellery in Berlin, where he was to tell the cheering crowd to "rally around his white necktie."

But Otto Abetz believed that the young people of France and Germany were the ones to effect a genuine understanding between the two countries; and that, only in this manner, would it be possible to wipe out all the old, accumulated hatreds and antagonisms, and perhaps also to right the wrongs which his country had suffered.

He had written to Paris and subscribed to periodicals expressing views similar to his own. This was how he had come to read Jean Luchaire's articles in *Notre Temps.*

In July he finally arrived at his destination—Paris—and immediately made his way to the offices of *Notre Temps.*

That very morning, Abetz said, while he was waiting in the hall, Jean Luchaire was conferring in his office with a group of French students who had been planning to meet German students during their long vacation.

Abetz was enthusiastic about the idea and urged the organization of a summer camp in the Black Forest, where young Frenchmen and young Germans would find the opportunity to know each other.

To me—and to the other Frenchmen at the table—Abetz's friendly voice seemed to promise brighter days to come. We lifted our glasses and drank a toast to Friendship and to the Future.

The young people of France—with only very few exceptions—were heartily in favor of such a sentimental foundation for an everlasting peace.

Together with the great majority of my generation—I quite naturally turned toward the Left, politically, toward those parties that preached a policy of reconciliation with the former enemies and the establishment of a lasting peace based on universal disarmament.

As far back as I can remember, I had always wanted to be a newspaperman. In my first years at school, I began getting up little news bulletins for my classmates—written by hand, at first, and later I learned how to make carbon copies. I never once considered the possibility of taking up any other profession.

But my father, a businessman, was of the opinion that only misfits and blackmailers went in for journalism. To put it mildly, he disapproved. Nevertheless, one day when I was supposed to be at school—I was fourteen at the time —I got a job with the *Journal du Peuple*, the mouthpiece of the unions. Naturally, the job was a very modest one. I would go to the *Bourse de Travail* (Employment Center) for the announcements issued by the different unions, and would then make a digest of this news as well as I could. My salary was 100 francs a month. I was very proud indeed.

Then and there—and to my family's dismay—I decided to leave school and to devote myself entirely to the profession which attracted me irresistibly.

Gradually, going from one newspaper to another, from one department to another, I began to learn my trade. I served as a cub reporter; then I covered sports; then theatrical and screen news; then I was just plain reporter, covering the widest field of news; I worked on dailies and on weeklies; and after a while I began to get some understanding of what was going on behind the scenes in Paris.

Some few of the men of my generation achieved success at an early age—as playwrights, novelists, composers, journalists, etc. They formed a group known as "Under Thirty." Hopefully, overconfidently, I wanted to found a publication which was to be the worthy mouthpiece of this group of brilliant young men. I was seventeen. The periodical—a weekly—was to be called *Illusions,* a name intended to express our reaction to the rampant materialism of the time. Naturally, I had no money for any such undertaking. Not a centime. But I was lucky enough to find a printer who took us seriously, and I readily obtained a promise from a number of these talented young men to contribute material free of charge.

The staff was selected by Henri Béraud, a writer of controversial articles (a Leftist writer at the time). In our first issue we ran a long article protesting—in the name of Science—against the planned destruction of the hangars at Friedrichshafen, where the German Republic had requested permission to resume construction of Zeppelins. (Parts of Germany were still occupied by our troops.)

It was in this manner that I became acquainted with young French Leftists who favored working toward a lasting peace by fostering friendly relations with the youth of Germany.

Illusions published almost 40,000 copies a week, which was very good. Unfortunately, this success lasted only three weeks, as the printer suddenly insisted upon payment in full before the fourth number was to appear. *Illusions* folded. Without financial backing, it had been an impossible undertaking. What worried me most, however, was that I had incurred debts. I saw myself landing in jail. And then one evening at the Olympia, the big music hall of the day, someone asked me why I was so sad, asked me to tell what was wrong—it was Yvonne George, the famous singer of sailors' ballads and torch songs. I told her my sad story. And I don't know how she did it—she certainly wasn't wealthy in her own name—but the following day she brought me salvation in the form of a check with which to pay off my printer. Such spontaneous acts of generosity and *camaraderie* were not uncommon, at the time, in those somewhat Bohemian circles.

I was anxious to settle this debt as soon as possible. I

therefore gave up the idea of playing the role of editor and resumed the normal activities of a newspaperman.

At the same time, I became more and more interested in the problems of Franco-German relations. I did not actively join the group that had been organized by Jean Luchaire; but I was delighted to hear that a month after the conference with Otto Abetz the summer camp had actually been opened at Sohlberg, in the Black Forest. The attendance was not very large. There were not more than thirty democratically minded young men from both sides of the Rhine, sleeping there in tents and preparing their food over campfires. Among those present were: Bertrand de Jouvenel, who had already made a name for himself as a journalist, and whose father was Henri de Jouvenel, the French Ambassador at Rome; and then, of course, Jean Luchaire and Otto Abetz.

At about the same time, André François-Poncet, member of the Chamber of Deputies, directed the newspaper *L'Avenir,* which represented the interests of the Comité des Forges, the French steel cartel (later, when the international situation became tense, he was appointed French Ambassador to Berlin and then to Rome). I got a job with *L'Avenir.* And one evening I heard André François-Poncet, who was an expert on German affairs, speak of a new Party that was rapidly gaining strength in Germany. The leader of this Party, he said, was a young agitator, a war veteran by the name of Adolf Hitler. We all looked at Monsieur François-Poncet in some surprise. The name he had mentioned had scarcely ever been heard. Then one of the staff, a specialist in foreign affairs, exclaimed: "Oh, yes, Hitler. He's the man of the Munich *Putsch.* But his movement isn't to be taken seriously." "No," André François-Poncet replied, dryly, "not to be taken seriously for the moment. No more so than the name of Jesus Christ was to be taken seriously—a year before his death."

Chapter Five

From Bluff to Blackmail

ONE of the first newspapers on which I was regularly employed was called *Le Soir*. The director of this paper also owned a weekly called *Le Courrier des Pétroles*, a trade journal, and naturally devoted to the cause of a few big companies. The management of *Le Soir* hit upon something new: in theaters and motion-picture houses, the paper was distributed free, together with the program. This did, of course, increase the circulation, but it was difficult to see how this device could contribute to the paper's income. And there never was any advertising to speak of. Well, then, how did *Le Soir* manage to exist? I was soon to find out. One of my bosses soon enlightened me. "You know, Lazareff," he said, "when I was your age I actually thought that all you had to do was write a good article, and that then some newspaper would be only too glad to pay a good price for it and to feature it. That's what I used to think. Young fellows like you ought to be told just how matters stand. For instance, I just wrote three articles on Rumania. Really good articles, full of sensational revelations, carefully checked—articles in which I may say I boldly attacked the strange conduct of some of the Rumanian Ministers. Since we wanted to make absolutely sure of the authenticity of all the statements in these important articles, I submitted them for final checking to the Rumanian Minister (in Paris). He kept the manuscripts for a few days, then asked one of our managers to come to see him. The articles were very interesting, the Minister said. He added that the Rumanian Government was very grateful for this valuable information. The Government requested, however, as a personal favor, that we postpone publication of this material, for the time being. Then, in conclusion—and quite incidentally—the Minister informed our manager that the Rumanian Government had decided to give our paper a rather handsome contract for advertising the beautiful scenery of the Rumanian countryside. . . . So you see, Lazareff, what happened. For these three articles which will never be published, I received more money than I ever received for any published material in my life. And, thanks to this windfall, I'll be able to pay you your salary at the end of the month. So you see what goes on in this business."

Such shameless bribery might be the practice among the smaller journals, but on one of the big, really important newspapers, things would be different. So I thought, at least.

At the time, there were five big newspapers in Paris: *Le Petit Parisien, Le Journal, L'Echo de Paris, Le Matin, Le Petit Journal.* They were all morning papers, with circulations ranging from 250,000 to 1,500,000. All five were controlled by the Agence Havas.

In a passage that has received too little attention, Honoré de Balzac pointed out that the Agence Havas was a serious menace to the independence of the French press:

> The public may believe that there are several newspapers. But there is, in fact, *only one paper.*
>
> On the Rue Jean-Jacques Rousseau in Paris there is an office directed by Monsieur Havas, ex-banker, ex-co-proprietor of the *Gazette de France,* ex-co-associate in an enterprise formed to exploit the licenses granted by Napoleon at the time of the Continental Blockade. Monsieur Havas has seen many Governments come and go. He has a profound respect for facts, and has expressed little regard for principles. He has faithfully served each succeeding Administration. The men may be different, but he knows that the human mind never changes, and

that public opinion is always to be molded in the same direction.

No one—no Minister and no newspaper of the Opposition—can derive any benefit from exposing the Agency of Monsieur Havas. That is why Monsieur Havas has correspondents all over the world; he receives all the newspapers from every country on earth, and he is the *first one* to receive them. Furthermore, his offices are on the Rue Jean-Jacques Rousseau, opposite the General Post Office, so that not a minute is lost. *All* the newspapers of Paris, for the sake of economy, have decided to forego incurring the expenses which Monsieur Havas is already undertaking, notably in view of the fact that he now has a monopoly; and *all* the newspapers have abandoned their custom of translating from foreign newspapers and of maintaining their foreign agents, since they now pay Monsieur Havas monthly sums to supply them, at stated times, with all foreign news. Without their knowing it, the newspapers receive only such information which the Premier is willing to have them publish. . . . If there are twenty newspapers, and if they pay an average of 200 francs to Monsieur Havas, he receives *4,000* francs monthly from his subscribers. But he receives *6,000* from the Ministry. . . . Do you now understand the reason for the pathetic uniformity of the *foreign news* in all our newspapers? Each paper merely colors up, in white or green or red or blue, the news item received from Monsieur Havas, the Jack-of-all-trades of the press. In this respect, therefore, there is only one newspaper, prepared by him, and serving as the source of information for all the others. . . .

Similarly, Monsieur Havas provides for the provincial press. Thus, as there is only one newspaper in Paris, there is only one in the Départements. Monsieur Havas is the dummy for the Ministry. And that is the way this immense machine, known as journalism, works. It is as simple as the mechanism of a *rôtissoire* turned by a trained poodle.

The people, which considers itself to be the most intelligent in the world, is being duped in the crudest manner.

This page from Balzac, which still applied in 1940, had been written precisely a century earlier—in 1840.

In 1835, Havas had had the idea of establishing a service offering translations of foreign newspapers. His clients were the banks as well as the newspapers. Expanding his idea, he organized (1840) a regular dispatch service by carrier-pigeons between Paris, Brussels and London. In this manner, messages arrived from England in ten hours, from

Belgium in four. From 1850 on, Havas had a special correspondent in every capital city. After the invention of the electric telegraph, he naturally gave up the use of carrier-pigeons.

Gradually, the Agence Havas opened up offices in all the principal cities in France and abroad, made contracts with all the big advertising firms throughout the world, and signed exclusive contracts, calling for an interchange of news, with all the big telegraphic news agencies which had sprung up everywhere—Reuter in England, Wolff in Germany, Stefani in Italy, Belga in Belgium, Fabra in Spain, Rador in Rumania, Tass in Russia and the Associated Press in the United States.

Naturally, it was to the advantage of the French Government—regardless of its politics—to maintain control over the news issued by the Agence Havas. To this end, the Government was prepared to grant increasingly large subsidies, which ultimately reached the sum of 30,000,000 francs annually. Furthermore, Havas handled the publicity for foreign Governments, for the big business enterprises, financial publicity, both private and official (the French Budget). In addition, Havas handled propaganda campaigns on behalf of various French products as well as of Government stocks and bonds.

Through its grip on the distribution of news and advertising, the Havas Agency was able to exert control over the biggest newspapers in France, and gradually acquired an actual interest, either direct or indirect, in these properties. No other advertising agency could possibly offer any serious competition. Nor was any other news agency ever able to organize effectively in France, although two did manage to eke out a modest existence: L'Agence Radio and L'Agence Fournier. They had to content themselves with playing a strictly secondary role. Havas, and Havas alone, transmitted bulletins to the newspapers by means of tickers and printing machines.

A number of foreign agencies have made sporadic and timid attempts at offering their services to French newspapers (United Press and International News Service, among others). But these attempts, doomed to failure, were always soon abandoned.

From the days of Balzac down to the present, this state of affairs has consistently grown worse and worse. It has happened more than once that the Havas Agency, receiving grants of tens of millions of francs from the Government and officially appointed to handle French propaganda abroad, has directly and openly attacked the policies of the Government—at the request of certain important clients. Better than that: Havas occasionally gave financial support to various newspapers openly hostile to the regime.

A mere dispatch from Havas was enough to start a panic on the Bourse, or to set in motion a movement in the Parliament which might lead to the Government's fall, to rioting, or even to war. Who, then, would have dared to attack these evils? Who was in a position to denounce them? Of all the poisons which exerted their influence on French public opinion, the Agence Havas was surely one of the most virulent. And this poison often fell on favorable ground.

At one time, I wanted to work on *Le Matin*. I went to see Georges de Porto-Riche, the famous playwright, whom some called "the contemporary Racine." He had frequently spoken of Bunau-Varilla, a veritable colossus in French journalism and director of *Le Matin*.

"Don't you ever do any writing for this man," Porto-Riche said. "Once I wanted him to publish an article about an old writer—a man who had shown considerable talent—but who was now very badly off. We wanted to call the public's attention to this case. Well, at that time *Le Matin* was waging an active campaign on behalf of the Armenians, who had been cruelly persecuted by the Turks. I was promptly shown in to the highly impressive office which Monsieur Bunau-Varilla occupied—and still occupies. When I commenced telling him my story, he immediately stopped me. '*Mon cher maître,*' he said, '*Le Matin* is always more than willing to serve any good cause. We shall be glad to mention the case of your friend, and since he appears to be a writer worthy of the greatest respect and consideration, we shall charge you no more than we have been charging the poor Armenians.' "

Georges de Porto-Riche saw that I was not completely convinced. He asked me to meet a friend, a man who had had an important position on *Le Matin.*

This gentleman said to me: "To know what *Le Matin* really is, you should read a little book which is almost impossible to find (Bunau-Varilla bought up all the copies he could lay his hands on). This book is entitled *Du Bluff au Chantage* or *Comment On Fait L'Opinion Publique en France* (*From Bluff to Blackmail* or *How One Forms Public Opinion in France*). It was published by Powelle and written by Monsieur François Mouthon, former editor-in-chief of *Le Matin,* and now in charge of its strongest competitor, *Le Journal.*"

In 1897, Maurice Bunau-Varilla had acquired *Le Matin* after its owner and president, Edwars, had been involved in a truly Parisian scandal: the suicide, during a cruise on his yacht, of his mistress, the beautiful comédienne, Lantelme. Edwars had been obliged to retire from public life.

Shortly after Maurice Bunau-Varilla had taken over the direction of *Le Matin,* the Panama scandal broke, involving his brother, Philippe, an engineer and contractor. After the scandal had quieted down, Maurice Bunau-Varilla initiated a series of newspaper campaigns "entirely devoted," as he wrote, "to the public welfare and without hope of any reward other than the satisfaction of knowing that one's duty has been done. . . ."

These altruistic campaigns, however, were occasionally marred by questionable incidents. In 1900, *Le Matin* had opened a nation-wide subscription intended to endow Paris with an opera at popular prices. In ten days, the readers sent in 500,000 francs. But during the next three years, no one ever found out what had been done with this money. Finally, one of Bunau-Varilla's associates, by the name of Poidatz, was arrested, following a complaint filed by a number of exasperated subscribers. *Le Matin* made good use of its connections. The Court found that there was no ground to prosecute, and Poidatz was released. But he severed his connection with the newspaper.

Then, after a while, *Le Matin* started a violent campaign against the King of the Belgians, Leopold II. He was accused of being "cold-blooded, egotistical and cruel, greedy of gain, looting the Congo of ivory and rubber, held in contempt by the sovereigns of Europe, an unworthy monarch and an unnatural father." The paper went so far as to incite the Belgians to revolt. Then, all of a sudden, this campaign ceased. An agreement had been reached, in the meantime, between the Compagnie du Chemin de Fer Congolais and the Congo State, which belonged to the King of the Belgians. The Congo State surrendered its right to reacquire the railroad concession, purchasing the outstanding capital shares at par. This would not have been to the advantage of the railroad company, since the shares had risen constantly. And, by a strange coincidence, the brothers Maurice and Philippe Bunau-Varilla were members of the Board of Directors of this railroad company. Certain newspapers called attention to the fact that *Le Matin's* anti-Leopold campaign had ceased abruptly when the Congo State and the railroad company reached an agreement, and that the director of *Le Matin* was also a director of the corporation.

Then there was the story of the post offices. A campaign was launched against Léon Bérard, Under-Secretary of State, protesting against the lack of cleanliness of the post offices. Monsieur Bérard, in turn, protested. Monsieur Jules Madeline, Chairman of the Board of Directors of *Le Matin,* went to see him.

"Monsieur le Ministre," Madeline said, "I have come to show you a specimen of the signs which we intend to put up in every post office in France."

"In the post offices? Impossible!" Bérard said. "Why, it's illegal. Besides, we can't put up placards for you and not for your competitors."

"No," Madeline replied. "These signs are designed to be displayed in post offices and, naturally, to be the only ones so displayed. You see what's written on them: 'Buy *Le Matin,* the only French newspaper with direct wires to all the world capitals.' "

Monsieur Bérard was adamant. Thereupon, *Le Matin*

resumed its campaign, and some score of post offices were invaded by crews of cleaners. A scandal! Shortly afterward *Le Matin* was granted permission to display its placards in the post offices of France.

Obviously, Maurice Bunau-Varilla had mastered the technique of creating the impression that he was defending the interests of the public.

Le Matin proclaimed: "The power of our newspaper is unlimited. Whatever it wants done, is done." And it liked to dazzle the public by manifestations of this power.

For example, *Le Matin* persuaded the Army to detail 2,000 soldiers and 200 officers, each wearing arm bands bearing the name of *Le Matin*, and coming from all parts of France; these men carried out a "patriotic" march of forty kilometers. In the course of this performance, one man died and twenty-five were injured. But it didn't cost *Le Matin* one centime.

At a later date, *Le Matin* persuaded the Navy to supply an escort, consisting of seven destroyers and two cruisers, for the Algiers-to-Toulon motorboat race, sponsored by the newspaper. This little manifestation of *Le Matin's* power cost the French Government several hundreds of thousands of francs.

In his dealings with the air arm, however, Maurice Bunau-Varilla was somewhat less successful. In 1906, at the time of the first experiments with dirigible balloons, *Le Matin* offered a prize of 100,000 francs to the winner of a Paris-to-London race in dirigibles, the race to take place in 1908. He had felt confident that no such machine would be able to accomplish this feat within the time limit—only two years after the very first experimental flights. But he was wrong. In 1907, three dirigibles were ready and well able to undertake the flight—and win the prize. But 100,000 francs represented a lot of money in those days. And *Le Matin* saw fit to make the following announcement: "Our attention has been called to the fact that it would not be in the best interests of the national defense to attract too much attention to one of our war industries. Therefore, we do not hesitate . . . The race will not take place. To all the other satisfactions, we prefer the one of feeling that we have done our patriotic duty." Most regrettably, however, two months later, *Le Matin* ran an article which must have escaped the editor's vigilance. The article said, in part: ". . . There are no more secrets connected with a military dirigible balloon than with an automobile in which the Minister of War follows the armies."

Maurice Bunau-Varilla never changed. When attacked, he would reply contemptuously, and reaffirm not only that he was an honest man, but that he was a benefactor of mankind.

He lived the life of a mighty autocrat either at his sumptuous Château d'Orsay near Paris, or in his apartment on the Avenue Henri IV, or on his estate d'Agay on the shores of the Mediterranean. The Premier of France and Cabinet Ministers eagerly sought his invitations.

After the first World War, he became passionately interested in a new pharmaceutic product. He had bought the formula—for a few hundred francs. Synthol, it was called. And he had this lotion made up in vast quantities, and more or less forcibly introduced it into the Army, hospitals, schools, Colonies, etc. He always insisted on presenting every one of his guests with a small bottle. Synthol had become a real obsession.

This strange character—and his newspaper—was destined to play an evil role in the period between the two wars. We have already seen that, following the occupation of Paris, *Le Matin* became the first Nazi newspaper in France. We shall now see how the groundwork for this treachery was laid.

Chapter Six

The "Big Five" versus *Le Quotidien* and *L'Ami du Peuple*

UNTIL the end of the last war, the combined efforts of the five big dailies and the Agence Havas had succeeded in thwarting the expansion of *L'Oeuvre,* which had been transformed by its proprietor, Gustave Théry, from a weekly into a daily. The public had been favorably inclined toward this newspaper because it was aggressively independent.

Finally, however, *L'Oeuvre,* was obliged to "play ball" with the Agence Havas.

In 1923, Henri Dumay, of the *Petit Parisien,* denounced the venality of the press and the monopoly enjoyed by the Havas Agency. He declared that he was going to launch a newspaper that would be really independent. This newspaper, "never sectarian, never neutral," was to be called *Le Quotidien.*

Henri Dumay's program was enthusiastically welcomed. He announced that, instead of relying on powerful sponsors and hidden resources, he intended founding his newspaper in a truly democratic manner. Sixty thousand subscribers eagerly put their savings into *Quotidien* shares. Henri Dumay collected twenty-two million francs.

Throughout France placards announced the birth of this newspaper. Furthermore—and never before had such a thing been done—every citizen of France received a copy of a pamphlet explaining just what this newspaper was going to be and just why it was being published. The public impatiently awaited the appearance of *Le Quotidien.*

The five big dailies, sensing the threat of serious competition, now took the offensive. At the very last minute, the *Petit Journal,* which had contracted to print *Le Quotidien* in its plant, forfeited the guarantee and broke the contract. Not one of the large printing establishments was willing to undertake the work. Henri Dumay was obliged, therefore, to postpone publication until he could get a plant of his own. When the paper was coming off the presses, Henri Dumay learned that the newspaper dealers throughout France had been warned not to handle *Le Quotidien*—under penalty of losing the privilege of selling the five big newspapers.

The merciless boycott continued. By means of series of placards, Henri Dumay kept the public informed of the methods employed "to prevent publication of the truth." The public response was overwhelmingly favorable. The circulation continued to increase steadily, but funds were beginning to run low. *Le Quotidien* had been obliged, by the action of its competitors, to incur enormous and unforeseen expenses—the purchase of a printing plant, an office building, the distribution of placards in reply to the boycott, etc. The Havas Agency, which controlled the great majority of advertisers, naturally refused to allot any sums to a paper that had come out against deliberate lying, to a paper that was inclined to expose the Agency's own devices.

On October 31, 1924, the entire Board of Directors of *Le Quotidien* met to discuss the newspaper's financial condition. Addressing the meeting, Henri Dumay calmly made the following announcement: "I have recently received a proposition from important groups of coal-mining, insurance, textile, oil and railroad interests, offering us subsidies amounting to at least a million, annually. In return for these subsidies, they ask very little of us. They merely want us to show a bit of discretion."

There was an uproar. Georges Boris, secretary-general of the paper, violently attacked ". . . this baneful custom of having the newspapers of France accept sums of money from powerful interests—not in return for advertising which can be seen, but for secret accommodations and for maintaining a guilty silence."

Henri Dumay hastily beat a retreat. The proposed subsidies were unanimously rejected.

Several days later Georges Boris was called to the telephone to speak to an important representative of the big railroads.

"Cher Monsieur," the voice said, "certain notices have appeared in the press concerning the projected merger of the Compagnie d'Orléans and the Compagnie du Midi. In view of the agreement entered into with your newspaper, it is to be understood that you are not to mention this matter until further notice."

The man had hung up. What were those agreements he had mentioned? . . . Georges Boris asked the political directors and the editor-in-chief. No one knew the answer.

Why had Henri Dumay abandoned the campaign directed against the monetary policy of the Banque de France? Why had Henri Dumay wanted to revise the proofs of the account of the session of the Chamber of Deputies at which the oil monopoly had been considered? Why, under pretext of finding the article too long, had he, with his own pen, deleted all the passages which were hostile to the monopoly? And why had a director of a big insurance company said that *Le Quotidien* would never again attack their privileges? And why, finally, had Monsieur Henri Dumay so insistently requested his associates not to criticize the policies of the Poincaré Government?

Henri Dumay was called upon to explain. The 60,000 stockholders and the hundreds of thousands of readers of *Le Quotidien* were shocked and dismayed when they learned that all the principal collaborators on their beloved newspaper had resigned. The public was even more stupefied when a new publication appeared, *La Lumière,* a weekly, which had been founded expressly for the purpose of revealing the truth about *Le Quotidien.* The public then heard the true facts in the case: how Henri Dumay, seeing that funds were running low, had secretly solicited subsidies from financially powerful groups; and how these interests, only too glad to get their hands on *Le Quotidien* —this constant menace to monopoly and privilege—had speedily responded to Henri Dumay's request.

Naturally, *Le Quotidien's* circulation took a terrifying drop. The only thing left for Henri Dumay to do was to disappear. Which he did, after having sold—at par—his shares in *Le Quotidien* to Monsieur Jean Hennessy, of "Three Star" cognac fame. Hennessy had political ambitions. And, thanks to *Le Quotidien,* he became Minister, then Ambassador.

Since he was impervious to ridicule, Hennessy began to dream of the laurels of Hitler and Mussolini, and proceeded to transform *Le Quotidien* into the mouthpiece of the "Socialist-Nationalist" groups. This was the end. *Le Quotidien* went down, amidst gales of laughter.

Thus, the first attempt to give France a newspaper truly belonging to and serving the interests of the people had resulted in dissipating the savings of 60,000 good citizens who had shown too great a desire for honesty and decency and in transforming an ambitious businessman into a politician, a diplomat, and finally into an apprentice dictator.

The five big dailies were, of course, delighted. But they were not to be complacent for long. Another danger cloud soon loomed on the horizon.

François Coty, the perfume manufacturer who began as an obscure little chemist, had lofty political ambitions. Because he was born in Corsica, he considered himself a reincarnation of Napoleon. His megalomania increased from year to year.

After Coty had made hundreds of millions of francs out of his seductive perfumes, he decided to seek political power with the help of his enormous fortune. (In 1928, his American business alone was appraised at some 90 million dollars.)

In 1923, he presented himself as a candidate for the

office of Senator from Corsica. Coty was declared elected. But his opponents had no trouble at all in proving that he had bought and paid for a large percentage of his votes. The election of the perfume magnate was declared null and void. François Coty began to nourish an abiding grudge against the Republic.

In 1922, he had acquired two socially fashionable newspapers of Paris: *Le Gaulois* and *Le Figaro*. He had immediately discontinued publication of *Le Gaulois,* and had attempted to revive *Le Figaro,* intending to make it the official gazette of High Society.

But after his defeat in the Corsican elections, Coty decided that *Le Figaro* would not be a sufficiently strong weapon politically.

In 1927 François Coty laid his plans for a big, popular newspaper which he decided to call *L'Ami du Peuple*. And he decided to sell this paper not for 25 centimes, the price of all the other dailies, but for a mere 10 centimes. The gentlemen of the "Big Five" violently opposed this "demagogic" lowering of the price.

"I have the absolute right to do anything I like with my money and with my newspaper," said the perfume king. "I can sell it at any price, and I can even give it away if it amuses me to do so."

Thereupon, the "Big Five" plus the Havas Agency decided to deal with Coty as they had dealt with *L'Oeuvre* and with *Le Quotidien*. But the perfume potentate was prepared to fight. He plastered the walls of France with enormous proclamations, framed in the French colors, asking nothing more or less of the population than a plebiscite, and urging them to destroy "the feudal fortresses of venal opinion." The "Big Five," in reply, put up placards that were every bit as large, every bit as patriotically bordered in red, white and blue, and which solemnly warned of the danger of exposing the people's minds "to domination achieved by a selfish capitalist with his millions." As usual, the French could not resist a bargain; and the fact that it was priced at 10 centimes—instead of 25—made them buy *L'Ami du Peuple,* even though it was François Coty's newspaper. In short, Coty won.

But *L'Ami du Peuple* was a strange sort of newspaper—drab, boring, full of interminable articles in which Coty tirelessly proclaimed that what France needed was a Bonapartist Republic—amounting, in fact, to some vague sort of Fascism. He had the walls of his Château de Louveciennes strategically strengthened with concrete; the cellars were liberally stocked with arms. "To defend myself against an attack," he would say. "To prepare an insurrection," his enemies said.

The Havas Agency, naturally, refused to give *L'Ami du Peuple* any advertising, although the paper's circulation was close to a million daily. Furthermore, the Hachette Agency, which had a monopoly of the sale of newspapers in all the kiosks of Paris and in all the railroad stations in France, refused to handle a newspaper priced at 10 centimes.

"As for that," François Coty said, "I'm rich enough to take care of the distribution myself."

Since Coty could not win the friendship of existing journals, he simply decided to create some of his own. Coty not only founded *L'Ami du Peuple du Soir* and a satirical weekly called *Le Coup de Patte*, but he also gave financial support to innumerable publications of the extreme Right and created a number of war veterans' organs whose main function it was to speak highly of the benevolent Monsieur François Coty.

He now launched a violent campaign against Communism. He was making so much noise that he drowned out the voices of his enemies. The clamor he was making ran into sums which even the biggest fortunes could not afford forever. Coty lavished some 500 millions of francs on these various publications.

And now a new crushing blow was to be delivered, not from his competitors, but from his own wife. Mme. Yvonne Alexandrine Coty had married François Coty on the basis of community of property. Yvonne Coty had courageously stood by her husband during the difficult years. Now she did not intend to be deprived of her rightful share of their fortune. She wanted to rescue her share before Coty could waste it on his journalistic ventures. Coty was ordered by the Court to transfer to his wife the sum of 268 millions, of which he paid 39 millions on the day their divorce was decreed in New York. The following year he paid another 100 million, but from then on he claimed that he no longer had enough liquid assets, and proposed paying her the balance due in ten yearly instalments. Yvonne Coty insisted on immediate payment.

Coty, in a most embarrassing situation, tried to evade his legal obligations by resorting to the use of figureheads. Gabriel Alphaud, a former managing editor of *Le Figaro* and director of *Comédia*, asked Coty for his help in preventing the liquidation of a printing company of which he, Alphand, was manager and the largest stockholder. Coty felt sorry for the man, gave him a handsome price for the shares in the tottering company, and a contract for printing a part of *Le Figaro's* output. In return, Coty asked Alphand to subscribe, with this money, to an increase in the capitalization of *Le Figaro*. In reality it was clearly understood that Alphand was to return the shares in *Le Figaro* by mail—that, in other words, he was merely to lend his name to the transaction. Alphand received the money, subscribed to the new shares, but overlooked the detail of sending them back by return mail.

Then François Coty noticed something: his name was nowhere to be seen on the *manchette* of *Le Figaro*. A typographical error, he thought. But then his attention was caught by a paragraph on the front page—only a short paragraph—announcing that the Board of Directors had voted to discontinue the title of Director on *Le Figaro*. Coty was stunned by this blow.

On the following day, in *L'Ami du Peuple*, François Coty published the best article he had ever written—or at least signed—in his life. He crucified the Comte Beaupoil de Saint-Aulaire, former Ambassador, Grand Officier de la Légion d'Honneur, Chairman of the Board of Directors of *Le Figaro*—as well as his accomplice, Alphand. Addressing his remarks to the ex-Ambassador, he wrote: "You have apparently forgotten with what generosity I welcomed you and entertained you in my home at a time when your personality, already lacking in diplomatic manners, was about to founder in the scandalous Oustric Affair in which you, as manager of this bank, were declared in bankruptcy. You have forgotten that *Le Figaro* was a place of refuge for you after your correctional misadventures, and that you extracted an extravagant salary from me to regild your tarnished coat-of-arms."

But these reproaches did not alter the situation. The odor, so to speak, was not so sweet in the great *parfumeur's* house. *L'Ami du Peuple du Soir* and *Le Coup de Patte* had been discontinued. And Coty soon had trouble finding enough money to keep *L'Ami du Peuple* alive. As the result of a protest for non-payment, *L'Ami du Peuple* was put into receivership. The Havas Agency, which had been stalking its prey, immediately bought up the newspaper for 3,250,000 francs. And promptly raised the price to 25 centimes.

Shortly afterward, François Coty—broken by all these humiliations—died at his Château de Louveciennes.

Le Figaro was then taken over by Coty's former wife, who had married a Franco-Rumanian banker, Léon Cotnaréanu. Under the able political, literary and technical direction of Lucien Romier, Pierre Brisson and Pierre Lafitte, *Le Figaro* became one of the best newspapers in France.

But in the meantime, the "Big Five" had been confronted by a new enemy—*Paris-Soir*.

Chapter Seven

How *Paris-Soir* Was Born

Paris-Soir was founded in 1924 by Eugène Merle, a cheerful and adventurous scoundrel from Marseille. He had been administrator of *Le Bonnet Rouge* since the founding of that anarchistic paper in 1912. F. I. Mouthon, director of *Le Journal,* knew an enterprising man when he saw one. Merle had little difficulty in persuading Mouthon of the advantages to be derived from a subsidiary newspaper which would serve as an evening edition. Thus *Paris-Soir* was born.

For many years *Paris-Soir* was published as a Leftist evening paper. It was more youthful, more enterprising than its principal competitor, *L'Intransigeant.* But its circulation never exceeded 40,000 to 50,000.

It was not until six years after it had been founded that *Paris-Soir* became a big newspaper, thanks to Jean Prouvost.

A wealthy textile man from the North, Jean Prouvost bought a small newspaper, *Paris-Midi,* in 1926. *Paris-Midi* was the only paper to fill the gap between the appearance of the morning papers at 5 A.M. and the evening papers at 3 P.M. Its circulation was only about 5,000.

At the time Jean Prouvost acquired *Paris-Midi,* I came to the paper as a substitute for a friend who was covering theatrical news. The entire staff of *Paris-Midi* occupied offices consisting of five or six rooms on the top floor of an old building. The copy was lowered to the ground floor, where the presses were, by means of an old basket going down the well of the staircase and manipulated by an antique rope-and-pulley device.

After I had been working there a short time as a substitute for a friend, I was summoned by Jean Prouvost. With hardly a preliminary greeting, he said:

"I think *Paris-Midi* is asleep. No life at all. I want to make some changes. This doesn't particularly concern you because you're not staying here—are you? But I want to tell you about it anyway, because I'd like you to remain here, in the office, just a few minutes longer. I've summoned all the editors to take part in a sort of *foire aux idées* (idea market). I intend holding such conferences every week. And as I want the theater to be represented, I'd like you to be present at these meetings until the head of the department returns."

A few moments later, the staff filed in. Each one gave his idea of what *Paris-Midi* should be like.

When my turn came, I advanced my opinions. The older employees glared at me, an utterly unknown young man, an intruder, who dared to voice what they considered to be revolutionary opinions. I went on until I had said everything I wanted to say.

As we were leaving, Jean Prouvost detained me.

When we were alone in the office, he said: "Where do you work?"

"I make 300 francs a month on the *Soir*. And I make about the same amount by writing articles for various newspapers and weeklies."

"I offer you 500 a month to work here," he said. "And you will be free to continue writing for other publications. If you do well here, you'll soon get a raise."

That was how I became regularly employed on *Paris-Midi*. I was not quite nineteen.

Within a few weeks, *Paris-Midi* underwent a complete change. Innovations were introduced, designed to attract every potential reader of a newspaper appearing at noon.

An entire page was devoted to racing. There was a page directed by a former professor of philosophy, A. L. Jeune, who revealed himself as an excellent news analyst and economist. I was given charge of a page devoted to Paris—the theater, night life—*la vie parisienne.*

The departments of foreign and domestic politics, of literature and of the arts—all were put into the hands of men who knew how to write concise, vigorous and clever articles.

I created a department featuring last-minute news dispatches. Previously, *Paris-Midi* had merely repeated and expanded the news items published by the morning papers. *Paris-Midi* had had one particularly humiliating experience the day Paul Deschanel, the President of the Republic, suddenly went out of his mind and threw himself out of the window of the special train that was taking him to the little town of Montbrisson for an inauguration. And while the President, in pajamas and bare feet, was identifying himself to a track-walker, *Paris-Midi* was calmly publishing the official description of the ceremony: ". . . the President, Paul Deschanel, was welcomed in Montbrisson by the local authorities. A little girl recited a poem in the President's honor, and then presented him with a bouquet of red, white and blue flowers. . . . The local band played the 'Marseillaise'. . . . Then came the official procession. . . ." The account would have been accurate down to the smallest detail—if the ceremony had taken place.

To avoid the possible repetition of any such journalistic disaster, we abandoned the practice of running prepared "news." We were the first paper out with the evening news from the United States, for when it was midnight in New York the Paris morning papers had long since published their final editions.

Paris-Midi, with its limited facilities, showed so much initiative that the circulation increased 1,000 percent within six months. Within one year the circulation increased from some 5,000 to over 100,000.

Jean Prouvost was the youngest child of very wealthy parents, and had increased his inherited fortune by marrying a wealthy cousin. Returning home after the war, he had found his textile plants in the North totally destroyed. With the war-reparation sums received, he had completely rebuilt his factories along the most modern lines. He had even opened a plant in New York and another in the new Czechoslovakia. His approach to journalism had been that of a dilettante; he had wanted, primarily, to cut a figure in Parisian society; but he soon became deeply involved in his avocation.

The Havas Agency, however, was greatly displeased, and tried to stop Jean Prouvost. But this time the wrath of the Havas Agency caused no alarm, for the investment in *Paris-Midi* was relatively small for a man of Jean Prouvost's resources.

He said to me one day: "I believe that a newspaper should be prepared to do everything in its power to get the largest possible circulation. When this circulation has been achieved, no one can do the paper any harm, for, if there are enough readers, the advertisers will want to buy space, regardless of boycotts and regardless of the cost of this advertising. Then, progressively, the investment is amortized, and from then on the profits can be considerable."

I considered this attitude to be infinitely more sound than the apostolic announcements made by scoundrels who then sold criticism and praise to the highest bidder. Jean Prouvost was unable to believe that a newspaper could possibly make a living from anything besides normal receipts—that is to say, from sales and from admittedly paid advertising. He refused to accept subsidies from foreign embassies, and informed the ministries that he would not accept any sums from the "secret funds." From that time on, he was looked upon—in political and business circles—as a strong man and a dangerous one. No one could believe that the director of a newspaper could be guilty of plain, unadulterated honesty.

Jean-Louis Malvy, the Minister of the Interior, said to me one day: "What does your boss really want? It isn't easy to figure him out. Why, he doesn't even want the *Légion d'Honneur*. Do you think he may have bought

Paris-Midi with the object of somehow benefiting his textile business?"

In the meantime, Eugène Merle had had a great deal of trouble with Mouthon, with the result that the management of *Le Journal* finally decided to take over *Paris-Soir*. Mouthon chose Alexis Caille, the former director of *Le Soir*, to head *Paris-Soir*. But he was not equal to the task. The paper was running such a deficit that *Le Journal* began looking around for a customer for *Paris-Soir*. Jean Prouvost was approached. His friends warned him that no evening paper could possibly hope to compete with *L'Intransigeant,* which had firmly entrenched itself.

In 1924, when the circulation of *L'Intransigeant* was beginning to fall off, the paper was bought by Léon Bailby, a journalist of the Right. He failed to reawaken public interest in the newspaper. But soon after the beginning of the war, the General Staff found it useful to publish an official communiqué at three in the afternoon. The public, therefore, eagerly bought the evening papers. Léon Bailby took advantage of the situation. He developed a special kind of sentimentality—a special *"Intran"* style—intimate and pathetic, designed to appeal to "the noncombatants."

L'Intransigeant was willing to go to any lengths to please and to reassure its public. During the four years of World War I, *L'Intransigeant* outclassed all its competitors in the gentle art of *bourrage de crâne* (misleading reports about the war, conditions at the front, etc.).

After the Armistice, Léon Bailby increased his circulation by introducing the first small classified advertisements at low rates—with very special rates for demobilized veterans in search of employment. *L'Intransigeant* was also the first French newspaper to give sports and motion pictures the attention they deserved. All in all, Léon Bailby and his newspaper enjoyed extraordinary prestige. *L'Intransigeant* was considered to be *the* Parisian newspaper.

Jean Prouvost decided to go and see this "Napoleon of the evening press" in the ultra-modern building which housed *L'Intransigeant.*

"I suggest," Jean Prouvost said to Léon Bailby, "that

we jointly take over *Paris-Soir.* We'll limit the circulation. In that manner, you'll do away with all possible competition."

Léon Bailby snorted. "My dear sir," he said, "I'm not in the least interested. Can't you see that *L'Intransigeant* is an impregnable fortress? We have nothing to fear."

This overconfidence irritated Jean Prouvost. I believe it was because he was annoyed and because he wanted to challenge Bailby that he bought *Paris-Soir.* He had no definite plans for the paper.

L'Intransigeant and *Paris-Soir* were not the only evening newspapers published in Paris: there were *Le Temps, Le Journal des Débats, La Liberté* and *Le Soir.*

And *Le Soir* was no longer a sheet that was handed out free with programs in theaters and movie houses; it was now sold, normally and respectably, in kiosks and by newsboys. The paper had been put under the direction of two politically minded young men, Georges Bonnet and L. O. Frossard. Their general line was best described by the expression "To the Left, always to the Left. But never beyond that." (Daily circulation: 25,000.)

La Liberté belonged to a group of the Right, and was directed by a gentleman who specialized in promoting business deals. (Circulation: 15,000.)

Le Journal des Débats, very solemn and erudite, was the last stronghold of the old journalistic traditions. Its director, Henri de Nalèche, forbade the use of typewriters, ordered his secretaries to use goose-quill pens when answering all letters, and even refused to permit the installation of a news ticker in the offices, claiming that the noise made by such a machine would disturb the meditations of his editors. When he was accused of having accepted subsidies from foreign Governments, Henri de Nalèche replied, curtly: "I accept money only from such Governments of whose politics I approve." And everyone thought the explanation was quite satisfactory.

Le Temps was considered the unofficial mouthpiece of the Third Republic. Each successive Government favored it with first news, despite the fact that this newspaper had been frequently embarrassed and compromised by unsuppressible scandals.

Le Temps had a stilted and solemn tone which was quite impressive. Former and future diplomats, professors, men with political inclinations—all these considered it a great honor to appear in *Le Temps,* even anonymously. Every self-respecting upper-middle-class Frenchman was automatically a subscriber to *Le Temps.* And, outside of France, *Le Temps* was mentioned and quoted more than any other French newspaper. Senator Adrien Hébrard, who had founded *Le Temps,* had understood that a sufficiently austere appearance and dreary tone would be likely to inspire profound respect and, of course, complete confidence.

When the scandalous Panama Canal Affair was investigated, it was revealed that Senator Hébrard had shared in the loot to the extent of over a million francs. When the subsidies granted to the French press by the Czarist Government were published, it was seen that *Le Temps* was among the newspapers that had most unashamedly profited by his shower of rubles. And during the war, in 1916, Minister Keratof sent Isvolsky, the Russian Ambassador in Paris, a telegram which commenced in the following manner:

> On instructions from his editor, the Petrograd correspondent of *Le Temps* has raised the question of an annual subsidy of 150,000 francs to be granted this newspaper for a period of twelve years. The newspaper is prepared to undertake publication of seventy telegrams from Petrograd annually, designed to clarify questions concerning our foreign policy in a manner to be approved by us. (Telegram No. 3934, dated 29 August 1916, No. 410,403.)

Having solicited money from the Czarist Government, *Le Temps* did not, of course, hesitate to accept subsidies from the Soviets at a later date. There was a scandal when a Ukrainian, named Markoutum, was deported from France in September, 1928. Markoutum's attorney, Le Provost de Launay, Member of the Municipal Council of Paris, exposed the secret in an open letter—which only a few small political papers saw fit to publish: the order of deportation had been obtained by *Le Temps* after repeated appeals to the Prefecture of Police. Motive? *Le Temps* wanted to get rid of an embarrassing witness and a costly intermediary. For Markoutum had introduced two prominent executives of *Le Temps,* named Roels and Tavernier, to the Soviet Ambassador, Krassine. These gentlemen had then signed a contract, according to which *Le Temps* was to receive a subsidy of 520,000 francs for publishing, within a period of eight months, a series of articles on Russia that were to be favorable to the Soviet regime; furthermore, the paper's editorials on foreign relations were, naturally, to harmonize with the pro-Soviet articles. It is to be noted that these editorials were written by Jean Herbette, who was soon to be appointed French Ambassador to Moscow.

In February, 1926, a newspaper, *Les Documents Politiques,* published the contract signed by *Le Temps* and the Bulgarian Government, according to which *Le Temps* pledged itself to support the Bulgarian claims to former Bulgarian territory which had been awarded to Greece, Yugoslavia and Rumania, and to discuss the question of Bulgaria's outlet to the Aegean Sea, as well as the question of minorities. In addition to the formal contract, there was a letter specifically adding: "Needless to say, the support mentioned would be all the more effective if the agreement were kept strictly secret."

In November, 1929, *L'Action Française* published a copy of a letter from Monsieur Politis, Greek Minister to Paris. This letter revealed that *Le Temps* had been engaging in "impudent blackmail," threatening to launch a campaign against Greece unless, within a given time limit, the Government at Athens granted certain sums to be allotted to *Le Temps* "for publicity."

Finally, General Primo de Rivera, then Dictator of Spain, publicly stated in a speech delivered in January, 1930:

> It would be childish to attempt to conceal the fact that Spain maintains an organization charged with watching the nation's interests and its good name in the foreign press, and that this organization has been in contact with *Le Temps.*

This newspaper has willingly offered the hospitality of its pages to articles by writers with whom arrangements had been made. These relations have been interrupted, however, as the result of conflicting opinions as to the value of the services ever since—and possibly without the knowledge of its management—*Le Temps* has ceased to manifest the same good will toward the Spanish Government which had characterized its attitude during more than two years.

Hitherto, *Le Temps* had chosen to disregard all such exposures. This time, however, it could not pretend to ignore an affront publicly administered by the head of a foreign Government. Believing that the vast majority of its readers had not seen the various other exposures, which had been published only in newspapers with limited circulation, *Le Temps* calmly published the following declaration:

The Management affirms that no agreement of any kind whatsoever exists between *Le Temps* and any foreign Government. The political views of *Le Temps* are invariably and exclusively determined with regard to the interests of France. *Le Temps* has played a part in a publicity campaign, intended to offer information concerning Spain, but the publicity was of a general nature, having to do with economics and tourism, and in no way inhibiting the newspaper's freedom to express its own critical opinions. The Management of *Le Temps* has not, at any time, authorized any measures to obtain a continuation of or an increase in the terms and conditions relating to this publicity. In order to avoid all possible ambiguity, the Management of *Le Temps* deems it necessary herewith to announce, once and for all, that no one is qualified to enter—in the name of *Le Temps*—into any engagements whatsoever with any foreign Government whatsoever.

Thus, calmly, brazenly, *Le Temps* disavowed its own administrators and correspondents, and termed it a mere coincidence that its attitude toward certain countries had changed at precisely the times when these countries had either refused to contract for or to renew contracts for "publicity." Furthermore, when a foreign Government approached *Le Temps* and offered a subsidy of its own accord, the minimum sum to be paid for a campaign of "economic and touristic" publicity was quoted by the newspaper, and the prospective client was then duly informed that "nothing further could be promised at that price." In short, all other matters were to be discussed—discreetly, furtively—outside of the offices of the newspaper. The dignity and the integrity of *Le Temps* had to be preserved!

When Hébrard left *Le Temps* in 1929, Louis Mill succeeded him as director. He was a mere front for the big industrial interests of France. They were divided into two groups: le Comité des Forges, embracing all the important units of the heavy industry, and l'Union des Mines, uniting the biggest mining interests.

When Louis Mill died in 1931, the Comité des Forges and l'Union des Mines stepped out from behind the scenes and resolutely took the center of the stage. To represent their interests on *Le Temps,* they chose two of their employees—Etienne Miraux, who directed *Le Bulletin Quotidien d'Informations Economiques,* the house-organ of the Comité des Forges, and Jacques Chastenet, President of the Banque de l'Union des Mines.

Le Temps went on and on, never losing prestige, never losing any of its 80,000 faithful readers, who represented the élite of France.

When Jean Prouvost took over *Paris-Soir,* he wanted to give the élite an honest newspaper, and he wanted, above all, to give the masses a newspaper that was alive, well written, well informed and impartial.

Chapter Eight

The Rise of *Paris-Soir*

During the post-war years, most French newspapers gave consideration to the German problem in relation to the future peace of Europe. Their articles reflected the prejudices and political allegiances of the owners of the newspapers, rather than the facts themselves. *Paris-Soir* decided to study the facts at first hand. It sent not one but three reporters to Germany: Jules Sauerwein, who had specialized in foreign affairs; Pierre MacOrlan, a writer who had a special gift for making the man in the street talk; and Maurice Dekobra, a novelist of the international scene and an expert in the study of manners and customs. Jean Prouvost was to accompany them in order to study economic conditions.

Their featured reportage, entitled "Three Men in Germany," had a very great success. *Paris-Soir* had already achieved a daily circulation of almost 200,000. The circulation now took a mighty jump and increased about 100 percent. This was, surely, a noteworthy indication of the fact that the French appreciated being told the simple, dispassionate truth about their former enemy.

Aristide Briand, who represented to the world France's effort to achieve collective security, was a candidate for the Presidency of the Republic in June, 1931. At the last moment, the name of the austere Monsieur Paul Doumer, President of the Senate, had been put up in opposition to Briand. A week earlier, Briand's election had looked like a certainty, and no one had even expected to see any kind of serious competition. But the ranks of those who were expected to vote against Briand because of his stand for a united Europe were swelled by a considerable number of men who would normally have voted for him, but who now seemed unwilling to give the high office of the Presidency to such a strong personality. In a similar situation eleven years previously, Clemenceau, *"le Père de la Victoire,"* had most unexpectedly lost the election to the neurotic Paul Deschanel. Could Briand be defeated now?

I noticed one thing before the election: in the corridors and cloakrooms of the *Assemblée Nationale,* there was little talk about Briand's being the "Apostle of Peace." He was more bent than usual. He was very pale.

"I'm beginning to be worried," he said to me. "Many, too many, of my intimate friends are making a detour to avoid shaking hands with me."

Briand's faithful assistant, Peycelon, grumbled: "Despite all their promises, Tardieu and Laval, both of them, are betraying you. One is worse than the other. But all other signs point so definitely in your favor that I don't see how there possibly could be any doubt about the outcome."

Briand shrugged and said simply: "I'd like to see France take a plebiscite on the policy to be adopted toward Germany. If this is not done, the consequences may be very serious."

A few hours later, Paul Doumer was elected. I saw how Briand grew faint, almost staggered, when he heard the news.

The new President left for Paris, heading a procession that had been prepared for someone else. The *cortège* went from the Château de Versailles to the Elysée Palace, under a strong guard—which, incidentally, was now superfluous, since it had been ordered to protect Briand against the expected demonstration by the (Royalist) *Camelots du Roi.*

And, during this time, all the kiosks were selling the

magazine *L'Heure* featuring a front-page picture—faked, of course—of Briand sitting in the Presidential landaulet beside his predecessor, Gaston Doumergue. The editors had been absolutely certain of Briand's victory, and had wanted to publish a nice little scoop.

I saw Aristide Briand when he returned, for the last time, from a meeting of the League of Nations. Thousands of sympathizers had come to meet his train at the Gare de Lyon. A few groups from *L'Action Française* (Royalists) had also come to make a noisy display of their disapproval.

I followed Briand—he was Minister of Foreign Affairs, at the time—to his offices on the Quai d'Orsay. Only a few of his intimates were there, and Briand asked me to stay a few moments.

"Mon petit," he said to me, "I can only hope that things will turn out well. But the men of your generation must never forget that generosity and enthusiasm are essential to good statecraft; without generosity, one arouses hatreds, and without enthusiasm, one engenders weakness."

Aristide Briand died on March 7, 1932. Two months later, almost to the day, Paul Doumer was assassinated by a Russian fanatic, Gourguloff. The President had been inaugurating a sale of books written by war veterans.

These two unhappy events, I must say, served to strengthen the position of the new *Paris-Soir*.

I was in my office when one of our staff, who happened to be at a counter selling books for the War Veteran Writers, called me on the telephone. "Hurry up," he said. "Get this. The President of the Republic has just been assassinated!"

"You'll have to do better than that," I said, laughing.

I must explain that this was an old joke in all editorial offices. Whenever the editor in charge was away or came on duty late, and whenever the last edition was printed too early, or when an unnecessarily big headline was given to some relatively unimportant bit of news—there was always somebody who saw fit to say: "And what would you do now if the President of the Republic were assassinated?"

But the man on the wire wasn't joking this time. "Paul

Doumer has been rushed to the Hôpital Beaujon. Let me speak to a stenographer. I'll give her the story."

Now I was convinced. A quarter of an hour later, *Paris-Soir* was the first paper to appear with the incredible story. In the meantime, one of our photographers had come back to the office—unashamedly radiant with joy. But he had a good, professional reason for being happy: he had wanted to take a picture of the President in the act of buying a book, and at that very moment Gourguloff had committed the crime. A perfect picture. We gave it to the whole front page. It was more eloquent than any detailed narrative could ever have been. Everybody bought a copy of *Paris-Soir* that day.

The rise of *Paris-Soir* continued without interruption. Following "Three Men in Germany," we published an impressive series of stories by star reporters. Stories were wired to us from all over the world by experienced journalists or by well-known writers. These stories were illustrated with pictures—transmitted by cable or wireless.

We began to present news in a more direct manner, and did not rely on reprinting or rehashing the dispatches given out by the Havas Agency. We gave such a variety of material that *Paris-Soir* appealed to every member of the family. We made a strong bid for women readers. We ran detective and adventure stories and a daily short-short story. Sports were given so much space that this department practically amounted to a newspaper within a newspaper. And a whole page was devoted to matters of interest to children between the ages of five and fifteen.

Shortly before the revival of *Paris-Soir*, *L'Intransigeant*, confident of its impregnable position, had decided to discontinue the practice of allowing the return of unsold copies. However, in view of our rapidly increasing circulation, *L'Intransigeant* promptly reversed this dangerous decision. But, although our circulation had already jumped to 600,000, *L'Intransigeant* had not lost many of its readers. The Paris morning papers had suffered the greatest loss. They had been put on sale in the near-by provinces on the evening of their appearance, and on the following morning in the more remote provinces. But now *Paris-Soir* was available at the same time—and with later news. Naturally, the provinces began buying *Paris-Soir*. But that was not why they continued to buy it—but because the more important news items were broadcast by radio, anyway, and the latest news was also more promptly available in the local press. The people in the provinces bought *Paris-Soir* for the simple reason that it gave them what no other newspaper did.

When the "Big Five" finally recognized the danger, it was too late. In the meantime, Jean Prouvost had found that the unexpectedly rapid success of his enterprise had outstripped his own financial resources. He had been obliged, therefore, to take in a partner—another extremely wealthy industrialist from the North, Henri Béghin, who manufactured sugar and also paper, and who thus became doubly interested in the expansion of *Paris-Soir*.

The "Big Five" newspapers did not undertake to meet our competition by improving and modernizing their publications. Instead, they tried to injure *Paris-Soir* by organizing a campaign of systematic vilification. With the aid of Minister Pierre Etienne Flandin, they had already brought a serious charge against *Paris-Midi* before the tribunal of the Chamber of Deputies. Flandin claimed that *Paris-Midi* criticized his policies because he had refused to grant the spinning mills of the North tax exemption on their imports. Pierre Etienne Flandin happened to represent Havas Agency as counsel.

For ten years, Havas reiterated the charge that Jean Prouvost and Béghin were pouring millions into *Paris-Soir* with the sole object of having a mouthpiece that was strong enough to defend their real interests—namely, the textile, sugar and paper business. As a matter of fact, *Paris-Soir* did, in the beginning, require an outlay of some hundred million francs—but the newspaper very soon became a much bigger and far more profitable business than either of the partners' industrial enterprises ever were. All the accusations were disseminated by a horde of blackmailing journals.

A notable exception was *Le Petit Parisien*, one of the cleanest newspapers in France. It belonged to the Dupuy family. The father, a Senator, had left it to his two sons, Pierre and Paul. Paul had died. And Pierre, who had been Deputy ever since coming of age (1902), directed the newspaper. Madame Paul Dupuy—an American, *née* Helen Brown—and her two sons, Jacques and Jean, were in charge of *Excelsior*, an illustrated paper, devoted half to news and half to Society. They also published numerous magazines dealing with sports, motion pictures, the outdoors, etc. All these publications belonged to the *Petit Parisien* group.

Le Petit Parisien, itself, was commonly known as *le journal des concierges* (the janitors' newspaper) because it always featured local news and human-interest stories, and ran serials in which virtue always triumphed over vice. Having adhered to this policy from the very beginning, *Le Petit Parisien* had won the right to run the following statement under its masthead: "The biggest circulation in France."

The offices were calm and peaceful. Editors received promotion according to seniority, and were perfectly contented to be pensioned and provided for for the rest of their lives. Initiative was frowned upon here. Elie-Joseph Bois, a journalist of the old school, was editor-in-chief. His political line was cautious and consistently pro-Government. He knew everyone of consequence in the Third Republic, and everybody showered him with attentions.

Prior to the revival of *Paris-Soir, Le Petit Parisien* had a staff of outstanding reporters, including the star of them all—Albert Londres, the man who had dared to expose conditions in France's penal settlement.

Albert Londres, with his ability and his devotion to his profession, served as a shining example to all of us. He used to say: "The only big reporting job left for me to cover is the story of France, for I've spent less time here than anywhere else."

On his way home from Ethiopia, Albert Londres died in the fire which destroyed the steamship *Georges-Phillipar.* A prize was then created in his name, to be awarded to the author of the year's best piece of reporting. Albert Londres' death was a very great loss to *Le Petit Parisien.*

While the circulation of *Paris-Soir* was rising rapidly, *Le Petit Parisien* lost some 500,000 of its readers. The inscription under its masthead had to be changed now. And this was done rather skilfully by avoiding mention of the word "circulation," and by substituting the claim: "The most widely read newspaper in the world."

Le Petit Parisien's political line was definite on only one point: *rapprochement* with Fascist Italy. But this was primarily a personal matter, a sort of hobby of the paper's owner, who was flattered by the honors Mussolini had shown him, and above all by the *Cordon de Grand Officier de la Couronne d'Italie.*

Le Petit Parisien had attempted to be at least relatively independent of the other members of the "Big Five" group. It had established its own organization for distribution, in order to free itself from the powerful Hachette Agency. Furthermore, for its provincial editions, it had wanted to set up printing plants in a number of the larger cities of France. But its competitors cried "trust" and warned the provincial press. Finally, the Government ordered *Le Petit Parisien* to give up the idea and to conform.

Le Journal was affected even more than *Le Petit Parisien* by the sensational rise of *Paris-Soir.* When it was founded, in 1892, *Le Journal* also felt the enmity of its rivals. For, in those days—before the "Big Five" formed a united front against all independents—they used to spend their time fighting one another. No sooner had *Le Journal* been born, than it was subjected to a boycott, directed by *Le Petit Journal* and *Le Petit Parisien.* These newspapers threatened to withdraw their business from newsdealers who handled *Le Journal. Le Journal* started a suit, but then discreetly came to a friendly understanding with the opposition. In the beginning, *Le Journal* was a literary daily, but soon turned into a newspaper devoted to news and politics.

During World War I, two of its directors—Lenoir and Duval—were, in turn, arrested on the charge of having accepted money from the enemy. Lenoir was involved in the famous Bolo Pacha case; Duval, in the Dessouches affair. Both were shot. When Charles Humbert succeeded to the now somewhat shaky chair of *Le Journal,* he saw fit to publish—without delay—the following praiseworthy announcement:

> *Le Journal* will be engrossed, first and last, in serving the interests of the nation. Our readers know me. They know that my past is a guarantee of my future. They know that, under my direction, *Le Journal* will be a glass house, open to inspection by everybody.

But the walls of *Le Journal* must have been made of opaque glass, for the readers were stupefied when they later found out that the big campaign—"Guns—Munitions"—undertaken by their favorite newspaper, ultimately led to the indictment of Monsieur Charles Humbert on the charge of traffic with the enemy.

To make the public forget this long series of disasters, Charles Humbert was replaced by F. I. Mouthon, already mentioned. He was an able and shrewd journalist. He knew better than to expose himself to criticism or to allow the suspicions of his enemies to be confirmed by proofs. He always acted through intermediaries.

When Mouthon died, the Havas Agency placed its own man at the head of *Le Journal*—Pierre Guimier, chief of the Havas advertising department, a man for whom journalism represented little more than a vantage point for furthering his private business and his social aspirations. He made an excellent move, however, when he appointed a splendid journalist and an honest and highly cultured man—Jacques de Marsillac—as editor-in-chief. He selected a staff of brilliant young reporters, who injected new life and color into *Le Journal.* But, as a result of disputes and jealousies—office politics, in short—this group soon broke up; and we, at *Paris-Soir,* were thus able to get the most promising of these men. *Le Journal,* on the other hand, was falling more and more under the domination of the big monied interests, and was pursuing an increasingly reactionary line, thus driving many of its readers away.

Chapter Nine

Monsieur Alexandre, Alias Stavisky

"JUST name your own figure, Monsieur Lazareff. I'm anxious to obtain your services at any price, and I'm quite prepared to pay you an advance right now. You'll have an entirely free hand in getting up the newspaper. You'll be given all the necessary equipment and facilities to carry out your ideas."

Serge Alexandre was trying to make it sound very tempting.

A friend, an advertising man, had more or less prepared me for this speech. "Serge Alexandre is a very important financier," he had told me. "He controls a lot of money. He wants to start a new big-circulation newspaper, using the very latest modern improvements. It won't do you any harm to speak to the man."

Serge Alexandre didn't look in the least like the classic picture of a financier, but rather like a dancer.

"Great fellow, don't you think so?" my friend asked, later.

"He makes me uncomfortable," I said. "He talks too big. He's too generous. Where does he come from, anyway? Where did he get all that money?"

"Business, my boy. He swings those big international deals. He knows everybody—all the Ministers, all the Ambassadors."

Two days later, I received a copy of a paper called *La Bonne Guerre* in the mail. This was notoriously a blackmailing sheet. But I couldn't help noticing one big headline: "The swindler, Stavisky, alias Serge Alexandre, mysteriously immune to arrest." The author of this article, Jean Sartori, stated that the so-called Serge Alexandre was no one else but the gang leader—real name, Alexandre Stavisky—who had been arrested, together with his accomplices, in 1927, charged with an assortment of larcenies. Suddenly, Stavisky had been freed on bail; then the trials had been postponed again and again, with the result that none of the cases, in which Stavisky was a defendant, was ever brought before the Court. And the article went on to say that Stavisky had then changed his name and identity, and had proceeded to collect a new set of victims. In conclusion, the article said that ". . . three issues of this newspaper will be sent to everyone who might now be in touch with Serge Alexandre, for the purpose of informing everyone as to the true nature of this man."

This article served to make up my mind: I was going to undertake a thorough investigation of this Alexandre. I instructed two of the ablest reporters on *Paris-Soir* to probe into the man's past, and a third one to investigate his more recent activities. Within a very few days, I had all the information I wanted.

Alexandre Stavisky came from a respectable family. His father, born in Russia, was a dentist. At an early age, Alexandre became the black sheep of the family. He exploited his charm, was supported by women. He soon had his first encounter with the authorities, being charged with fraud and embezzlement. But that was only the beginning. In 1927, he was entertaining his friends one evening in a delightful villa he had rented at Chatou, in the suburbs of Paris. They were at dinner when the police broke in and arrested everybody. His guests turned out to be his partners in crime.

The police searched the homes of all involved, to recover some of the loot (the crimes had included forgery, boosted checks, issuance of worthless securities, organized card games with marked cards and even felonious assault). The search was in vain. Stavisky, in the meantime, offered his services as informer to the police officer who had arrested him, Commissaire Bayard. Bayard was interested in the proposition, for Stavisky had been shrewd enough to make his offer sound quite enticing by gratuitously throwing in a few choice bits of information about certain important personalities.

Stavisky was well aware of the antagonism between the Sûreté Nationale and the municipal police; he decided to use it to his advantage. He sent word to the ex-Prefect of Police, Hudelo, informing him that the Sûreté was about to search his, Hudelo's, home. Stavisky did not add that the search was being undertaken at his suggestion. The ex-Prefect was alarmed. But Stavisky soon reassured him: there would be no further investigation and no search if he, Hudelo, used his influence to have Stavisky freed and the case adjourned. In a panic, Hudelo pulled all his strings. On the recommendation of Assistant District Attorney Prince, of the Financial Section of the Court of the Department of the Seine, Stavisky was released on bail.

Stavisky was then plagued by a swarm of blackmailers. Stavisky commenced paying them for their silence. But it was running into big money. Then he had an idea which was nothing less than a stroke of genius: he founded a company which bought up in advance the rights to the total annual advertising space of all the gossip and scandal sheets; and thus, of course, practically gained control over most of these publications. Those which did not see fit to come to an understanding with Stavisky were none the less silenced by the threat of returning blackmail with blackmail.

Alexandre Stavisky became Serge Alexandre. Discreetly he came to the aid of some Superintendent or Inspector of the Sûreté who was having trouble meeting his bills. He was provided with a new and synthetic identification card, as well as with a special card entitling him to admission to gambling clubs and casinos, from which he had previously been excluded, following an episode in which a card had dropped, regrettably, from his sleeve. Now Alexandre was ready to undertake the conquest of Paris.

In the rush of events, I was inclined to forget about Monsieur Alexandre. But every now and then I happened to run into him. At Easter, I went down to Cannes on the Riviera. I went into the gambling rooms. There was a big crowd about the baccarat table on which the highest game was being played. People were whispering that a man was losing a lot of money—that he had already lost over two million francs in a few hours.

It was, of course, Serge Alexandre.

Later I saw Alexandre at Maxim's in the company of a former Cabinet Minister, two Deputies, a newspaper director, a well-known writer and a number of dazzling beauties. Alexandre honored me with elaborate gestures of recognition. Some of the others at the table knew me, too, and also insisted that I join them. I promptly declined the invitation. Then, a few minutes later, the writer came over and sat down at my table.

"Why are you hanging around with that fellow Alexandre?" I asked him. "Don't you know who he is?"

"Of course I do," he replied. "And that's just why I find it amusing. After all, I'm a writer—an observer—and the man fascinates me. His game is perfectly obvious. What he does is simply to compromise new people all the time, with the result that they ultimately become his accomplices, willingly or otherwise. And he operates through his old cronies, the blackmailers. The politicians and men of affairs who have been compromised fall under his power. For services rendered, Alexandre demands his share. Thus he has wormed his way into the management of several corporations. But he is never openly active. He appoints very distinguished Boards of Directors, whose members are paid handsome salaries for doing absolutely nothing—nothing, that is to say, except to lend the full weight of their impressive names and titles. And why shouldn't these gentlemen accept the positions, since, after all, Alexandre had been recommended by members or ex-members of the Government and men of financial power?"

"In other words," I said, "it never occurred to anyone to look into the past of this Serge Alexandre."

"Why should they?" the writer replied, laughing. "The only thing they look for is which side their bread is buttered. As for how it is all done, Alexandre has a staff of very able assistants. There is Gaston Bonnaure, his attorney and general factotum. Then there is Albert Dubarry who runs a newspaper, *La Volonté,* a gossip sheet, *Le Carnet de la Semaine,* and a theatrical paper, *La Rampe.* These three publications live mainly on money supplied by Stavisky. This Dubarry, an old-timer when it comes to politics, knows everybody of importance by his first name, and, what is more important to him, by his past indiscretions."

Jean Chiappe, the Prefect of Police, was entering Maxim's at that moment. I saw Albert Dubarry go up to him, and the two men kiss on both cheeks. Dubarry then introduced the people at the table to Chiappe, and I witnessed the spectacle of the Prefect of Police shaking hands with Alexandre.

"I get the idea," I said to my friend, the writer. "Very clever work. But, tell me, how about those famous suits that are pending? They'll be brought to Court some day, and when that happens . . ."

"Not a chance. The judges are honest, but they're inclined to cater to people with influence. They go out of their way to help Alexandre. Stavisky's case has just been postponed for the eighteenth time."

"But, after all," I said, "he doesn't manufacture all this money, does he?"

"I understand that Alexandre founds some highly complicated corporations, in which the big insurance companies and credit banks take a part interest. Some people say that he's gone straight; that his present operations are all strictly respectable. Others seem to think it's all going to blow up, one fine day, in a terrific scandal. But I fail to see how there could be any scandal, since so many newspapers have accepted Stavisky's money, since so many judges have lied for him, since so many Ministers have more or less directly accepted political contributions from him. And then, of course, the fact that so many members of the Police and of the Sûreté have become his devoted friends—all this makes it rather difficult to picture him being denounced, not to say arrested."

Alexandre did not seem to be heading in the direction of jail. I heard stories of lavish receptions he gave in the de-luxe suite of the Hotel Claridge on the Champs-Elysées, and of the brilliant parties he was giving in the most fashionable mountain resorts and on the Riviera. There were rumors to the effect that he was a silent partner in the new Rightist daily, *Le Rempart* (the first French tabloid), and in *La Liberté,* another ultra-reactionary newspaper. Obviously, Stavisky cared little about the political coloration of his journalistic enterprises. A big music-hall near the Etoile—the Empire—was transformed into a theater for the production of operettas. I attended the dress-rehearsal of *Katinka,* a sumptuous production. To my great surprise, I saw Serge Alexandre sitting in a box, in the company of an active Cabinet Minister and of the President of the Authors' Association. During the intermission, he seemed to be playing the role of host to everyone.

"Why, of course," one of the authors of *Katinka* said to me. "Naturally he acts that way. He's the boss here."

"Do you know who he is?" I asked.

"Of course I do. Everybody who is seen anywhere near him immediately gets a copy of *La Bonne Guerre* in the mail."

"Isn't that enough to scare people away?"

"Not necessarily. They prefer to believe—or perhaps they really do believe—that those stories are all lies. They don't see how such a wealthy gentleman—a gentleman with such splendid connections and such a distinguished wife—could possibly be a crook."

"Well, tell me," I said. "Why do you think he put his money into this theater?"

"Very simple. Aside from the leading lady—who's an import, as you know—the rest of the cast is made up exclusively of young ladies who happen to be the protégées of various Cabinet Ministers, judges, police commissaires and attorneys."

That evening, Serge Alexandre plowed through the throng and came up to me.

"My dear Monsieur Lazareff," he said, "I've been so anxious to see you again. You remember that idea we were discussing the other day—about the newspaper? Well, I'm more interested than ever, and I'd really like to talk it over with you again."

"Thanks," I said. "I'm very much flattered. But I haven't the remotest intention of considering your proposition, Monsieur Stavisky."

He looked at me as though he really couldn't understand why I had called him by that name.

"Nevertheless," he said, after a moment, "I'll call you up some time." Then he retreated and disappeared in the crowd.

I was not to see him again or to hear anything more about him until December 28, 1933, when the scandal of the Bayonne Bonds exploded.

The Stavisky Affair served as the pretext for the first major assault against the French Republic and led to the exposure of the strongly organized anti-Republican conspiracy which was to culminate, ultimately, in the defeat of France. And yet, although the sums involved in the Stavisky Affair were considerable, they were no greater than the losses suffered by the public in two other financial scandals that had recently been exposed: the failure of the banker, Albert Oustric, and the downfall of Marthe Hanau, whose financial newspaper, *La Gazette de France,* had unsuccessfully fought the big banking interests. However, these two affairs had failed to arouse public opinion, although the losers had been small investors, whereas powerful financial establishments had been victimized by Stavisky. In any event, by the end of 1933, feelings had risen to white heat. All of France—and Paris, most particularly—was suffering a severe economic depression. Everybody was worried. There was an enormous increase in subversive propaganda, coming both from the extreme Right (encouraged by the triumph of Fascism in two neighboring countries) and from the extreme Left.

There was a disconcertingly rapid turnover in Ministries; but each change in Government was little more than nominal, for, as a rule, the same incompetent men were merely given different positions in the reshuffled Cabinet.

The President of the Council of Ministers, Camille Chautemps, was unlucky, too. His Minister of Justice was a Monsieur Raynaldi, and his Minister of the Colonies was Monsieur Dalimier. And, by a most regrettable coincidence, this Raynaldi had been involved in the irregular issue of shares in a company founded by a swindler. As for Dalimier, he had gone so far as to write a letter to various savings banks, recommending the purchase of the now famous Bayonne Bonds. Furthermore, the Attorney General, Pressard, who had indorsed the adjournments of the Stavisky suits, happened to be Camille Chautemps' brother-in-law. And the Premier, himself, had served as attorney to one of Stavisky's accomplices, General Bardi de Fourtou.

On New Year's Eve (1933), *Paris-Soir* commenced publishing a complete exposure of the life and the strange career of Stavisky. He had now disappeared. I received a phone call from our Swiss correspondent, telling me that a mysterious meeting had been held at St. Moritz, a meeting which had been attended by a number of prominent industrialists of various nationalities. At the conclusion of this conference, representatives had been sent to the heads of various subversive groups in Paris.

We were never able to obtain a complete list of the men who had attended the St. Moritz conference or to find out just what decisions had been arrived at or the identity of the men who had been sent as envoys. But the fact remained that the next issue of the official publication of the Association of War Veteran Officers featured a front-page drawing picturing the Palais Bourbon burning fiercely and, in the foreground, a number of Deputies hanging from the lamp-posts of the Pont de la Concorde. Obviously, the Reichstag-burning technique had won enthusiastic approval in certain quarters.

The New Year's holidays in no way lessened the tension. The newspapers which had been most seriously compromised by the Stavisky Affair now made the most noise.

On January 7th, we received a telephone call from one of the reporters we had sent along with the detectives who were on Stavisky's trail. The reporter was calling from Chamonix, the famous winter-sport resort.

"We've traced Stavisky," he informed me, "to a shelter up in the mountains. He's living there with someone whom he imagines is his right-hand man, but who's really an informer, according to confidential information I got from the Inspector of the Sûreté. Don't publish anything yet. I hope to see Stavisky tomorrow, having arranged for an interview with him through this informer, who comes down to the village every day for supplies and to confer with the police."

The following day, we heard that Stavisky had "committed suicide" in the mountain cabin, just as the police were breaking in to arrest him. His companion had also been arrested, but had soon been released. In view of the information our reporter had given us, we were inclined to entertain some doubts as to the manner in which Stavisky had actually been killed. Léon Bailby's *Le Jour* went so far as to state that Stavisky had been killed by the police—to keep him from talking. The paper gave a wealth of detail—largely fictional—by way of sensational exposure. Léon Bailby, apparently, had decided to get *Le Jour* off to a good start by exploiting the Stavisky Affair, as he had successfully launched *L'Intransigeant* by publishing the three-o'clock communiqués during the World War. And Léon Bailby's editorials urged the people of Paris to organize street demonstrations expressing disapproval of the regime "which was corrupting France, and which could not be whitewashed by any summary executions."

And the first street demonstrations did, in fact, immediately break out in Paris. The first organized groups to take part were the young men of the Monarchist Party (*l'Action Française*), the *Croix de Feu* and the *Jeunesses Patriotes.* The tension was not relieved by the arrest of Garat, Deputy-Mayor of Biarritz, of the Deputy, Gaston Bonnaure (Stavisky's attorney), of Camille Aymard, Director of *La Liberté*, of Albert Dubarry, Director of *La*

Volonté; nor did the resignation of Albert Dalimier, Minister of the Colonies, do much to quiet public opinion. On the other hand, Camille Chautemps' obstinate refusal to appoint an investigating committee merely allowed people to suspect the very worst.

The attitude of Camille Chautemps was exasperating. In the Chamber of Deputies this otherwise brilliant speaker, obviously confused to begin with, seemed to tie himself up hopelessly in the threads of his own arguments. . . . If he had nothing to hide, why did he persist in refusing to appoint a Parliamentary Investigation Committee? And why did he now urge a change in the law with respect to libel in the press—at the very moment when he was under attack in the newspapers?

The demonstrations in the streets had developed into parades and then into riots. These were met with the feeblest opposition on the part of the authorities, and the magistrates showed themselves to be strangely and extraordinarily lenient when any individuals of these disorderly groups were brought before them.

The Communists called upon their comrades to join in the demonstrations against Deputies and the Government. It had become practically impossible to walk through the quarters where the Ministries were located or through the Latin Quarter where the students lived without encountering street fighting.

When the Minister of Justice, Raynaldi, finally decided to resign, the entire Cabinet of Camille Chautemps went with him. They seemed to think that they were leaving of their own accord. In truth, the Cabinet fell like a piece of rotten fruit.

On February 2nd, Edouard Daladier formed his second Cabinet.

Chapter Ten

With Daladier on February 6, 1934

SPEEDILY—brutally, if necessary—we shall put an end to the blunders and evils which have convulsed the country. We, together with the people, demand that light be shed into the darkest corners. We are determined to act, speedily and drastically."

The heavy hand of Premier Edouard Daladier pounded his oak desk as he emphasized his determination to bring peace and quiet and order back to Paris.

Speedily and drastically . . . Two hours later, this forceful declaration was repeated in *Paris-Soir*'s blackest headlines. The Parisians were hopeful again. For weeks they had felt the pressure of secret forces, inciting them to rebellion.

I called upon Jean Chiappe, Prefect of Police, to find out whether Daladier's pronouncement had put an end to all street demonstrations.

"I've seen Daladier," he said. "He told me that the demonstrations, which had been planned for the coming Sunday by the War Veterans, were not to take place. Since it will be difficult to take strong measures against the cripples who are to be at the head of the procession in their little wagons and tricycles, I have asked the Minister of the Interior and the Minister of Pensions to meet me this evening and to confer with the leaders of the War Veterans. I hope to be able to persuade them to call off the parade."

During the meeting at the Ministry of the Interior, the representatives of the War Veterans—Lebecq and Jean Goy—commenced by putting on a show of great indignation. But Jean Chiappe took a firm stand. He would resign, he said, if the War Veterans insisted on staging their demonstration. Finally, Messrs. Lebecq and Jean Goy agreed to persuade their followers to postpone the performance.

Pleased with his success, Jean Chiappe returned to the Prefecture. There he received a telephone call from Premier Daladier, congratulating him and assuring him of the Government's "complete confidence."

This was on the evening of Friday, February 2nd.

The following morning—Saturday, February 3rd—Daladier telephoned Chiappe and informed him of his appointment to the office of Resident-General of Morocco, adding that Chiappe was to leave Paris and assume his new duties immediately.

Nervous and exhausted as he was, Jean Chiappe expressed his surprise in something like an outburst of temper. "The Government can relieve me of my duties at any time, but I can refuse to accept any other post offered me. As for Morocco, I say no! *Vous me couvrez de fleurs et vous me jetez à la rue où je serai ce soir en veston.*" ("You cover me with flowers and you throw me out into the street, where I'll be this evening—in shirt sleeves.")

Daladier, who had not yet consulted or even seen any of his new Ministers, promptly convened the Cabinet. He announced his decision to make some important changes: the Prefect of Police, Jean Chiappe, was to be named Resident-General of Morocco; the chief of the Sûreté Nationale, Thomé, who had failed to observe the involvement of any of his subordinates in the Stavisky Affair, was to be relieved of his post and transferred to the position of General Manager of the Comédie Française, replacing Emile Fabre, the renowned playwright, who was to be retired;

and, finally, the Attorney General, Pressard, Chautemps' brother-in-law and the man who had indorsed all the adjournments of the suits against Stavisky, was to be appointed Counsellor to the Court of Appeals, replacing Monsieur Pailhé, who, in turn, was to become Attorney General.

The assembled Ministers were dumbfounded. Albert Lebrun, President of the Republic, seemed to be the only one who had not been completely overwhelmed by Daladier's decision.

"Has Chiappe been notified?" one of the Ministers asked.

"Yes," Daladier said. "I spoke to him on the telephone."

"Has he agreed?"

"Oh," Eugène Frot, Minister of the Interior, sighed, "if you only knew what he said to the President of the Council!"

"What did he say? What did he say?" All the Ministers asked the question at once.

In a profoundly melancholy voice, Monsieur Frot replied: "He said that tonight he would be down in the street—in shirt sleeves—at the head of the demonstration."

The situation was growing worse.

As an old friend and political associate of Jean Chiappe, Minister François Piétri announced that, under those conditions, he would withdraw from the Cabinet; Jean Fabry, Minister of War, and Doussain, Under-Secretary of State, then announced that they, too, would resign.

Daladier held his ground; he insisted on going through with these changes in the Administration.

Daladier appointed Paul-Boncour and Marchandeau to replace the Ministers who had resigned.

I hastened to the Prefecture of Police, where I learned that Chiappe's successor, Bonnefoy-Sibour, Prefect of the Departement de Seine et Oise, had just left. The interview between these two men had been brief and colorful.

"My dear Chiappe," Bonnefoy-Sibour had said, "the Government has just given me your job."

"And you are taking it?"

"Yes."

"Then get the hell out of here!"

The anteroom to Jean Chiappe's apartment was crowded with friends: Parisians and Corsicans, Rightist Deputies, heads of various leagues and an assortment of indignant colleagues.

Jean Chiappe was in a state of extraordinary excitement. "It seems," he said, "that Frot stated that I'd be at the head of the demonstration tonight down in the street—in shirt sleeves. What an idiot! I merely said I'd be 'out on the street this evening.' They've seen fit to misinterpret me. They want to start trouble. Fire and bloodshed—that's what they want to see in Paris. And they've driven me out of the Prefecture—me—those people, those same people who, only yesterday, congratulated me and thanked me!"

It was a hard blow for Jean Chiappe. Fully aware of his great popularity, the outgoing Prefect was all the more angry. "They say that the Communists and the Socialists demanded my removal. I can understand that, as far as the Communists are concerned. I've always waged war against them, mercilessly. But those Socialists, those ungrateful curs—after all I've done for them!"

The news of the removal of the Prefect of Police had left Paris dazed. This reaction was being exploited to the full by the leaders of the anti-Republican leagues and movements who had, momentarily, been stunned by Daladier's forceful pronouncements. In *La Liberté* André Tardieu published a violent article entitled, "The Horse-Traders Cartel." Another evening paper featured a statement of Paul Reynaud, accusing Daladier of having sacrificed Chiappe in the hope of gaining more Leftist votes, since the Right refused to support his Government. In conclusion, Reynaud summarized the situation in one of his famous slogans: *"Daladier coupe des têtes pour avoir des voix."* ("Daladier cuts off heads in order to get voices—votes.")

Every one of these articles repeated the expression, "National Revolution," which had recently been imported from Germany and Italy.

The following day, street-fighting again broke out. And the police, under orders of their new chief, were extraordinarily mild in their attitude toward the troublemakers. But these clashes were merely preliminaries. The big show was being planned for February 6th—the day on which the Cabinet was to appear before the Parliament. Members of all the war veteran groups, of the quasi-military leagues, of the Rightist organizations and of the Communist Party—all received the same order: to assemble, on February 6th, in front of the Chamber of Deputies for a mammoth demonstration.

The press of Paris was running wild, publishing notices that were nothing more nor less than mobilization orders for a general insurrection.

On February 5th, Colonel de la Rocque led a sort of dress rehearsal through the streets. Numerous policemen and participants in the demonstration were wounded.

Paris-Soir published an appeal to reason, urged its readers to be calm. The Royalist organ, *L'Action Française,* stated that "numerous machine guns have been brought secretly to the Palais Bourbon." Worse than that, both *Le Jour* and *L'Echo de Paris* published a photograph of "a machine-gun company, rushed from the provinces, and intended to intimidate the citizens." I immediately looked into this. I learned that the photograph in question did, in fact, show a machine-gun company that had been brought to Paris—but this company was only one of several contingents that had come to pay military honors at the funeral of General Lefèvre. The funeral had been held that very day. But I also learned that this detachment had already left Paris and had returned to its barracks in the suburbs. . . .

On February 6th, I spent a good part of my time with the reporters who were being sent out to the various parts of the city where demonstrations were expected. Each one of these reporters had been given an assistant and a motorcycle-messenger, so that they might be in constant touch with the office. In each successive edition, we planned to give a true picture of conditions throughout the city.

The first significant bit of news was that Paul Guichard, Director of the Municipal Police, who had long been Jean Chiappe's principal assistant, had now claimed that he would be unable to attend to his duties, inasmuch as he was suffering from an attack of appendicitis.

Then news began coming in of the session of the Chamber of Deputies, at which Daladier was presenting his new Cabinet. As soon as the Premier began to speak, there were shouts from the extreme Left of "Long live the Soviets!" and "Chiappe belongs in jail." From the extreme Right came loud shouts of "Down with the thieves!" and "Chiappe belongs in the Prefecture!" In the meantime, scuffling had broken out among the Deputies.

But Daladier finally managed to read his declaration of policy, and at 5:15 P.M. he obtained his vote of confidence with a majority of over 100 votes.

At just about that time, we received a telephone call from the reporter we had sent out to cover the Place de la Concorde.

"They're shooting," he said. "No blank cartridges. Bullets. A young woman has just been killed. She was standing next to me on a balcony of the Hotel Crillon."

That was the beginning of a flood of gruesome bulletins. Calls came in telling that cafés were being transformed into first-aid stations; that women were being trampled; that dead bodies were being picked up in the streets. Pieces of iron were being thrown. Attempts had been made to set fire to the Ministry of the Navy. Newspaper kiosks had been burned down. Buses had been overturned. The Palais Bourbon was besieged. The barriers had been broken through.

Jean Prouvost insisted that we run an article branding the Government's attitude as infamous. Furthermore, he, himself, wanted to collaborate with his chief editors in writing this editorial.

I tried to reason with him. "Yesterday," I said, "we appealed to the people to be calm. Now—in the midst of an insurrection—we should not stir up emotions and hatred."

He looked at me angrily. "We must follow the crowd," he snapped, "if we want to keep their good-will and confidence."

I began to understand that Jean Prouvost, unfortunately, was lacking in strength of character, in fineness, bigness of spirit. He saw the direction in which public opinion was stampeding at the moment, and his one concern was to tag along. He did not have the courage to attempt to lead the public in another direction.

To avoid having anything to do with the moves he was planning, I suggested that I go to the Chamber of Deputies and cover the story of what Daladier was doing during the insurrection.

The first thing I saw was that a number of the salons and conference rooms were serving as infirmaries for the policemen and guards who had been wounded outside of the Palais Bourbon. "Infirmaries" is not quite the word, however, for no preparations had been made to take care of these unfortunate men. I saw four or five of them lying, unconscious, on a conference-table.

The Chamber was in session, but the commotion and confusion were indescribable. I looked for Daladier. There he was, slumped on his bench, his head bowed. He sat there, motionless, deflated, and almost as though he were unaware of what was going on around him.

The Basque Deputy, Ybarnegaray, had climbed up on his bench. "This is civil war!" he was shouting.

"Who gave the order to fire?" cried Scapini, the blind Deputy.

The distant sound of sustained gun-fire could be heard.

"They're killing each other," someone shouted. "Stop it! Stop it!"

Suddenly, a man rushed up to the Premier, shook a fist within an inch of his face. It was Franklin Bouillon, a Deputy. "You are contemptible," he cried. "You have broken your promises. Get out before the people kick you out."

Daladier did not even raise his head.

The younger Cabinet Ministers—Jean Mistler, Pierre Cot, Guy la Chambre—each, in turn, came up to him.

One of them said: "The mob is firing on 'our' guards, *Monsieur le Président.*"

Then, at last, Daladier looked up. As though in a daze, he stared at his colleagues. "But what are we going to do?" he asked. His voice was plaintive, pathetic.

"We must act," one of the Ministers replied. "We must do something. The Republic must be saved. We've just been given a big majority. That's all that counts."

Daladier appeared to be thinking it over for a moment. Then he made a broad and sweeping gesture—a gesture expressing utter helplessness. Barthe, the Questor of the Chamber of Deputies, came up and whispered a few words into Daladier's ear. Heavily, he got up.

I later found out that he had gone to confer—in one of the small private salons—with four members of the Municipal Council of Paris. These gentlemen had come to urge Daladier to resign.

One of them said to him: "We can guarantee to put an end to the demonstrations, provided we can announce to the people that you are stepping down."

Daladier shook his head. "The Chamber has just given me a vote of confidence," he said. "I'm not resigning. And if you can really exert some influence over the people, do so, unconditionally."

Returning to the Chamber, Daladier was handed a note: a telephone message from Eugène Frot, the Minister of the Interior. A moment later an usher brought him a copy of the latest *Paris-Soir*. Daladier barely looked at the headlines, then angrily crumpled the paper and threw it on the floor.

In the midst of confusion, the session was finally adjourned. I heard the President of the Chamber, Ferdinand Buisson, request the commanders of the Palais Bourbon guards that the men be given regular ammunition again—in an attempt to prevent undue incidents, the guards' ammunition had been withdrawn—but now the rumor was going around that the last barricades, defending the Chamber of Deputies, had been rushed by the mob.

"Turn out the lights," one Deputy cried, in panic. "Then at least they'll think there's nobody here any more."

Daladier was still hesitating, still had no idea of what he should do. He conferred, briefly, with some of his Ministers in one of the private salons. Then, escorted by a Superintendent of Police, they stepped into an automobile and were driven to the Ministry of Foreign Affairs, near by. A number of his colleagues and a few journalists followed him. During the short drive, Daladier covered his eyes with his hands, so as to be spared the sight of the battle that was raging on all sides—the charging mounted police, the men who were falling, the blood that was running—but he could not, at the same time, put his hands to his ears and avoid hearing the whistling of the bullets, the screams of the wounded, and the cries of "Daladier to the gallows!"

We had barely arrived at the Quai d'Orsay, when Daladier left. He had been summoned to the Elysée by President Albert Lebrun.

We then went to the Ministry of the Interior. Eugène Frot received us immediately.

"The riots are decreasing," he said. "And in any event, I want you to know that it's been definitely ascertained that the first shots were fired not by the police, but from somewhere out of the mob. The President of the Council will be here presently. We shall then, together with the Minister of Justice, the Attorney General, the District Attorney and the Prefect of Police—we shall then take all necessary measures to prevent the recurrence of any such demonstrations."

Having reported hurriedly to the President of the Republic, Daladier—still accompanied by Ministers Jean Mistler, Pierre Cot and Guy la Chambre—arrived at the Ministry of the Interior.

The assembled Ministers now rapidly came to a decision: the heads of various leagues were to be arrested. In addition, Daladier demanded an immediate investigation of the plot against the State.

"Have you proof of the existence of any such plot?" the Attorney General asked, dryly. "No? Well, then, don't confuse justice with politics."

Daladier promptly backed water. And, a few minutes later, he again backed water when the Minister of Justice refused to declare a state of siege without consulting the Parliament.

In conclusion, the Ministers agreed to reinforce the troops in Paris.

At 3 A.M. Daladier left for the Ministry of Foreign Affairs. His head was still bowed.

I went up to him. "What are you going to do, *Monsieur le Président*?" I asked.

And then, for the first time that day, this man who had been unable to foresee or to forestall anything, who had been unable to take command in the moment of crisis, now abruptly resumed his strong and determined manner. He squared his shoulders, took a deep breath, and then blustered: "You'll see what I'll do. I'll save the Republic."

But the tone of the morning papers was not at all reassuring; nor were the long lists of the dead and wounded . . . Everywhere the people were calling for the removal of the Daladier Cabinet. And there were reports of new street demonstrations.

Toward noon, I was informed that a provisional revolutionary government was to be proclaimed that very afternoon at the Hôtel de Ville (City Hall). Placards appeared on the walls, demanding the dissolution of Parliament.

And in the meantime, Daladier—under constant attack from all sides—was still unable to make up his mind. But at 11:30 the news was finally announced that Edouard Daladier was on his way to offer his Cabinet's resignation to the President of the Republic.

Ferdinand Buisson, President of the Chamber of Deputies, had been instrumental in helping Daladier come to a decision. Here is what he said, more or less in confidence, to one of *Paris-Soir's* reporters: "You'll never guess what finally decided him to resign. It wasn't the prospect of a continuation of the slaughter in the streets. Not that. But he was afraid that a civil war would inevitably lead to a crisis in the nation's finances."

I had asked Maurice Icart, our Toulouse correspondent, to get an interview, as soon as possible, with the former President of the Republic, Gaston Doumergue, who had retired from politics and who was living in the little village of Tournefeuille. There the ex-President was living contentedly and obscurely with his wife—a writer of stories for young girls—whom he had married secretly in his late seventies.

In France, the name of Gaston Doumergue stood for mellow wisdom, for gentleness and peace. And it occurred to me that this was the man best suited to draw impartial, and constructive conclusions from the unhappy events through which we were living.

Beginning with the 2 P.M. edition, *Paris-Soir* ran Gaston Doumergue's statement, in which he placed himself over and above all political partisanship. Throughout the afternoon, he received telephone calls—from the President of the Republic, from the Presidents of the Chamber of Deputies and of the Senate—urging him, pleading with him—and at 6 P.M. the news came through that Gaston Doumergue had agreed to leave his peaceful retreat and to come to Paris to form a new Cabinet.

His coalition—or, rather, "reconciliation"—Cabinet included members of all Parties, with the exception of the extreme Right and the extreme Left. And even while these consultations and conferences were being held, pillaging, looting and smashing of shopwindows was still going on throughout the night. Then, on February 9th, the city was again shaken by the big Communist uprising which was almost as bloody as the riots of February 6th had been. And on February 12th, a huge demonstration by Socialists and Communists—accompanied by a "general strike of protest"—culminated in an enormous gathering of proletarians at the Cours de Vincennes. This, however, was to be the last spasm of the reaction to the Stavisky Affair.

On February 15th, Gaston Doumergue appeared before the Senate and the Chamber of Deputies and presented his new Cabinet. He received a majority of almost 300 votes.

Tardieu was named Minister of State. Edouard Herriot was also Minister of State. Louis Barthou was Minister of Foreign Affairs. Pierre Laval, Minister for the Colonies. And Marshal Pétain became Minister of War.

The streets of Paris were quiet again.

Chapter Eleven

A Suicide and a Murder

Two committees from the Chamber of Deputies were appointed: one to investigate the Stavisky Affair and the other to examine the consequences of that scandal. Independently, parallel investigations were being carried on by the regular judicial and administrative agencies.

On February 21st I received a telephone call from our correspondent in Dijon.

He said: "You remember Councilor Prince, don't you? The man who indorsed the first adjournments of the case against Stavisky? Well, his body has just been found on the railroad track at Combe-aux-Fées. He had been drugged and then bound to the rails."

Here was the Stavisky Affair in the news again with another tragedy. Minister of the Interior Albert Sarraut, announced officially: "The Councilor Prince has been the victim of a Maffia which we shall apprehend and duly punish."

The death of the Councilor seemed shrouded in darkest mystery. It was known that the magistrate had left his home on February 20th at 11 A.M., after having told his wife that he had received a telephone call summoning him to Dijon immediately to see his sick mother. At Dijon he had taken a room at a hotel—not, however, at the hotel where he usually stopped. Then he had gone to see his friend, Durand, the District Attorney. They had conversed for some time, discussing matters of no special importance. But Prince had not visited his mother; nor was she ill. She was, in fact, enjoying the best of health.

Those were the only known facts covering the last hours of his life.

But the long fingers of the politicians reached out for this corpse, and clung to it as something to be exploited. With a total disregard for the facts, they supplied an interpretation of the mystery that suited their own purposes.

Paris-Soir assigned no fewer than fifteen reporters to the job of getting at the truth in the Prince Affair. The Sûreté Nationale, officially entrusted with the case, did not feel entirely free to act, for the Sûreté, itself, was under attack. It was being widely rumored that Camille Chautemps had instructed the Sûreté to execute Prince.

Inspector Bony ordered the arrest of two notorious gangsters in Marseille—Carbonne and Spirito—who were known to have ordered the underworld of Marseille to vote for Parties of the extreme Right. With regard to the Prince Affair, however, the only thing known against Carbonne and Spirito was that they had been seen in Dijon during the month of February. As soon as I heard of their arrest, I went to the headquarters of the Sûreté Nationale. I had a long conversation with the chief of the Criminal Brigade, Mondanel. He seemed inclined to doubt that the murderer or murderers would ever be apprehended. Furthermore, I learned that Inspector Bony had acted on direct orders from the Minister of the Interior, Albert Sarraut, by whom he had already been entrusted with a number of secret political missions. I was told that these gangsters, Carbonne and Spirito, were connected with the Corsican groups that were friendly with Jean Chiappe. As I left the Sûreté, I felt quite certain that some new complications were to be expected as the result of Inspector Bony's move.

A Mademoiselle Cotillon, a well-known adventuress, offered me "a document against Inspector Bony," as she put it. Since the lady's past did not inspire too much confidence, I refused to take her remarks at all seriously. She left in a rage.

Several days later, *Gringoire* published Mlle. Cotillon's story, considerably rewritten, and made use of the article against the Free Masons and "the corrupt politicians." At Marseille, the Rightist Deputy, Simon Sabiani, presided over indignation meetings and demanded "the immediate release of Carbonne and Spirito." These gangsters had suddenly been promoted to the rank of martyrs.

At *Paris-Soir,* we received thousands of letters, urging us to cast all possible light on the affair. We organized an entire department, devoted exclusively to the investigation of the Prince Affair. We requested all Frenchmen, who might have any kind of information on the subject, to communicate with us. We were overwhelmed with theories submitted by experts and cranks, "eye-witnesses" who were hundreds of miles away and publicity-seekers. We were getting nowhere.

Jean Prouvost then had an idea. "The French police are not making any headway at all," he said. "We'll call on the police who are considered the best in the world, and they'll help us get at the bottom of this case."

Our London office was instructed, therefore, to ask Scotland Yard to lend us the services of two of their very best sleuths. They were to come at our expense. Sir Basil Thompson had already been engaged by us. Two retired English detectives promptly arrived in France. Both of them had achieved extraordinary reputations during their careers. They got to work without delay.

The three detectives left immediately for Dijon. A few days later, they returned to Paris with an exhaustive report. A catastrophic report! The English investigators had arrived at the definite conclusion—based on what they considered incontrovertible evidence—that Councilor Prince had committed suicide. Motive? He had been ashamed of his involvement in the Stavisky Affair. For religious reasons and out of consideration for the honor of his family, he had chosen to commit suicide in such a manner that it would look like a murder.

"We cannot, we simply cannot publish anything like

this," said Jean Prouvost in a panic. "We cannot go against public opinion. The people believe that a crime has been committed, and they don't want to be told that a crime has not been committed. If we say that it was merely a suicide—why, they'll think we're playing politics. And that will be bad for circulation."

He begged the men from Scotland Yard to continue their investigation. He tried to make them reverse their opinion and even offered them large sums of money to change their minds. The English detectives stood their ground. Only after Jean Prouvost had told them that if they insisted on publishing their report it might very well lead to civil war in France did they agree to the compromise of publishing the results of the investigation minus the conclusion of suicide.

Several weeks later the suicide theory was confirmed. The Government had sent Commissaire Guillaume—who, it must be noted, belonged to the Prefecture and not to the Sûreté—to investigate the case. Guillaume had an excellent reputation as a detective. I heard that his report was to be read to the Parliamentary Investigation Committee, and was to be accepted as correct and final.

"If we should be able to get hold of the Guillaume report, which is an official report, would you favor publishing it?" I asked Jean Prouvost.

Embarrassed by the manner in which he had handled the report of the English detectives, he gave his consent.

I instructed one of the political specialists on *Paris-Soir* to get hold of a copy of the Guillaume report at any price. Our man asked one of his friends, the private secretary to one of the members of the Investigation Committee, to let him see the report as a matter of curiosity. As soon as he got his hands on it, he rushed it over to *Paris-Soir*.

We stopped the presses. I asked our typographers to make a special effort to set up this report—which was to cover four full pages of *Paris-Soir*—just as quickly as possible, since we were to return the document to the secretary before the Investigation Committee resumed the hearings. Two hours later *Paris-Soir* was on the streets with the sensational report of Commissaire Guillaume's findings in the Prince Affair. The report revealed that Councilor Prince had long been leading a double life; that he had been subject to acute spells of neurasthenia and depression; that he had told a number of his colleagues that he was constantly harassed by worry and fear that his name might become involved in some scandal; and that he had finally decided to commit suicide.

The public was now willing to accept Commissaire Guillaume's conclusions. Most people were relieved at having the affair finally settled, for they were getting to be increasingly aware of the dangers inherent in the quasi-military leagues which had become even more aggressive and arrogant since Gaston Doumergue had been named Premier.

Then a far more important event was to relegate the Stavisky Affair and its various implications and complications definitely into the background.

The Minister of Foreign Affairs, Louis Barthou, in order to make an impressive demonstration of his foreign policy—notably, the policy of collective security and of defending the integrity of the smaller nations—had formally invited King Alexander of Yugoslavia to visit France. A series of elaborate ceremonies and celebrations was planned to welcome the king.

Paris-Soir sent a special reporter to Marseille to cover the story of the king's arrival. We awaited his call, but it didn't come. I knew that arrangements had been made for him to have a special wire installed on a balcony on the Place de la Bourse, overlooking the procession. At last René Barotte, our special reporter, was on the telephone.

"Well, old man," I said, "is everything O.K.? Have you sent in anything yet?"

"Yes," he said, "I've sent in a few preliminary paragraphs . . . Here comes the procession now. It's getting closer and closer . . . What a lot of noise. . . . But, wait a minute, something has happened, something . . . A man jumped on the running board of the car and . . . He just fired . . . The king has collapsed . . . I can't see very well . . . But, wait, I think Barthou has been hit, too, and General Georges, too. He's in the car . . ."

"What are you talking about?" I demanded.

"I'm not joking. This is no time for jokes. Our photographer is right here, next to me. I think he's managed to take some sensational pictures. He's gone to have them developed. Says he'll wire them in at once . . . Wait a second, people are saying that King Alexander is dead."

I handed the telephone to our chief news editor, a calm and deliberate man. I hurried away to give the necessary instructions. And as I left the room, I heard the news editor make the classic remark on the telephone: "Listen, Barotte, I'm warning you, if the king isn't dead—you're out on your can."

Our entire front page was taken up by a headline announcing the death of the king and of our Minister of Foreign Affairs, together with a splendid picture that spoke for itself. And, thus, the people were provided with another alarming incident, with another reason for sorrow and indignation.

And the political repercussions were to bring on changes of the very greatest international importance. For, at Marshal Pétain's formal request, the Council of Ministers chose Pierre Laval, Minister for the Colonies in the Doumergue Cabinet, to become Minister of Foreign Affairs. Henceforth, under the leadership of Pétain and Laval, our country was to enter upon a new phase in its foreign policy.

Chapter Twelve

Pierre Laval

THE first time I interviewed Pierre Laval, he told me of his childhood and youth, and he cleared up the myth perpetuated by his biographers.

"No," he said, "it's not true. My father was not a butcher, even if people do keep on saying so. I don't trouble to deny the story; it does me no harm. But the truth is that my father was a peasant from Auvergne—not wealthy, but quite comfortable. We had a large house—partly a farmhouse and partly a café—and a few servants who were treated like members of the family. I went to the primary school because there wasn't any other in our village. As far back as I can remember, I always wanted to make a name for myself. That's why I was always so anxious to learn. People have said that I used to deliver meat from my father's store in a wagon. On days when school was closed I did, in fact, drive a cart, loaded with vegetables and animals, down to the station for shipment to the city. Since it was quite a long drive and the horse was an extraordinarily peaceful one, I used to wrap the reins around my legs—and read. I was studying, learning. One day I met the village priest on the road. He asked me if I could take him in to the station. He climbed up and sat beside me and commenced reading his breviary. That gave me an idea. I asked him if he would teach me Latin. He was a good man. He said he would."

Pierre Laval laughed and revealed his tobacco-stained teeth.

"That good old *curé*, he really had reason to be annoyed with me, I'm afraid. One day," he said, "I was carrying the cross in a procession. But my surplice was so long that it was dragging in the mud. My father called to me and told me to lift it up a bit. But I went right along and acted as though I hadn't heard him. Then he came up to me and started shaking me. So I simply put the cross down and ran home. They tried to get me to take my place in the procession again, but it did no good. At that age I was already as stubborn as a mule."

In this manner, going from one anecdote to another, Pierre Laval told me the story of his career.

He had been such a fine scholar that his father willingly made sacrifices to send the boy to a good school in the nearest city. He had taken his bachelor's degree, but his family's finances had not permitted him to continue his studies beyond that point. He had then decided to look for a position as a tutor in a public school, but since he had no references and no influential friends his applications were regularly turned down. However, the Headmaster of the Saint-Ambert Lyceum at Lyon had been so favorably impressed in the course of his first conversation with the young man—had been so struck by the intensity of his enthusiasm and by his manifest desire to succeed—that he promptly employed him.

From the Saint-Ambert Lyceum, Pierre Laval had gone on to the Ampère Lyceum. There he had become acquainted with a brilliant young history professor, a man who had already made quite a name for himself—Edouard Herriot. The two had not, by any means, been attracted to each other.

"Even then," Pierre Laval said, "I had no desire for literary success, and I suppose Herriot was provoked with me because I didn't attend his lectures. I was strongly attracted by the fermenting social movements—the organization of trade-unionism, the workingmen struggling for their rights. Therefore, as soon as I had passed my examinations and had been admitted to the bar in Paris, I decided to specialize in labor questions."

Pierre Laval had opened an office in Aubervilliers, a town in suburban Paris, inhabited largely by the working classes. There he gave consultations to unions as well as to individual workers. His charge for legal advice was one franc, two francs, sometimes three francs. He was beginning to make a name for himself. There were numerous strikes at the time; militant labor leaders were frequently arrested.

In 1914, Aubervilliers sent its Socialist candidate, Pierre Laval, to the Chamber of Deputies.

Faced with a threatening international situation, Pierre Laval passionately espoused the pacifist cause in the Chamber of Deputies. War was declared on August 4, 1914. Because of the views he had expressed, the name of Pierre Laval was down in the famous *Dossier "B"* of the Sûreté Nationale—listed among those who were under suspicion. Tirelessly and boldly he advocated an immediate separate peace with Germany. He was one of the clique of defeatists who surrounded the ex-Premier Joseph Caillaux.

In 1917, it was Pierre Laval who stood up in the Chamber of Deputies and read a report drawn up by Marshal Pétain on the mutinies that had broken out in the Army. This report had arrived at the Ministry of War that very morning. How the document ever got into Deputy Pierre Laval's hands no one knew.

"Make peace at once!" Pierre Laval cried. "For if you don't, the soldiers will come back from the front with their guns in their hands, and they'll force a revolution on you."

Contrary to Pierre Laval's predictions, the war ended in victory and without a revolution. In the first post-war elections, the Socialists were swept away and Pierre Laval lost his seat in the Chamber.

In the meantime, however, he had made some valuable connections. Joseph Caillaux had introduced him to men high in Parisian society and to certain big industrialists. These gentlemen—including François de Wendel, head of the powerful Comité des Forges—did not fail to recognize Laval's cleverness as an attorney, and readily gave him their legal business. Thus Pierre Laval was no longer defending the cause of the workingmen and of the unions, but of big business.

He had been waiting, apparently, to break the bonds which held him to the political discipline of one group. When the Congress of Tours ended in an open break between the Socialists and the Communists, Pierre Laval speedily resigned from his Party. Running as a so-called Independent Socialist, he was elected Mayor of Aubervilliers by a large majority.

In 1924, when the question of Franco-German *rapprochement* arose, the Leftist *cartel* won a majority of seats. Then, in turn, the Rightists came back to power as the *bloc national.*

Pierre Laval had been re-elected in the meantime. Painlevé named him Minister of Public Works. More and more Pierre Laval continued to drift toward the Right. He was now a successful corporation lawyer.

As early as 1930 he said: "I believe that people can best be cared for without consulting their wishes."

Over a period of time he had acquired, successively, a large coal business and a mineral-water enterprise (whereupon hospitals, steamships and dining-cars were ordered to serve this invaluable spring water). Laval took over a chain of provincial newspapers. He was highly successful in numerous real-estate operations, and proved himself to be an extraordinarily skillful trader on the Bourse.

During his stay in Rome, Pierre Laval had paid an official visit to the Vatican, and had been honored with the title of Papal Count.

His daughter, José, married a descendant of Lafayette—René de Chambrun.

In 1930, Pierre Laval was elected Senator from the Seine, largely by the votes of the Moderates. Throughout his term of office, he was greatly feared by the successive heads of the Government because of the influence he wielded in the cloakrooms and corridors.

At the special request of Pétain, Pierre Laval had been named Minister of Foreign Affairs in the Doumergue

Cabinet. He held the same portfolio in the following Cabinet—Pierre Etienne Flandin's. Then, in June, 1935, he was made Premier.

Slowly, cautiously, but stubbornly, he worked toward his objective—to become absolute head of his country. France, at this time, was faced by three grave dangers: the acute internal political crisis, the deepening financial depression and the international tension brought on by Hitler's accession to power.

One of Laval's first moves was to ask Hitler to have a frank, direct talk with him. But the Führer had not yet reached the point of summoning the heads of foreign Governments to Berchtesgaden. Hitler sent Pierre Laval his trusted von Ribbentrop, the former champagne agent who was now traveling salesman for Nazism. Laval told von Ribbentrop that he was desirous of improving relations with Hitler's Germany along the lines previously discussed with the Bruening Government. And—as Ribbentrop was proudly to tell his French friends before leaving—Pierre Laval took advantage of the occasion to express his admiration for "the great man who is in Germany," and to hint rather broadly that certain modifications might very well be made with regard to the Treaty of Versailles.

Pierre Laval went to Rome in January, 1935, in order to eliminate certain points of friction between the two countries. He had known Mussolini when both of them had been militant Socialists.

The agreement which Laval brought back from Rome was well received. In return for some slices of African desert, for some shares in the Djibouti-Addis Ababa Railroad and for some favors to be granted the Italians living in Tunisia, Il Duce solemnly undertook to insist upon the integrity of the frontiers of Austria and to oppose unauthorized rearmament on the part of Germany.

Our political editor, who had gone to Rome with the Laval mission, had learned something else from one of Mussolini's closest collaborators. According to our usually well-informed editor, Mussolini had asked the following question: "Supposing Italy wanted to deal with Ethiopia as France has already dealt with Morocco—what would the attitude of France be?" And Pierre Laval is said to have replied: "I'll see to it that France will look on without saying a word. We won't have any trouble on that score." This brief dialogue was, of course, as important as the formal agreement. And, through some leak, the story got around to many newspapermen. But not one paper published it. Why not? Some said that they did not want to "embarrass the Quai d'Orsay's foreign policy." Others—including the most violently anti-Laval papers—said that they refrained from publishing the item because they were perfectly satisfied so long as Germany was encircled. The majority, however, were silent because Laval wanted them to be. Most of the owners or directors of the big Paris newspapers were his friends or his clients—or both. There was Pierre Guimier, notably, of *Le Journal.* And Bunau-Varilla—Laval had done him many favors in the past. And the directors of the big provincial newspapers were Pierre Laval's colleagues; he had repeatedly intervened on their behalf and had obtained facilities for them from the Government.

On March 1st, the Plebiscite in the Saar gave a 90 percent majority in favor of returning to Germany. France had in no way attempted to influence the vote—no propaganda whatsoever—lest someone be offended. A fortnight later, Hitler introduced compulsory military service throughout the Reich. France, England and Italy did nothing more than enter a formal protest. No, that's incorrect, they did something more than that: they requested summoning the League of Nations for an extraordinary session. The failure of the Sir John Simon-Hitler interview had seemed alarming, even to Pierre Laval. He recognized the necessity for holding certain trump cards with which to impress the German dictator, who, clearly, was becoming more and more obstreperous. A conference was called, therefore, at Stresa. Here, the principles of Locarno were reaffirmed; the idea of an Eastern Locarno was suggested; and it was decided to hold a congress of the Danubian States at Rome.

Shortly afterward, Pierre Laval left for the Soviet Union. He had commenced to be concerned about the Communist activities in France. Furthermore, among the papers left by his predecessor, Louis Barthou, he had found the draft of a Franco-Soviet treaty which needed only to be signed. On this trip, Laval was accompanied by a large suite. And newspapermen, who went along, told me how flattered Laval had been by the demonstrations staged in his honor, and also how surprised the Russians had been when they saw that Stalin really seemed to like his guest.

When Laval returned to Paris early in May, he brought back not only a Franco-Soviet pact and the bugbear of an Eastern Locarno to intimidate Germany, but also a statement from Stalin obliging, in effect, the French Communists to revise their attitude completely. The master of the Kremlin thoroughly approved of the French rearmament program, and the mere expression of this opinion on his part served as an order to the Communists to cease their opposition to the law providing for two years of military service in France.

On his way back from Russia, Pierre Laval had stopped off at Warsaw. There, with Marshal Pétain, he had represented France at the funeral of Marshal Pilsudski. Germany had sent Marshal Goering. After the ceremony, Pétain, Laval and Goering had a long conversation; and that evening the conversation had been continued—without Marshal Pétain—late into the night (at Goering's hotel).

Playing both ends against the middle—and moved most especially by his desire to appease the Germans—Pierre Laval had once again demonstrated his talents as a horse trader. Had he, in fact, gone to Moscow in the first place with any other object in mind? The Pact was to go into effect as soon as ratified by the French Parliament. After his lengthy conversation with Goering, however, Laval decided that there was no hurry at all about having the Pact ratified.

Forestalling English criticism, Laval took the first opportunity to accuse British diplomacy of similarly deplorable behavior. Sadly, as though profoundly disillusioned, he said to a group of newspapermen (who were, of course, to write appropriate articles on the subject): "England has just struck a terrible blow at the Stresa Front by signing a naval agreement with Germany. The Reich is thereby permitted to build a navy up to 35 percent of the British tonnage—that is to say, a navy that is just twice as strong as the one authorized by the Treaty of Versailles. Neither France nor Italy was consulted before this document was signed—this document, which, you will note, constitutes the first formal approval of an infraction of the Treaty of Versailles—the Treaty which the English, at Stresa, promised to defend."

Laval had remained in direct—although secret—contact with Il Duce. On October 3, 1935, when Italy launched her offensive against Ethiopia and feelings ran high again in France, Pierre Laval calmly continued to play his game, in which his personal stand was diametrically opposed to his official attitude. To keep from being ousted by Parliament, he openly favored the policy of sanctions by the League of Nations; and at the same time he was secretly trying to arrange an Anglo-Italian *entente* which was later to be notorious as the Hoare-Laval plan.

In the Chamber of Deputies, Paul Reynaud attacked Pierre Laval, and declared that "France must choose between Italy which has broken the covenant of the League of Nations, and England, the guardian of the covenant which is the strongest rampart against aggression."

"France is losing her prestige among the smaller States," Paul Reynaud said to me. "The covenant is their only protection. And it was France that created these States, promising to protect them, for they are our first line of defense against Germany. Now we're playing—and losing—an incalculably dangerous game."

I told Paul Reynaud how alarmed I was at the sight of so many German, Italian and Russian agents—all trying to create disunity and confusion in France. "There is a lot of talk about Rightist leagues and Communist agitation. What ought to be done," I said, "is to investigate those hidden hands that are pulling the strings."

"Yes," said Reynaud, "I know. But the French have been taught to look at foreign policies through the glasses of domestic politics. Their vision is distorted. And, as a result, the invasion has already started."

This was early in 1936.

Chapter Thirteen

Otto Abetz, Nazi Agent

IS IT true that you've become a Nazi, Otto Abetz?" I asked.

He had changed considerably since I'd last seen him. He wasn't the provincial little drawing teacher any more, in a sweater and espadrilles. He looked like a gentleman now. He still claimed that he was working for Franco-German rapprochement, but now it was to be through the National Socialist Party, which he had joined.

Since 1932 Joachim von Ribbentrop had tried to interest Abetz in the Hitler movement.

After Hitler had come to power, von Ribbentrop had redoubled his efforts to enlist Otto Abetz. For this young man, who had made so many friends in France and whom no one could possibly suspect of bad faith, would surely make an ideal agent for the Führer. He was indispensable.

Glittering promises were held out to him. He would be rich, he would be showered with honors, and his mission would bring him fame and glory. . . . His wife had just given birth to a second child. They were so poor that his wife had written to Paris, asking for some cast-off clothing for her son and for some things for the infant girl . . . Abetz finally accepted the Nazi proposition.

Now he was installed in Berlin, in the so-called Ribbentropburo, in charge of the French department. The former Christian Democrat was entrusted with the job of spreading Nazi propaganda in France.

He returned to Paris. He was, in truth, more of a Francophile than ever. He saw all his old friends—writers, newspapermen, political figures. He even attempted to keep the annual Franco-German youth camps going, but the meeting during the summer vacations of 1934 was a complete fiasco. The youth of France were beginning to get suspicious. Nor were they reassured when the story got around that, at the station to greet the handful of French guests at the camp, Otto Abetz had been decked out in a brown shirt with a swastika arm band.

Otto Abetz continued to make more and more connections in France. The Leftists, it is true, had become slightly less enthusiastic about Franco-German *rapprochement* since Hitler's accession to power, but they continued to see Abetz. Since they were primarily pacifists, they enjoyed hearing a German and also a Nazi affirm that they need not fear a war of aggression. The men of the political Center and the Right fondly saw in the new German regime the only effective rampart against Communism.

The doors of the most exclusive *salons* were opened to Otto Abetz. He had charm. He would tell the most fascinating anecdotes about the mysterious man who was now the master of Germany. He would reassure his listeners that they had nothing to fear from the new Chancellor's rough words and abrupt actions or from the threats against France contained in *Mein Kampf*.

As early as 1934 Otto Abetz was taken to see Pierre Laval by his old friends, Jean Luchaire, Bertrand de Jouvenel and Philippe Boegner, whose father was the head of the Protestant Church in France. From 1934 on, Abetz was in touch with the leaders of the powerful War Veteran groups, and with the organizations which had taken a prominent part in the bloody February uprisings. Evidently he convinced them of Hitler's desire to rely upon the War Veterans of 1914 to maintain better relations between the two great continental Powers. The leaders of the Veteran groups were vociferous patriots and embittered politicians. They were disappointed because they were not playing roles of the first magnitude in the politics of their country.

Toward the end of 1934, two of them—Jean Goy and Henri Pichot—founded the *Comité France-Allemagne,* which was the counterpart to the Germany-France Committee, recently inaugurated in Germany by Hitler.

Otto Abetz had become particularly friendly with a French journalist by the name of Count Fernand de Brinon. This gentleman, who was not lacking in ability and tact and shrewdness, had always been looked upon as a man of doubtful character. He had commenced his career as editor of a racing paper, and had then been promoted to the rank of manager of the racing stables belonging to the king of the Paris bookmakers, Elie Heliopolos. He had already divorced his first wife, an actress in the Comédie Française, and had married a wealthy Jewish girl, a granddaughter of the Grand Rabbi of Strasbourg. He found employment with a group of financiers as director of publicity and advertising for new issues of stocks and bonds. These financial affiliations inevitably led him into political circles.

Despite the fact that his wife was a Jewess, he had been playing with the idea of offering his services to the new regime in Germany. The leaders of the so-called Radical Party—notably Daladier and Georges Bonnet—found good use for Fernand de Brinon. But it was especially with Pierre Laval that he had allied himself politically.

Then Fernand de Brinon's career really began to take shape. His good friend, Otto Abetz, took him to Berlin and arranged an interview for him with the Führer. Fernand de Brinon returned from this trip with an eloquent appeal from Hitler himself—from a German war veteran to all the veterans of France—an appeal for understanding and co-operation between the two countries. This manifesto was published by *Le Matin,* and was immediately followed by an invitation to the French War Veteran groups to attend a celebration in honor of the German War Veterans. An impressive contingent of French veterans arrived in Berlin. They were loudly cheered by the population. And when these men returned to their homes, they were convinced of the Third Reich's friendly and peaceful intentions.

Following the example of Jean Goy and Henri Pichot, many other prominent French veterans—including Major L'Hospital, former *aide-de-camp* of Marshal Foch; Scapini, the Deputy who had been blinded in the war; Henri-Haye, then Deputy from Versailles—all joined the *Comité France-Allemagne* and came into direct contact with the Nazis.

In Berlin, the sumptuous mansion in the Hildegardestrasse, occupied by the Franco-German Society, was always crowded with guests. The enterprising Otto Abetz had transformed a dozen or so of the rooms into luxurious bedrooms for transient visitors, and had engaged the services of one of the most celebrated chefs on the Continent. Among the distinguished Frenchmen entertained here were Henri Bordeaux, of the French Academy, Alphonse de Chateaubriand, winner of the Prix Goncourt, and the novelist, Drieu la Rochelle. Former Communists—such as Ramon Fernandez—also paid their respects, and even certain Jews, such as Emmanuel Berl.

When Otto Abetz invited us—my wife and myself—we rather emphatically declined. But he was quite persistent, and thought he might get us to change our minds by saying: "If it's because you're Jewish, why, you're making a big mistake. We'll be glad to declare you honorary Aryans."

Early in February 1936, one of my associates on *Paris-Soir,* Bertrand de Jouvenel, was awakened early in the morning by a telephone call.

"Hello, Bertrand? . . . This is Otto Abetz. . . . I've just arrived in Paris. Listen, you're still on *Paris-Soir*?"

"Yes. Why?"

"Well, listen," Otto Abetz went on. "You've been wanting to interview the Führer for a long time, haven't you? Well, I've arranged it for you. But you must go to Berlin with me immediately."

Bertrand de Jouvenel notified me at once.

He was received without delay at the Chancellery. Hitler first spoke of de Jouvenel's father, the former Ambassador and Minister, then, briefly, about Bertrand, himself. And then, abruptly, he came out with a sensational statement. What Hitler said was that he would be willing to sign a twenty-five-year non-aggression pact with France—*provided* the Franco-Soviet Pact were abrogated by France—for he could not have complete confidence in a country which was allied with "destructive Communism."

Bertrand de Jouvenel was asked to write up his report of the interview on his way home on the train. Otto Abetz would look over the article on behalf of the Führer. There was to be no delay.

All the circumstances were suspicious: the haste, the secrecy and, above all, the fact that Hitler had seen fit to make this highly important proposition to the Government through a newspaperman and not through the customary diplomatic channels. Jean Prouvost immediately sensed the motive: the idea was to publish the interview in the most important newspaper in France in order to stir up public opinion, which, in turn, would influence the Deputies who were going to be asked to vote the ratification of the Laval-Stalin pact. Since we had agreed to publish the interview, we were obliged to do so; but, we decided to publish it in *Paris-Midi,* which, of course, had a much smaller circulation than *Paris-Soir.* Furthermore, our lengthy discussions and deliberate shilly-shallying had the net result that the report of the famous interview was not published until the very day the Russian pact was to be considered in the Chamber of Deputies.

Otto Abetz came to see us. He was foaming at the mouth. "Everything has been ruined," he exclaimed. "You've made a Franco-German alliance impossible."

"Now look here," I said. "You wanted to influence public opinion in this country against the pact with Russia. We can't permit ourselves to get involved in any such interference on the part of a foreign country in our own affairs. What would you say if, for example, the head of our Government were to appeal to the German people in some such manner—advising them to oppose a plan of Hitler's?"

After a moment Abetz said, smiling cynically: "You

seem to overlook the fact, *mon cher,* that in my country the press is strictly controlled."

German agents in France were becoming more and more daring. By studying Abetz's methods, the whole pattern of Fifth Column activities became clear. First, there were the spies whose duty it was to acquire information concerning the country's military and industrial establishments, and who reported directly to Goering's headquarters. Second, there were the propaganda agents, under Dr. Goebbels. Then, third, there were the agents under von Ribbentrop, whose function it was to create discontent and unrest in the country to which they were assigned. Finally, there were the Gestapo agents, under Himmler, whose primary function consisted in watching all other agents. Not only did these four branches operate independently, but the individual agents did not, as a rule, even know one another.

Von Ribbentrop supervised two departments: the organizations of Germans living outside of Germany and, the agents engaged in influencing public opinion in the country to which they were assigned, usually officials from the Wilhelmstrasse or members of the famous Ribbentropburo.

Von Ribbentrop's men were specialists who had studied the history, language, customs and political and social life of the countries in which they were to operate. In each country, the outstanding agent was assigned the exclusive task of taking "psychological soundings." The reports sent in by this super-agent enabled Headquarters to outline a general plan of attack against the given country from within and to specify the individual duty of each agent, permanent as well as transient.

Otto Abetz was the man who was taking the "psychological soundings" in France. He did not engage directly in espionage. His role was to charm, to persuade, to convince. It was up to him to find out how a given individual could best be approached and won over.

In France, the methods used were flatteringly subtle. A writer, for example, would be offered a handsome sum for the translation rights of a book which had never been a conspicuous success in the first place. An industrialist would receive an offer of a share in an important Franco-German corporation which was about to be launched. Or a journalist would receive an invitation to come to Germany and get a close-up view of the Hitler regime in all its glory. Or, in the case of a gentleman who enjoyed hearing the sound of his own voice, a series of lectures would be arranged. If the gentleman should happen to be a disappointed politician, he would be told that it was surprising that a man of his caliber had not achieved the very highest rank—but that, after all, what could one expect under "the corrupt regime in France"—and that he would be given the actual means with which to organize a new political party of his own, etc., etc.

And it worked!

In this manner, Otto Abetz succeeded in injecting Nazi poison into the French bloodstream. Of all the men who were, in effect, Otto Abetz's accomplices, not one in a thousand was an agent paid to sell out his country; most of them, in fact, allowed themselves to be persuaded that they were acting in the best interests of France.

In 1936, a German agent by the name of Hans Slatten[1] came to the offices of *Paris-Soir* and gave me an outline—drawn up by Hitler himself, he said—of the strategy of the propaganda to be applied to France. The French Military Information Department did not want to have anything to do with him. He finally left for London. I don't know what became of him.

Here are the outlines for the propaganda campaign:

French public opinion is to be molded, until the French are convinced that:

1) they have everything to gain by making an alliance with Germany; and that if France does not soon enter into such an alliance, England will; and that such an Anglo-German alliance would constitute a real danger for France.

2) that Germany has no claims against France; that Germany wants only one thing—to be permitted to live; that it would be to the great advantage of France to authorize the

[1] For obvious reasons, this is not the German agent's correct name. This is the only fictitious name in my book.

abrogation of the Clauses of the Treaty of Versailles, which are strangling Germany; and that Germany wants only to re-incorporate her mistreated national minorities, and will forever renounce her claims to Alsace and Lorraine and will not consider the Germans there as representing such minorities.

3) that France today is not strong enough, either demographically or militarily, to play the role of a Great Power; that she would be unable successfully to defend the small States, created by the Treaty of Versailles, with which she has neither a common frontier nor, in fact, any common interest. . . . The agent is to stress the point that France must direct all her energies toward preserving the integrity of her Empire. In this connection, the agent is to say that Germany's demands for the return of her lost colonies are of no immediate consequence; and that, in any event, these questions will never lead to war, insofar as Germany is concerned, since they will, in time, be discussed diplomatically on a strictly economic basis.

4) that Hitler has urged, and France has opposed, disarmament; and that Germany was obliged, therefore, to proceed with a rearmament program on a vast scale, giving her an overwhelming preponderance of military power. . . . The agent is to stress this point. The French are to be frightened. But at the same time all the latest reports on German rearmament are to be denied or at least to be minimized—and to be made the subject for lively controversy.

5) The French are to be terrified by the threat of Bolshevism. The agent must stress that Germany, and Germany alone, can effectively defend France against the Soviet menace.

6) Constantly stir up quarrels between political factions. Create and encourage discussion of internal political questions. Support all anti-democratic movements, *including those which are also anti-German.* Support all anti-Fascist movements, in order to drive a wedge between France and Italy.

7) Support all pacifist movements and give them—discreetly, indirectly—all possible aid. Also supply them with arguments. The Leftist pacifists cannot possibly be suspected of being on our side. *They are, therefore, our most valuable allies.*

8) Wherever possible, put our watchwords and slogans into the mouths of Frenchmen belonging to all classes, and especially of men prominent in political circles, in society, journalism, administration, in the Army and Navy, and in trade unions. Naturally, these Frenchmen are to repeat and spread our slogans in good faith and spontaneously. Each man must, therefore, be approached and converted according to his individual tendencies, idiosyncrasies—either along lines of ideology or of religious conviction, or with special regard for his obsessions, his ambition or his vanity.

9) Incite to anti-Semitism. Organize anti-Semitic campaigns —to be as violent as possible. At the same time, spread the news among Jewish circles, notably among the financiers, that the Decrees of Nürnberg are not intended for export. Stress that anti-Semitism could arise in France only as the result of a war against Germany, or if the Jews should try to push France into such a war or into the arms of the Soviet.

10) Spread the idea, gradually, that it would be best for France to give Germany a free hand in the East. Satisfying her need for expansion in this direction, the Reich would simultaneously be ridding Europe of the threat of Bolshevism.

11) The agent is to arrange for publication of newspaper articles intended to arouse the French against: a) England, by showing that France is under the domination of this selfish nation; b) Bolshevik Russia, by showing that Russia is trying to incite France to wage a war against Germany, in order to eliminate Germany as a danger to Russia—a war in which Russia would take no part; c) the United States, by showing that isolationism is gaining ground there and that the Americans will not again be dragged into a European war by Allied propaganda (furthermore, stress the war debts, which place France in an awkward position in its relations with the U.S.); d) the South American countries, by showing them to be pro-German; e) Italy, by stressing their territorial ambitions in Africa, thus conflicting with the interests of France.

I had ample occasion to observe that the Nazi agents in France did, indeed, operate precisely along the lines indicated in this document.

Two other documents—definitely authenticated documents which were both published later and attracted little if any attention—corroborated the document given me by Hans Slatten. The first of these was a letter written in 1932 by Hitler to von Papen, in which he emphasizes his intention of holding France responsible for the failure of disarmament; the second document was a note of the Führer's to the effect that a wedge should be driven between France and Italy. The Nazi Party tried in vain to prevent publication of this note in the foreign press.

This Hans Slatten was the only Nazi agent who ever came to us with an offer to work against his Party.

Hans Slatten also volunteered the information that Nazi Germany had informed Messrs. Pierre Etienne Flandin and Pierre Laval, who were then in power, that she would consider it to be an "unfriendly act" if General Weygand were retained as Generalissimo beyond his retirement age.

Weygand's plans provided for an offensive army. His idea was to expand the professional Army; this nucleus of highly trained specialists would enable France to constitute expeditionary corps with which to defend the smaller States. Hitler, of course, knew of Weygand's plans; and he also knew that Gamelin, Weygand's probable successor, was fanatically in favor of a purely defensive army. Skillful propaganda had portrayed Weygand as a reactionary general who was quite capable of staging a *coup d'état,* and whose military theories justified the accusation that France was "imperialistic." Gamelin, on the contrary, had many followers among the Leftists, who approved of his defensive theories. And so, on January 21, 1935, when Pierre Etienne Flandin replaced Weygand with Gamelin "to avoid irritating Hitler," the Leftist majority in the Chamber of Deputies was delighted—almost as delighted as was Herr Hitler himself. *And, despite Weygand's reputation as a soldier, there was practically not a word of protest in the entire press.*

I spoke of Otto Abetz to Hans Slatten. He had heard Abetz's name mentioned, but did not know just what he was supposed to be doing in France. Hans Slatten had been working under Dr. Schmoll, Press Attaché at the German Embassy. I had originally met Slatten with Dr. Schmoll. Whenever Otto Abetz pointed out that a certain newspaper director might readily be "persuaded" to support the German viewpoint, Dr. Schmoll would make his appearance. But he would never directly and grossly dispense favors and rewards. Hitler's Germany was too shrewd to leave any evidence of out-and-out corruption. The usual procedure was that representatives of the given newspaper would be put in touch with the advertising managers of big German firms, notably I. G. Farbengesellschafft and Bayer, the big chemical and pharmaceutical interests. These corporations had branches in France. And it was through these French companies that the newspapers received their subsidies in the form of advertising contracts at very fancy prices. However, more often than not, this advertising matter was never published after the contract had been signed.

It was also from Hans Slatten that I first heard about the banker Hirsch, who served as a middle-man for the distribution of German money in France, and whose special function it was to spread corruption in industrial and private circles.

I was surprised. "Isn't this Monsieur Hirsch a Jew?" I asked.

"Why, of course," Hans Slatten replied. "He's a naturalized refugee and pretends to be violently anti-Nazi. That's why no one could ever possibly suspect him. You haven't any idea of the number of German refugees who are working for us. We've got them in the palm of our hand. And it's an easy matter to keep them that way. For one thing, many of them have relatives in Germany, and are afraid of reprisals. Others hope to be able to rescue some of their property. And some even want to go back to Germany. Well, after all, it's their home, it's their country."

Chapter Fourteen

The Führer's Social Brigade

EXCLUDED from wielding any power officially, the social leaders among the women of France exerted an influence that was as dangerous as it was subtle and insidious. One might almost assert that, before the outbreak of the Second World War, the fate of Europe was being decided in the mansion of Madame Marthe de Fels, in the white and red *salons* of Countess Madeleine de Montgomery, in the drawing rooms of Madame Horace de Carbuccia and of Marie-Louise Bousquet, at the teas given by Jeanne de Crussol, at the luncheons of Marie Laure de Noailles, at the dinners of the Duchess Antoinette d'Harcourt and of the Baroness Philippe de Rothschild, and at Lady Mendl's lavish parties in Versailles.

Who are—or were—these ladies? You weren't much of a Parisian if you didn't know who they were, and you were certainly not in the swim if they didn't know you. If, by any chance, you weren't aware of the fact that the Countess de Montgomery's nickname was "Minou," you were a rank outsider, and you were an even worse outcast if you didn't know that Madame Horace de Carbuccia always liked to be called "Adry."

Each *salon* had its habitués, its stars and its own special customs. Paul Reynaud—walking almost on tiptoe to appear taller, and with his hands in the arm-holes of his vest—was regularly to be seen and heard orating at "Minou" de Montgomery's.

This lady, intelligent and patriotic, divorced from an immensely wealthy industrialist, was the heiress of the owners of the famous Noilly-Prat apéritif. Slender, graceful, high-strung, with ash-blonde hair and aquamarine eyes, her beauty and personality stimulated the gentlemen to engage in interminable tournaments of ideas and lofty flights of eloquence. As a hostess, she was an artist. Ambassadors William Bullitt of the United States, Lucasiewics of Poland and Carcano of the Argentine were among "Minou's" regular guests; prominent French political figures, such as Georges Bonnet; directors of big French and foreign newspapers, such as Jean Prouvost (*Paris-Soir*), Pierre Guimier (*Le Journal*), and Lord Camerose (*London Daily Telegraph*); renowned *couturières*, such as Chanel and Schiaparelli; members of the international social set, such as the Duke and Duchess Jean d'Ayen, the Honorable Daisy Fellowes and Lady Mendl; bankers, big industrialists, and so on. "Minou" directed a women's magazine and did some work for charitable organizations, but she still found time and energy to establish contacts with the greatest variety of personalities, to further the careers of people in whom she had confidence, and to strengthen the position of her friends in politics. The general public knew nothing about her.

Except for an occasional new face and for the star performer, the *salons* all put on the same show with the same cast; the only real difference lay in the scenery and lighting effects. You met the same crowd at "Minou's" as at Countess Marthe de Fels' sumptuous mansion. (*Née* Mademoiselle de Cumont, she was married to the youthful and enormously wealthy Deputy, André de Fels.) A large, buxom woman, hearty and friendly, she moved her pawns subtly and shrewdly on the chessboard of politics and diplomacy. The brightest star of her *salon* was the Secretary-General of the Ministry of Foreign Affairs, Alexis Léger. He held his audience spellbound when he discussed his views on foreign policy, speaking with great charm and with truly poetic imagery.

If you really "belonged," your social calendar for one week might very well include a luncheon at Marthe de Fels', a dinner at "Minou's" and a late supper in the ultra-modern cellar apartment, with black-and-white marble flagstones, of the ravishing Florence Jay Gould (an American by marriage). During this week, you would also find time to attend a dance or a garden-party given at Versailles by Lady Mendl. (This octogenarian interior decorator, who persisted in being youthful, was an American by birth and had married an English diplomat.) Then, late in the week, there would be just one more dinner to attend: in Madame Paul Guillaume's spacious apartment near the Bois de Boulogne.

Where else besides in the homes of these charming ladies could our politicians and our diplomats have met and talked, informally and without restraint? There was always a chance of making some valuable contacts at these gatherings. One might, in the course of a whispered conversation, discover a valuable political ally. Or one might succeed in coming to a friendly understanding with a powerful newspaper director. One might even extract from a foreign diplomat some significant hints as to his country's fundamental foreign policy.

Otto Abetz had soon succeeded in making his way into these circles, as had also another German agent, Friedrich Siebourg. The latter, a writer of talent, who spoke French perfectly, had for many years—since long before Hitler—been Paris correspondent of the *Frankfurter Zeitung*. As a young man, he had established his literary reputation with the book, *Dieu, Est-Il Francais?* He was handsome, witty, and had a beautiful wife. He had gained distinction as a Don Juan when, out of love for him, the wife of a Parisian author had committed suicide.

In these salons, Abetz and Siebourg could not only spread the Nazi Party "line," but they could also overhear many a state secret, for, in order to impress the ladies or merely out of carelessness, some of the French politicians spoke too freely, and told of what had occurred at ministerial conferences and secret committee meetings.

It is well known today that Hitler undertook all his major moves contrary to the advice of his military leaders. This was true in the Rhineland, in Austria and in Prague; in each of these instances Hitler's decisions were based on information of a political nature, and were made in defiance of warnings from the Reich's leading technicians. Who had supplied Hitler with this accurate political information? Unquestionably, Hitler permitted himself to make certain moves against France because he had been informed that highly influential Frenchmen—Cabinet Ministers, owners of powerful newspapers, high officials—had said, over the dinner table, "No, we won't fight for Austria . . . No, not for Prague . . . No, we won't try to prevent the remilitarization of the Rhineland."

These casual, informal—but highly significant—remarks had been promptly transmitted to Berlin. It was of incalculable value to Hitler to know that certain political leaders of France were beginning to break under the strain of the war of nerves or were, perhaps, beginning to change their minds and their attitudes for other reasons. Information of this kind certainly served to open the road to Paris. And this information was supplied by Abetz, Siebourg and a handful of fools, snobs and unwitting traitors who belonged to Otto Abetz's so-called Social Brigade.

In all fairness, it must be said of the women who held these social *salons* that, as a rule, the role they played in the tragedy of France was only accidental. Some of them even sensed the danger, and soon closed their doors to those whom they suspected of subversive activities.

The name of Madeleine de Montgomery should be mentioned as outstanding among these clear-sighted women. As she became increasingly aware of the dangerous undercurrents, she devoted herself more and more to making use of her great influence with owners of newspapers and numerous political personalities.

Attempts were made, however, to change her mind. Since it was known that she was passionately interested in hunting, she received a personal invitation from Marshal Goering, asking her to attend the International Hunting Congress to be held in Berlin. The Duchess Antoinette d'Harcourt received a similar invitation.

Goering went to extravagant lengths to entertain his distinguished guests. There was an endless round of sumptuous entertainment. The Marshal wore his most dazzling uniforms.

When the Countess Madeleine de Montgomery had returned to Paris, she said: "He tried too hard. It was easy enough to see that there was method in his madness. I'll never allow any of these Germans to enter my house again. Never!"

But the Duchess Antoinette d'Harcourt was less discerning. She was manifestly impressed by Goering's elaborate show. Following her return from Germany, she became a fervent supporter of the *Comité France-Allemagne*, and saw to it that her husband, a young Deputy, was named as one of its directors.

A number of French noblemen were readily persuaded to support the Nazi propaganda drive. The worst of these was a fat, flabby, bald-headed young man of distinctly mediocre intelligence, but of an excellent family—Thierry de Ludre. The de Ludres had long been established at the Château de Richard-Mesnil, on the banks of the Moselle, a few miles from Nancy. They were connected with all the old families of the province—the Princes de Beauveau, the Comtes d'Alsace, de Scitivaux, the Marquis de Lambertye—all members of what was known in heraldic terms as "the little and the big horses of Lorraine."

Thierry de Ludre's father had been a cavalry officer, Nationalist Deputy from Nancy and a friend of the great Lorraine patriots—Briand, Poincaré, Louis Marin and André Maginot. His mother was a granddaughter of Marshal Count Berthier, Napoleon's aide-de-camp. Thierry de Ludre was expected to grow up in the old tradition. But he hated all that. All Lorraine had the most deeply rooted feeling of mistrust of Germany. Thierry de Ludre soon came out with pro-German sentiments. As early as 1928, when he was twenty—and shortly after the death of his father—he conducted an electoral campaign by advancing ideas diametrically opposed to those advocated by his late father. He claimed that Poincaré had been responsible for the war; he violently attacked Clemenceau and "French militarism," and was lavish in his praise of Stresemann. As a matter of fact, Thierry de Ludre looked very much like the German Chancellor, and was proud of this resemblance. He would attempt to justify his infatuation for Germany by repeating that he had some genuine Wittelsbach blood in his veins. His great-grandfather, Marshal Berthier, had married a Princess of the reigning family of Bavaria. Naturally, Thierry always made a point of mentioning this fact when conversing with Germans.

When the Nazis came to power, Thierry de Ludre began spending more and more time in Germany. He was frequently to be seen at the Hotel Stephanie in Baden-Baden and at the home of Frau Haniel, who controlled the great Rhine River navigation interests. There Thierry de Ludre would meet Gauleiter Wagner, coming from Karlsruhe with Otto Abetz, Rudolph Hess and von Papen. The latter would take them to the races, together with Frau von Papen and her two daughters. The von Papens entertained Thierry de Ludre at the estate of the Villeroys (Frau von Papen's parents) in the Saar, and also in Berlin. Thierry de Ludre was the first to welcome von Papen in Paris.

The Germans were quite naturally pleased with the amiable young Thierry de Ludre. What they wanted was to gain entrée into French society, and the friendship of this young French nobleman was all the more welcome since there were not so many people in Paris, in those early days, who would even consider receiving a von Papen, a von Ribbentrop or a Lersner, the Reich's usual envoys at the time. In short, the Nazi agents had not, as yet, made much headway. And during this stage of the game, when von Ribbentrop came to Paris, he would stop, modestly enough, at the Hotel Bristol, on the Rue Saint-Honoré; Lersner and von Papen regularly stopped at the Hotel Lancaster, Rue de Berri. They barely managed to see the Marquis Melchior de Polignac, President of the French Wine Association, who, as owner of Pommery Champagne, had been von Ribbentrop's boss. They occasionally saw

Count Jean de Castellane, whose wife was a German; André Germain, the son of the founder of the Crédit Lyonnais; Fernand de Brinon; and, on a few rare occasions, Maurice Bunau-Varilla, the director of *Le Matin.*

Thierry de Ludre, considerably more naive than the others, was certainly much easier to handle, especially since he was pro-German to start with. He even went so far as to invite the von Papens to Richard-Mesnil, the ancestral estate in Lorraine. Marshal Lyautey, whose estate was only a few kilometers away, indignantly refused young Thierry's invitation to meet the German Vice-Chancellor.

Thierry de Ludre was the perfect defeatist. To begin with, he had no great love for France. He was a failure at home; but in the great country across the Rhine, he was respected. He had received hints to the effect that high honors were to be bestowed upon him some day. Besides, Thierry de Ludre was afraid. He was afraid of losing his property. He was afraid to fight. He was afraid of the Germans. And the Germans were well aware of his weaknesses.

On his return to Paris from one of his trips to the Reich, Thierry de Ludre, equipped with an elaborate fur coat, an automobile and a chauffeur, assumed the airs of an important personage. He gravely announced that there was a possibility of war. And he went on to show just how this war might be avoided—namely, by coming to an understanding "with the charming statesmen of the Reich who are so anxious to effect a sincere *rapprochement* with us."

In 1934 Thierry de Ludre was in Sarrebruck at the very moment when the Saar returned to the Reich. He was in the company of Stanislas de la Rochefoucauld, who wired his congratulations to Hitler. In March, 1936, when Hitler reoccupied the Rhineland, Thierry de Ludre had just returned to Paris from a visit to Berlin.

Shortly before this *coup* of Hitler's, Thierry de Ludre had overheard a highly significant remark uttered by no less a person than the French Minister of War. Someone asked General Maurin, the Minister of War: "What would we do if Hitler wanted to re-militarize the Rhineland?"

"Not much," the General replied. "I doubt whether we'd

do anything about it at all. I know the way most of my colleagues in the Cabinet feel about this question. In my opinion, the country wouldn't want us to force the issue, wouldn't want us to go to war to prevent the Germans from being masters in their own house. Besides, it would mean a real war—a war we should have to fight alone—for the English wouldn't stand by us."

Hitler felt reasonably certain that he had nothing to fear. On March 7, 1936, German troops marched, undisturbed, into the Rhineland. Later, however, when it became known that German rearmament had by no means been completed at the time of the Rhineland affair, and that two French divisions could have put an end to Hitlerism once and for all, several members of the Government, wishing, no doubt, to minimize their own responsibility in the affair, told me the details of the momentous Cabinet meeting of March 7th, in the course of which it was decided to do absolutely nothing.

I first heard the story from Albert Sarraut at a luncheon given by Jean Prouvost. His story coincided essentially with the versions I subsequently heard from Pierre Etienne Flandin and from General Maurin, who, in the meantime, had joined *Paris-Soir*.

Albert Sarraut said: "When the Council opened, the atmosphere was tense, nervous. I immediately presented the case to my colleagues. Mandel, who was Minister of Postal and Telegraph Service, was the first one to speak.

" 'If we permit this provocation to go unanswered, Hitler will feel confident that he can try anything with impunity. And he will try everything. A year ago, he reestablished compulsory military service. Today he is erasing the last of the Military Clauses of the Treaty of Versailles. Be careful! The decision we are called upon to make will be a historic one, for if we tolerate the Chancellor's present move, we shall be denying ourselves the right to intervene in the future. We shall then no longer be in a position to give aid to the States we have promised to help. And we shall be obliged to reorient our entire foreign policy.'

"That was what Mandel said. And I agreed with him, as did a number of the other Ministers.

"Pierre Etienne Flandin, who was then Minister of Foreign Affairs, did not contradict us. He merely said, in effect:

" 'We must either drive the German troops out of the Rhineland, or abandon the idea of trying to stop them when they will turn on Central Europe. England will have to help us. This contingency has been especially provided for in our treaties. I know, however, that she won't help us very willingly, and that she will disapprove of our resolute attitude toward Germany. The United States will accuse us of imperialism. And the Germans, of course, will hate us all the more.'

" 'That doesn't make any difference,' Mandel cried. 'If we don't act now, both England and the United States will change their minds, sooner or later, and then they'll be accusing us of cowardice and blaming us for the disaster which will have befallen Europe and perhaps the entire world. Besides, a military setback would almost certainly have serious repercussions within Germany—and that might very well mean the beginning of the end of Hitler.'

"I then asked our Minister of War, General Maurin, to tell us under what conditions a number of divisions, stationed near the frontier, could swiftly be moved into the Rhineland.

" 'I have consulted General Gamelin,' General Maurin replied. 'He answered, definitely, that our military system is so organized that we cannot proceed with any troop movements without ordering a general mobilization. No provisions have been made for a partial mobilization. And he added that we must expect far greater resistance than certain Ministers seem to believe. Therefore, gentlemen, if you are determined to oppose this *fait accompli*, the Council of Ministers must—today—issue the order for general mobilization.'

"Everyone was shocked. Finally, the heavy silence was broken by Jacques Stern, Minister for the Colonies. He could not understand, he said, why the Cabinet and the diplomatic service had not previously been informed of this point by the Army.

"The Minister, Francois Piétri, then exclaimed, 'How shall we explain it to the people? We'll be dragging them into a war without having been directly attacked.'

"But it was Marcel Déat who really swung the balance. He was Minister of Aviation at the time, and he most emphatically expressed his opposition to Mandel's stand. 'Hitler's decision was inevitable,' he said. 'The man must use his military power to accomplish his political ends. And if we decree General Mobilization tonight—within two months of the elections—we shall be thrown out by the Parliament tomorrow, if not before by a popular uprising. In addition, we shall be playing the hateful role of war-mongers. The Great Powers will withdraw their moral support, and we shall be risking disaster, both moral and material.'

"Nevertheless," Albert Sarraut went on, "I continued to insist that we could not allow the Führer's move to go unchallenged. I requested General Maurin to consult the General Staff again, and I decided to telephone General Gamelin, myself.

" 'I can handle the operation easily enough,' the Commander-in-Chief told me, 'but certainly not unless you give me adequate means, and such means call for a General Mobilization.'

"Flandin, in the meantime, had again consulted the English. He reported that they were now more and more inclined toward accepting the *fait accompli*. And the great majority of the Ministers now also took this stand. And I want to add," Sarraut said, "I want to make it clear that it was Flandin who was instructed to write the speech I was to deliver that evening—the speech designed to reassure the public in view of the German move. And Flandin—not I—was the author of the phrase for which I've been rebuked so often. You know, the famous phrase about Strasbourg and the German cannons!"

Regardless of their authorship, these words—"We shall not permit Strasbourg to remain within range of German guns!"—were cleverly exploited; and this vigorous declaration, which was not followed up by any action, was more sternly criticized in the French press than was Hitler's march into the Rhineland.

On this occasion Otto Abetz, Dr. Schmoll and the entire crew of German agents displayed a wealth of ingenuity in minimizing the enormous strategic and psychological advantage gained by Hitler's move. They insisted that it was "a mere incident of no great consequence—fundamentally justifiable—and something which could never have been prevented." They even went so far as to say that the entire situation had been greatly improved, and that the remilitarization of the Rhineland "had eliminated a point of friction between Germany and France."

Within a few days the public forgot all about this danger signal flashed from abroad—this move which was to foreshadow the defeat of France. Now Hitler knew the full extent of our weakness.

People were thinking and talking about only one thing: the *Rassemblement Populaire*, a group of Leftist parties, formed to combat the movements of the extreme Right. The platform, which this political coalition offered the electorate, included the forty-hour week without reduction of salaries, revision of the prices of agricultural products, Bourse reforms, etc.

The elections were almost at hand, now. Everybody knew that the Sarraut Ministry was only transitional.

Chapter Fifteen

The Front Populaire in Power

(From my notebook)

1936 (Day not recorded)

Poor Monsieur Albert Sarraut! People are beginning to believe that he has the evil eye. He was Minister of the Interior when President Paul Doumer was assassinated, and when King Alexander and Louis Barthou were murdered. He was again Minister of the Interior when the body of Councilor Prince was found. And he had to be Premier when Hitler re-militarized the Rhineland.

Albert Sarraut was often to be seen at the home of Madame Paul Guillaume—the young widow of the dealer in paintings who discovered the custom's official, Rousseau, and Negro art. There Albert Sarraut was in his best form. The Sarraut dynasty has been ruling France since the beginning of the century. Albert Sarraut and his brother, Maurice, are the grand pontiffs of the so-called Radical Party. Maurice withdrew from Parliament to devote himself to the management, direct and indirect, of his Party, and of its principal organ, *La Dépêche de Toulouse,* the big newspaper of the South of France, with a circulation of some 300,000. The paper exerts a powerful influence over the Party with the greatest representation in both the

Chamber of Deputies and the Senate, for most of the Radical members of the Parliament come from the South.

Albert, as Minister of the Interior, is his Party's representative in the Cabinet. The Ministry of the Interior is a political Ministry, *par excellence,* since it controls the electoral machine through the Prefects and Under-Prefects in the ninety Departements. This portfolio also makes him virtually Minister of the Police.

Why does Sarraut allow Russian, German and Italian agents to do as they please in this country? He had made an excellent name for himself as Governor-General of Indo-China. He had proved himself an alert and resolute leader and a forceful administrator. Is he incapable of dealing with the present situation? Is he incapable of cleansing France of these elements? Is he incapable of trying, at least?

Sunday, May 16, 1936.

Has the country ever gone to the polls in an atmosphere of such nervous tension? A crowd of some 10,000 has been standing patiently in front of the *Paris-Soir* building. Beginning early this afternoon, the Communists have been sending contingents of shock troops, singing the *Internationale* at the top of their voices. These elections are going to decide the destiny of France during the next four years. Are we going toward reaction or revolution? Toward war or peace?

In addition to our special editions, we have been posting up the returns as they come in, and also announcing them by loudspeaker. We have engaged the actor and singer, Saint-Granier, to serve as our announcer.

The election returns indicate a Leftist Coalition victory, despite the polls and surveys taken by the big newspapers, all of which indicated precisely the opposite trend. So far, the Communists have gained a few thousand votes. Notwithstanding the valiant efforts of a great part of the press, the perpetrators of bloody Sixth of February are now being recognized—after two and a half years—as the greatest enemies of democracy. Between the two evils, the people of France will choose the one they fear least.

After dinner, Jean Prouvost brought two friends—a banker and a big industrialist—to the office to look at the returns. The gentlemen spent several hours examining and analyzing the figures. By 2 A.M. they seemed to have given up all hope. And the industrialist said shamelessly: "It looks as though it were about time for me to be transferring my money to America."

May 23rd.

The *Front Populaire* is in. The Socialists got 2,000,000 votes and are thus the Party with the greatest number of Deputies in the Chamber. . . . Wonder what *Le Matin* will have to say? The Communists got 1,500,000 votes—seventy-two Deputies out of 610. (And the official membership of the Communist Party of France is no more than 276,000!) The Radicals have lost a few seats. As a whole, the Coalition of the Left gained thirty seats.

(Day not recorded)

It seems that the Soviets want to exploit the situation in France. Léon Blum has been named to select a Ministry, but the Communists are not to agree to enter the Cabinet, according to these reports. They are to stay outside the Government and are to exert constant pressure, for their seventy-two votes will be absolutely essential to the maintenance of a Leftist Ministry. In this way, they won't be burdened with any of the responsibilities and they'll really be in control.

We've received an outline of the instructions given by Moscow to the French Communists: "Immediately demand and insist upon the most sweeping, demagogic reforms for which credit will be yours. But maintain complete independence, enabling you to criticize the Government bitterly when the sentiment of the masses indicates such action. Whenever possible, create internal dissension and disorder, but simultaneously exert every effort toward getting France to take a hostile attitude toward Germany. Germany must be eliminated as a potential threat to the Soviets."

It is most enlightening to compare a recent issue of

L'Humanité, the official Communist newspaper, with a copy of the same paper, published only a few months ago. *L'Humanité* was then violently anti-militarist. Every officer was then a *gueule de vache* (untranslatable). The flag of France was then, in their language, "a vile rag." And the word *patrie* (fatherland) was held up to ridicule. But now *L'Humanité* speaks in glowing terms of our Republican Army. Every one of its editorials concludes with a reference to "immortal France." Overnight the Communists have been transformed into super-patriots.

(Day not recorded)

We have just celebrated the formal inauguration of our new building.

Enormous, all white, it was designed to include all the departments of *Paris-Midi* and *Paris-Soir.* Ours is the most modern establishment of its kind in France and in all of Europe.

Architects: the men who had planned the National City Bank Building in New York and on the Avenue des Champs-Elysées . . . Hidden staircases. Big elevators of steel, looking like massive safes. On the sixth floor there's a restaurant and a bar for the editors. If they want a drink, they don't have to leave the building. They're much less likely to get lost, this way.

June 1st.

Will *Paris-Soir* come out today? None of the morning papers appeared, except for a few copies of the strictly political newspapers: *L'Humanité* (Communist), *Le Populaire* (Socialist), *L'Action Française* (Royalist). The wave of strikes has reached the press now.

Beginning May 26th, almost all the metal workers of the Paris zone stopped work and started a sit-down strike, refusing to leave the factories until all their claims were granted. Here's the beginning of the Communist campaign. They want to show Blum that they're stronger than he is, and that he'd better toe the mark.

The workers, clerks, drivers of the Messageries Hachette trucks—all are out on strike and are preventing publication of the Paris newspapers. Pickets have been posted at every entrance to *Paris-Soir*. Others have literally barricaded themselves within the building in the shipping department. The police seem primarily interested in protecting the strikers.

We've appealed to the authorities in vain. Some of the business managers and I went to see the new Minister of the Interior, Roger Salengro.

We pointed out that the new Government could not afford to tolerate this dangerous situation. The people of Paris were cut off from their regular sources of information and were exposed to unscrupulous agitators. The public might thus readily misinterpret the situation, and might even be incited to action by inflammatory slogans. . . . The Minister seemed to agree. He promised to do something about it. Nothing has been done, however.

Our editors, typographers and press-men have done their work. The paper has been written, set up and printed. Nobody was on strike here. Bundles of newspapers were ready to be shipped out, but many of our linotypers and printers—out of solidarity with the Hachette strikers—actually helped them prevent the newspapers from leaving our plant. In other words, our men refused to permit the distribution of the newspapers which they themselves had willingly set up and printed! There was some fighting. To avoid any serious trouble, we decided to give in. . . .

Now the pickets are stopping everybody leaving *Paris-Soir*, searching them to make sure that *not a single* copy of the paper reaches the street. Bertrand de Jouvenel tried to smuggle his copy out by hiding it in an inside pocket. They found it and tore it up. He protested. He reminded them of the fact that he was "the defeated candidate, it was true, but nevertheless the candidate of the *Front Populaire* in the Corrèze."

The leader of the pickets replied: "Listen, brother, if you knew what we thought of your God-damned *Front Populaire*, you'd shut up."

(Day not recorded)

One of our staff, who had managed to smuggle a copy of *Paris-Soir* through the picket line last night, went to a restaurant on the Champs-Elysées for dinner. There he proudly took the paper out of his pocket and exhibited it as a trophy. Everybody seemed anxious to get a look at it. They hadn't seen a newspaper all day.

One especially enterprising lady finally went up to our man's table and said: "Ah, Monsieur, that is a rare and precious thing you have there. . . . My husband and I would be so grateful if you'd let us look at it for just a minute."

The lady took the paper, hurriedly brought it to her husband; and the two of them hungrily pounced on it. They did not look at the news on the first page, nor at the items on page 2 or page 3. They turned immediately to page 4. And the lady, quickly bringing forth a pencil, cried: "I was so afraid we'd miss the crossword-puzzle this evening."

(Day not recorded)

L'Humanité is coming out again tomorrow morning. No other paper. Not even *Le Populaire,* the organ of the Party in power, the paper whose nominal Director is Monsieur Léon Blum, Premier of France since yesterday. . . .

(Day not recorded)

The Italians maintain terroristic and espionage organizations in France, but these cannot be compared to the similar Nazi organizations. The Italians have never been able to conduct successful propaganda on behalf of their country or of Fascism. Nevertheless, all the newspapers are being swamped with material, free of charge, from Italian and pro-Italian agencies. At least once every week we receive a tempting invitation to attend some artistic or "cultural" function in Italy. And there seems to be no limit to the number of writers and journalists who come streaming into the office, generously offering to supply us with the latest on the innermost thoughts of Il Duce, himself.

Italian money has flowed freely in the direction of various newspapers. During the Ethiopian War, the *Manchester Guardian* published an enlightening list of the sums spent by Italy to influence the French press. Not one of these newspapers has ever dared to deny the charge or to sue the *Guardian. Le Matin* was prominent on this list, as was also *Gringoire,* where Henri Béraud, its principal editorial writer, published his famous article: "England must be reduced to slavery!" This article aroused considerable indignation in France, but it also set in motion a wave of anti-British sentiment. *It is to be noted that, prior to writing this article, Henri Béraud had spent many weeks in Italy. It is known that he was constantly entertained by militant members of the Fascist Party and by some of Mussolini's closest collaborators.*

The heads of the official Italian Press Service in France are M. Landini, officially connected with the Embassy, and a man by the name of Pettinati, who directs a small news agency. This Pettinati suddenly appeared on the scene immediately after the assassination of King Alexander and Louis Barthou. He successfully silenced most of the newspapers which had been pointing to collusion between Italian officials and the true instigator of the assassinations, Dr. Ante Pavelitch. These newspapers had been stressing the point that Italy probably considered it to be to her advantage to "rub out" the two outstanding defenders of the Little Entente. (Ante Pavelitch was chief of the Croatian terrorist sect known as the *Oustachis*—to which the murderer belonged. Pavelitch lived in Milan. His extradition was steadfastly refused by the Italian Government.) The adroit Signor Pettinati even succeeded in persuading the majority of French newspapers to feature the claims of the Croatian Separatists.

But of all Italian agencies, the Ovra—the Fascist version of the Gestapo—is most active in France. These sleuths of the Duce operate mainly in anti-Fascist circles. Many of them came to France in the guise of political refugees.

Roger Salengro committed suicide this morning in his bachelor apartment in Lille.

Gringoire had been waging an incredibly vicious campaign against the Minister of the Interior. They accused him of having deserted during the war; more specifically, they claimed he had deliberately allowed himself to be captured by the Germans.

Gringoire devoted eight columns in every issue to calling Salengro a deserter. He tried to clear himself. His former superior officer and a number of his comrades came forward and testified to his gallantry on the field of battle. They explained the conditions—unfortunate, but by no means unusual or irregular—under which he had been made prisoner of war. *Gringoire* simply ignored all this testimony. They went right on with their campaign, produced conflicting evidence. Ultimately, the Salengro Affair reached the Senate and the Chamber of Deputies. Then finally all the newspapers were obliged to mention it.

I went to see Roger Salengro, and asked him if he wanted us to publish an interview on the subject. He seemed completely bewildered.

"I'm going to speak to the Premier," he said. "I don't know what to do . . . This is all too unjust—too terrible."

He seemed to have lost all poise, all self-control. His eyes were full of tears.

Salengro was more or less of a hermit, a very sensitive man, by no means equipped to be in a position of power or to take part in violent controversies.

When Roger Salengro arrived at the Ministry of the Interior the other day, the sentinel didn't recognize him, and therefore didn't present arms. Without saying a word, the Minister passed the soldier several times. Finally, Roger Salengro entered the building and went to his office. There, in front of one of his assistants, he burst into tears. "The Municipal Guards refuse to honor me with a salute," he sobbed. "They believe *Gringoire*. I can't stand this any longer. I'll never be able to convince them. Never . . ."

The following morning, without telling anyone, he went to Lille. There he killed himself.

When Hervé Mille heard of it, he said: "This time Roger Salengro really did desert."

Léon Blum lives in an old house on the Left Bank, facing Notre Dame. From his windows, there is a magnificent view of the Ile de la Cité. His political enemies have been trying to make capital out of the sumptuous luxury of his apartment. This talk is exaggerated. The home of the chief of the Socialist Party is furnished in excellent taste, but by no means luxuriously. The apartment is comfortable, charming, but small. A policeman and a plainclothes man were detailed to guard the entrance to the building following the assault on Léon Blum by the aristocratic gangsters, *Les Camelots du Roi,* after Jacques Bainville's funeral. Blum was severely clubbed. This attack by organized reactionaries had greatly enhanced his popularity, just prior to the elections.

Léon Blum advanced his ideas of what a really free press should be, suggesting his program for reforming French journalism.

"I am speaking to you as a colleague," he said to me when I called on him. "I am speaking to you as a journalist, who, prior to assuming the guidance of his own Party's organ, wrote extensively for the general press, as a man who is well aware of the damage which the big newspapers are capable of doing."

He knows how to differentiate between journalists and the men who direct the newspapers. He knows the plight of the working newspaperman. He wanted to do something about strengthening his position, guaranteeing his rights, etc.

Léon Blum elaborated a complete program for reforming the press. He wants to break the Havas Agency's monopoly. He wants to institute a rigid control over the subsidies allotted to the newspapers, strict regulation of financial publicity and advertising, and compulsory publication of balance-sheets.

He asked my opinion on various points. I told him, perfectly frankly, what I thought. Before leaving, I said, "*Monsieur le Président,* if you really go ahead fearlessly with this, it'll be a difficult task."

He smiled and said, "All the tasks I have to face will be difficult."

The Blum Government is introducing reforms that were, obviously, long overdue—vacations with pay, the forty-hour week, collective bargaining, etc. But why is it that these measures all seem to be forced on the country by almost revolutionary action on the part of the Communists?

The atmosphere is bad. Despite rigorous control, gold and securities are streaming out of the country. The cost of living is rising constantly. . . . Foreigners have come to *Paris-Soir* to complain. Their cars were stopped in the streets, they say, and they were practically forced to contribute to strikers' funds. The Government intends to make much of the International Exposition to be held in Paris next year (1937), but work on the project has hardly been started and has constantly been interrupted by strikes.

There's some talk of devaluating the franc. The Communists are opposed to it.

The league of the *Croix de Feu* has been dissolved. Immediately, however, Colonel de la Rocque reorganized it under the name of the *Parti Social Français,* giving it legality as a political party. An even more reactionary party has been founded by Jacques Doriot, former head of the Communist Party in France. *Le Parti Populaire Français,* he calls it. He's being backed by big industrialists.

No one seems to be giving a thought to the foreign situation. Blum's blindness, in this respect, is alarming. Speaking at a banquet given by the American Club, he announced his faith in a policy of determined pacifism. He said, in part: "We do not believe—as did our forefathers in 1792 and 1848—that there can be some good to war, nor that war can be an instrument for Liberty or for Revolution. We were freed of this illusion years ago by a great man named Jean Jaurès." Léon Blum then went on to tell how he had once asked Jaurès whether he thought Lamartine had been wrong in refusing help to the Poles and the Italians in 1848; and that Jaurès had replied: "No. He did the right thing, the best thing possible. Whenever war can be avoided, it must be avoided. Peace—not war—is truly revolutionary."

Just before Hitler's accession to power, Léon Blum had written in *Le Populaire*: "France can now proceed along the path of disarmament, and can even take her place at the head of an international movement in that direction."

When Hitler became Chancellor, Blum wrote:

"Now that Hitler is at the head of his Government, it is infinitely less likely that he will engage in direct provocation, either against France, or against the Powers to the East." (1933)

And then, in 1934, he wrote:

"The Socialist group has never voted for military credits in times of peace, and will not vote for them now."

Chapter Sixteen

The Tragedy of Spain

EVER since the beginning of war in Spain, life on *Paris-Soir* was intolerable. The Spanish conflict created violent repercussions all over France.

When hostilities broke out on July 17th, everyone had already taken his definite stand. The Right, instantly, automatically, came out for Franco (twenty-four hours previously, practically no one had ever heard of him). The Left, naturally, came out for the legitimate Government.

Jean Prouvost agreed that we should send special correspondents to both camps. As we were discussing it, Louis Delapré came into my office, with the latest agency bulletins clenched in his hand.

"We've tried to get in touch with Madrid by wire and telephone," he said, "but the city doesn't answer. I want you to send me down there. Let me go right away."

Louis Delapré had been with us about a year, ever since he had brought us a forty-page manuscript—an extraordinarily gripping and vivid picture of conditions in Sing Sing Prison. On the strength of this article alone, we had immediately given him a job on the paper. He was of French West Indian descent, born in Brittany, slender, sallow, with splendid dark eyes, long eyelashes and finely chiseled features. Coming from Nantes, he had found his first job on a Paris newspaper in 1928. He had done well from the very beginning, first on Léon Bailby's papers, then on others. He had far too much self-respect to adapt himself to the policies of some of the newspapers, with the result that he was often out of work. One day he was reduced to walking the streets of Paris as a sandwich-man, carrying a placard on his back proclaiming that: *"Able-bodied man, Bachelor of Arts, married, father of four children, for rent. Any kind of work."*

He had already been editor-in-chief on two Paris newspapers; he had already published a number of important *reportages,* notably on the United States and Greece, as well as countless articles in which his warmth and generosity and his genius for concise and vivid expression were revealed.

It was several days after the sandwich-man episode that Delapré came to see us at *Paris-Soir.* We all became immensely fond of him. Jean Prouvost had immediately taken a great liking to him and had also been greatly impressed by his ability. He soon appointed Delapré, together with Hervé Mille and myself, to the task of creating a new weekly, *Paris-Soir Dimanche,* the first Sunday paper ever to be published in France. Unquestionably, it was Louis Delapré, with his enthusiasm and his inexhaustible supply of fresh ideas, who contributed most to the success of this new paper.

For *Paris-Soir Dimanche* was another big success for the Jean Prouvost chain of publications. But when Louis Delapré wanted to leave all this in order to go to Spain, I understood that there was no use trying to stop him. Here was a big job of reporting to be done.

The following morning at dawn—in the company of foreign correspondents Sefton Delmer of the *Daily Express,* H. R. Knickerbocker of the *International News Service* and a photographer from *Paris-Soir*—he left by plane.

Running out of gas, the plane made a forced landing. Our reporters, who had set out for the Loyalist camp, found themselves in Burgos, the site of Franco's General Headquarters. Fortunately, Madrid had been able to re-establish telephone and telegraph communications, and we were again getting reports from our regular correspondent there.

In the meantime, it had become almost impossible to discuss this war impartially. Léon Blum, faithful to his pacifist principles, had declared adherence to the policy of non-intervention. Under considerable pressure from England, Blum even refused to permit shipment of arms to Spain—arms which the Spanish Government wanted to buy for cash. The French Communists launched a tremendous campaign in favor of intervention. The extreme Right kept accusing the Blum Government of secretly favoring the "Reds," as they persisted in calling the Spanish Loyalists. There was a new wave of strikes. And labor was calling for "guns and planes for Spain."

In its attempts to mislead and to incite the public, the press actually surpassed the record it had achieved during the Ethiopian War.

When Louis Delapré returned to Paris from Burgos to bring us some uncensored articles, he told us that he had seen some horrible, some profoundly shocking things, but that he had been thrilled, too. "They're men, I tell you," he said. "They're brave, all of them, on both sides." And then he added: "It would be like a religious war, if it weren't for the women and children and old men who are dying—dying without knowing what for. As it is, it's difficult to say whether it's all horrible or merely dreadfully stupid."

While Delapré was in Paris, our regular Madrid correspondent informed us that he wanted to leave the threatened city.

"I'm going there," Delapré said.

It would have been useless to try to talk him out of it.

"I want to see both sides of this terrible war," he said. "I want to see as much of it as possible, so that I'll be able to write a book about it later. It's going to be an absolutely impartial book which will make it impossible for any such thing to happen again." His eyes were shining even more than usual.

We sent two other reporters to the Franco side. We were

trying our best to handle the story objectively. Every day we received a flood of letters from readers. Some of them complained because we published articles written from the Franco side; others criticizing us for the articles written from the Loyalist viewpoint. And we received offers—open, direct offers of subsidies from both sides—in return for which we were to abandon our policy of impartiality.

The Loyalist agents operating most actively in French journalistic circles were the Catalonian writer, Dalty, and a former German newspaperman, Simon Katz, known as O.K. Simon. Franco was represented by Juan March's men, working through certain French banks, and also by German and Italian agents who dealt directly with the French press.

The highest Catholic circles were divided. Cardinal Baudrillart was 100 percent for Franco because he looked upon Franco as a defender of the Church. But the Archbishop of Paris, Monsignor Verdier, on the other hand, refused to identify the cause of the Church with that of the Nationalist rebels. The distinguished French Catholic writers, François Mauriac and Jacques Maritain, rejected the idea of a Crusade; while Henri Massis believed that France must inevitably take part in this so-called Holy War.

Some of our newspapers persisted in denying that there were any Italian or German troops fighting for Franco—and continued to deny it, even after the Nazis and the Fascists had begun to publish official communiqués from the front. Another section of our press denied that there were any foreign Communist leaders on the "Red" side, despite the fact that the French Deputy Marty had already been broadcasting over the radio in the role of Chief of the International Brigades.

The chief of the French Navy, Admiral Darlan, called the Premier's attention to the fact that, if Spain should fall into German or Italian hands, France would be cut off from her Empire and would thus be in very grave danger. Furthermore, Darlan was instructed to go to London—unofficially and in utmost secrecy—to present his views to the English. They were not especially interested;

they told him, in fact, that what was really important was to see to it that the Communists did not get a foothold at the very frontiers of France. Darlan, whom no one on earth would ever accuse of pro-Soviet sentiments, is said to have been considerably annoyed by his reception in London.

In order to arrange for speedier transmission of our special correspondents' articles, I went down to the Basque coast, near the Spanish frontier. Under the surface of gaiety, the real business went on—the traffic in bootleg munitions, the plotting and the spying. For special entertainment, one could run over to the frontier and get a good view of Hendaye in flames and hear the rolling thunder of the big guns from over Saint-Sebastian way. At nightfall the lovely ladies of the French and Spanish aristocracy received visits from sinister individuals whom they would not have deigned to look at some few months ago. The GPU and the Gestapo had their best agents on the scene.

On my return to Paris, I found that Louis Delapré had come back again. The trip had been difficult, but he had decided to come, anyway. He complained about the censorship. He had been obliged to alter a number of his reports before being permitted to telephone them on to us.

"I have to write down everything in advance," he said, "and I'm obliged to add passages, here and there—absolutely useless tripe—intended to please the GPU agents. These fellows are now completely in control of the information and press services in Madrid. I'm like every other newspaperman in that I don't like to have my stuff cut. But in the future, when you come across some highfalutin, bombastic passages—material not at all in my usual style—why, you'll know I had to add those lines, and you'll be doing me a big favor by cutting them."

Louis Delapré asked me about his colleagues who had been sent to the Franco side. I told him we had had to recall one of them because he had become so enthusiastic that, during an attack one day, he had picked up a gun and commenced shooting.

"That doesn't surprise me in the least," Delapré said.

"Not in the least. We're all carried along by the action and the violent emotions of this incredible war."

Delapré went back to Madrid.

On December 1st, I asked Louis Delapré to return to Paris at once. We wanted him to be editor-in-chief of a new weekly we were planning to publish. He was to come by plane, together with one of his colleagues from *Le Journal*. He did get as far as the airport, but there he heard that some very big news was about to break. At the last moment he decided to stay on in Madrid for a while longer.

During a whole week, we were without any news from him. We were anxiously awaiting word as to when to expect him in Paris. Madame Delapré, a tiny woman, full of energy, had been coming to the office every morning and had waited hours for a chance to speak to her husband on the telephone for a few seconds. During those days, she waited in vain. We were worried, increasingly worried, but we tried to hide it from her.

Then, on December 8th, the Havas Agency sent us the following dispatch: *"The airplane of the French Embassy, in which your special correspondent, Louis Delapré, had booked passage to Toulouse, was shot down by an unidentified plane shortly after taking off from Madrid. Louis Delapré suffered minor injuries to one arm."* We almost felt relieved.

But we wanted to get the details. Through the Quai d'Orsay, I managed to get in touch with the French Legation in Madrid by telephone. And then we learned the whole truth: "Louis Delapré had lain for hours, without medical attention, at the scene of the accident. He was then brought in to Madrid in an old truck along a sunken road under heavy shell fire. He had abdominal as well as arm injuries, and had suffered a great loss of blood by the time he finally reached the hospital in Madrid." We received additional reports later.

Everyone who knew and loved Louis Delapré—newspapermen, artists, typographers, office boys, secretaries, clerks—everybody went around on tiptoe, everybody was quiet, waiting for the next telephone call which was to bring us news from Madrid. And after the report came through at 6 P.M., everybody tried to give an optimistic interpretation to the few words which left little room for genuine hope.

A great physician, Professor Desmaret, consulted, over the telephone in my office, with the physician who was treating Louis Delapré in the hospital in Madrid. He even offered to go down there, himself; and the Spanish physician heartily welcomed the idea and asked him to bring along certain drugs which were beginning to be very scarce in the beleaguered city. But the following morning, Georges Soria, the special correspondent of *L'Humanité*, called me from Madrid and told me that Louis Delapré was much better, that he was out of danger, and that Professor Desmaret need not trouble to take the trip. On December 11th, Madame Delapré left for Madrid, accompanied by one of our editors. And then, on December 12th, at 3 A.M., I was awakened by a telephone call from the Madrid correspondent of the Havas Agency. "Louis Delapré just died," he said, quite simply.

Steps were taken to have his body brought to Paris. They wanted to give him an impressive funeral. The Government even gave him a posthumous award of the Legion of Honor.

As for me, I didn't care what they did. His death meant too much to me personally. I had hoped that they would allow Louis Delapré to rest in peace. I had hoped the impossible might happen this time. But it didn't.

The Communists plastered the walls of France with huge placards, showing a picture of Louis Delapré with a caption in enormous letters: PARIS-SOIR HAS HAD ITS CASUALTY. The rest of the poster was devoted to extracts from an alleged telephone conversation between Louis Delapré, speaking from Madrid, and Hervé Mille and myself, in Paris. He was quoted as complaining bitterly because we had not published some of his articles about Mrs. Wallis Simpson. In another paragraph, and with reference to the death of another French journalist, Guy de Traversey of *L'Intransigeant*, at the front in Spain, Delapré was quoted as saying: "I don't suppose you'll be really interested again in what's going on here until *Paris-Soir*—like its competitor—can boast of a casualty." Needless to say, Louis Delapré never made any such statements. This campaign was admittedly sponsored by one of the 150 auxiliaries of the Communist Party—the so-called *Maison de la Culture*, whose President is the well-known writer, Louis Aragon.

Simultaneously, however, *L'Humanité*, the official organ of the Communist Party, ran a series of violent articles on the "Delapré Affair." This Soviet-controlled newspaper published parallel columns, intended to show the difference between the texts of Louis Delapré's articles as telephoned from Madrid and as published in *Paris-Soir*. Issue was made of the fact that, although the articles had not been revised, they had sometimes been cut, and that, occasionally, entire articles had never been published at all. All of which was quite true. But these deletions and omissions were undertaken for purely technical reasons, obviously—as was perfectly well understood by all newspapermen, including, of course, the staff of *L'Humanité*. But this campaign had a definite objective. In the first place, the idea was to alienate our very large following among workers and peasants—readers of *Paris-Soir* who were getting a diet that conflicted with the "Party line." In the second place, the Communists were planning to publish an evening paper of their own. And that was why they had decided to dance their war dance around the coffin of Louis Delapré.

The placards concerning the death of Louis Delapré, put up by the *Maison de la Culture*, had been replaced by other placards announcing a new "non-political" evening paper, *Ce Soir*. But by the strangest coincidence, the director of this new paper was to be none other than Louis Aragon, president of the *Maison de la Culture*.

What saddened me most was that a man like Aragon, who is a real poet, a powerful novelist and an idealist, should be an accomplice in such machinations. It has been proven since that the plane belonging to the French Embassy, in which Louis Delapré had left the Madrid airport, was shot down not by a Franco plane, but by a

Loyalist plane. The Loyalists say it was an accident, a deplorable accident, the result of a terrible blunder. Georges Soria, the correspondent of *L'Humanité,* brought to Paris the documents from the Madrid censors—the very documents on which the Communists based their entire campaign. It was Soria who called me from Madrid, the night before Delapré died, and lied to me, saying that my friend was well out of danger and that Professor Desmaret need not trouble to come down to Madrid.

Like Spain, France had become a battlefield. Behind the screen of their respective partisans, the Germans and the Italians, on the one hand, were fighting it out with the Russians, on the other. In France, however, the battle was being fought with far less courage.

Russian propaganda was as well organized as the German. Seventy-two Communist Deputies received their orders from Moscow. Moscow owned two big newspapers in Paris—a morning and an evening paper—not to mention eight magazines and literally thousands of house-organs in factories. Their "visible" activities also included the special schools for "the training of group leaders," courses in oratory, workers' universities, etc. But far more insidious than all that, the Russians, like the Germans, have learned how to make converts by playing on individual ambitions and by arousing envy and jealousy. French writers have had their books translated into Russian, and have then been invited to the U.S.S.R. to spend their royalties, for money cannot be transferred out of Russia. Scholars, scientists, politicians, union leaders and newspapermen have been asked to Russia and showered with honors there. *Mon Camarade,* a newspaper for children; *Regards,* an illustrated weekly; *Sport, Le Coupe-Papier, Le Paysan* and even *La Pêche,* the apparently harmless fisherman's paper—all were published by the Party. The Communists have made wide use of the technique employed so successfully in the C.G.T. (*Confédération Générale du Travail*): they set up organizations which are not strictly Communistic, but which soon come under Communist control through the various committee heads. It took the affair of *Ce Soir* to reveal that the *Maison de la Culture* was working exclusively on behalf of Moscow. And who would ever have guessed that the *Union des Jeunes Filles de France, La Fédération de l'Enfance, L'Association Internationale des Médecins contre la Guerre, Radio Liberté, La Fédération des Locataires* and even *L'Union des Auberges du Monde Nouveau,* chosen at random from among at least fifty, were, in effect, Communist action groups?

Working independently, the Russian Embassy and the GPU rounded out the activities of the Soviets in France. The public got a very fair idea of Russian procedure when the outstanding personalities of the "White" Russian colony in Paris—Generals Koutiepoff and Miller—were kidnapped and spirited away in broad daylight, although the Communist press insisted that the two Generals had chosen to disappear into thin air of their own accord. The big capitalist newspapers, like *Le Temps,* controlled by the most powerful industrial and financial interests and which are automatically anti-Communist, accepted subsidies from the Kremlin. Like Germany, Russia had its witting and unwitting agents among our journalists and among our Radical, Centrist and even Rightist members of Parliament. Even the *Front Populaire,* depending on Communist votes for its very existence, had its hands tied.

I have seen a little pamphlet, published by the *Comité de Vigilance des Intellectuels Antifascistes* and signed by names which evoke only the greatest respect and the fullest confidence, such as Langevin, the great physician, Paul Rivet, the famous anthropologist, and Alain, the eminent philosopher. The pamphlet is entitled: *No, War Is Not Inevitable.* In a text of some fifty pages, the distinguished contributors affirmed and reaffirmed that France could come to some agreement with Hitler and could persuade him to subscribe to the system of collective security, provided France was willing to consent *"aux sacrifices de souveraineté nécessaires . . ."* ("to certain necessary losses of sovereignty . . .") and provided Germany agreed to abandon her role of defender of Western civilization and her attitude of *refusing all contact with the U.S.S.R.*

Shortly after the publication of this pamphlet, the foreign policy of the Soviets underwent a change. Immediately, the *Comité de Vigilance des Intellectuels Antifascistes,* headed by Messrs. Langevin, Rivet and Alain, came out for a firm and uncompromising stand toward Hitler. If men like these have been misled and fooled, what could one possibly expect from hundreds of thousands of laborers, peasants and functionaries?

Americans were intensely interested in our *Front Populaire* movement, which seemed to remind them of their own "New Deal." But they could not know to what extremes the totalitarian powers were undermining France, Europe and the whole world.

Chapter Seventeen

Paris-Soir, Chief Link in a Newspaper Chain

Paris-Soir—after *Le Soir* of Brussels—was the most widely read newspaper in Belgium. In Switzerland, our circulation equalled that of the biggest newspapers published in the French-speaking Swiss provinces.

The Germans were alarmed by this penetration. They denounced it through their agents in Belgium as a dangerous foreign interference in order to conceal their own propaganda designs on the smaller European nations. They lost no opportunity to take advantage of the declining prestige of France, notably in Belgium. There Nazi agents were working tirelessly. They profited by the indifference of the changing French Governments, none of which wanted to bother about Belgium. The Nazis gave their support to the *flamingants* (Flemish nationalists), subsidizing their newspapers and their meetings, inciting them to redouble their demands for bilingual education (Flemish and French). The Germans succeeded in creating such tension among the Flemings that every pro-French gesture or word on the part of the Walloons was instantly interpreted as expressing the desire to have France dominate Belgium.

The same old complaints were still being brought up. After the sacrifice Belgium had made in 1914-1918, France, it was claimed, had not given Belgium any material or economic aid; France had not supported Belgium's claims against Germany and Holland; France had persisted in refusing to understand Belgium's domestic problems, etc.

Everything was working against France: Léon Degrelle, the young leader of the Rexist movement whose newspapers and other enterprises regularly went bankrupt, managed, somehow, to increase the number of his publication and the frequency of his organized meetings. He denounced France as "a country in disorder, under Communist control . . ." This served to terrify both the Catholic *bourgeois* and the Socialist workers in Belgium.

I was introduced to Léon Degrelle by his principal associate, Pierre Daye, one of the leading journalists in Belgium. Degrelle was a young man who seemed immensely pleased with himself. His appearance was ordinary; he was talkative and, to my taste, utterly without charm.

He commenced by protesting too much. "I love France," he said. "My wife is French. I love the French and I feel sorry for them because they're being dragged toward Bolshevism by your unspeakably rotten politicians. . . . But, of course, I must first think of Belgium. Here we must have our National Revolution."

"Something on the order of Hitler and Mussolini?"

"Naturally. There's no reason for me to conceal my admiration for what these two men have done for their countries. Personally, I'm not looking for power. I'm loyal to my King. But I'll fight to clean up our country."

No need for wearing kid gloves with this man, I thought. "Tell me," I said to him, "is it true that you are being paid by the Nazis?"

Léon Degrelle laughed hysterically. "Hi hi hi! . . . I know that's what they're saying about me. Well, let them try to prove it. I haven't concealed my trips to Berlin and Rome. I went there because I wanted to see for myself how splendidly these regimes are getting on since they got rid of those leeches, the parliamentarians. But I went to

France, too. Is anyone going to accuse me of being subsidized by the *Front Populaire* as well?"

He was shouting and making wide gestures, as though he were standing on a soap-box instead of sitting on the quiet terrace of a café.

"Take it easy," I said. "People are looking at us, listening . . ."

"All right, all the better," he cried. He was putting on an act now for the benefit of anyone within reach of his voice. "The more they look at me and the more they listen to me, the better."

Previously, he had confessed that he was taking lessons in oratory from an old actor. "Hitler took lessons, too," Degrelle said to me, by way of explaining himself. "Hitler learned the art of oratory from an old actor in Munich—Frederick Basil. Rudolph Hess told me so."

Paris-Soir maintained a close observation of developments in England. Our London office was a rendezvous for Continental correspondents. Lord Beaverbrook and Jean Prouvost were personal friends. The *Daily Express* and *Paris-Soir* had had an almost parallel rise to popularity.

At the end of the First World War, Beaverbrook paid some $85,000 for a newspaper which was losing money at the rate of $2,000,000 a year. It was the almost defunct *Daily Express.*

By every device, new and old, even the one of paying people to read his paper, Beaverbrook brought the circulation of the *Daily Express* to 2,500,000 readers and an annual profit of over one million dollars.

Jean Prouvost admired Lord Beaverbrook, especially because he was a self-made man. Their rise in the newspaper world was simultaneous and, just as Lord Beaverbrook dominated the field in England, so Jean Prouvost became the colossus of French journalism.

So great was the success of *Paris-Midi* that all the other papers issued at noon disappeared. No one could any longer hope to compete with *Paris-Soir* successfully. *Ce Soir*'s circulation was falling off steadily. And as for *L'Intransigeant,* its immensely wealthy owner, Louis-Louis

Dreyfus, was obliged to sell the paper hurriedly to Jean Prouvost, to avoid being wiped out. Jean Prouvost, in turn, re-sold *L'Intransigeant* at the first opportunity: namely, when he found a group which agreed to confine the paper's circulation to 200,000, maximum. Jean Prouvost started a big new weekly, *Marie Claire,* which, within three months, was being read by just about every woman in France. It launched fashions which became the rage. The number of French baby girls to be named "Marie Claire" increased tenfold within a year after the first appearance of this magazine.

The Jean Prouvost chain of publications included: a Sunday paper, *Paris-Soir Dimanche*; a movie magazine, *Pour Vous*; a sports magazine, *Match*; a daily devoted to horse racing, *Paris-Soir Courses* (and all the other racing papers in Paris belonged to Monsieur Béghin, Jean Prouvost's associate); and then there was also Jean Prouvost's radio station, Radio 37.

We, on *Paris-Soir,* were constantly introducing improvements, many of which had been suggested by features used in the United States and England. Since Jean Prouvost insisted that we take no part in political conflicts—and since these could not very well be ignored—we ran a new department, "Free Opinions," open to contributions from outstanding figures of the Left and Right, drawing the line only at Communists and Royalists. We decided to include articles by prominent English Parliamentarians, for the destinies of France and England were linked, and the course of public opinion across the Channel might have major repercussions on our own political life. We regularly published divergent views—ranging from those of Léon Blum to Pierre Etienne Flandin in France, and from those of Clement Attlee, the English Labor leader, to Winston Churchill, the Conservative. In this manner, we offered our readers an unprecedented coverage of the political scene, unprecedented both as to scope and as to quality.

As a reward we received an avalanche of insulting letters. Every article by a Rightist leader elicited abuse from our Leftist readers, and every contribution by a Leftist brought the maledictions of the Right upon our heads. After a while, however, our readers apparently became accustomed to reading, with more or less calm, the opinions of their political adversaries. Some of our readers actually seemed to be grateful. They understood that it required some sort of self-discipline to read opinions with which they violently disagreed, and that this was beneficial and enlightening. Our readers were also grateful to us for sending qualified observers to cover important events anywhere and everywhere in the world.

When the Revolution broke out in Greece, our reporter, Titayna, left for Crete in our plane. She was a young woman who boasted, not of never being afraid, but of never allowing fear to stop her—which is even better. Twenty-four hours passed without a word from her. We were worried. At 11 A.M., Titayna wired us her interview with Venizelos. Her plane had been machine-gunned and had made a crash-landing. But she had not been hurt. And if she had arrived one hour later, she would have made the dangerous trip in vain. For, at noon, the cable was cut and Venizelos was in full flight. Titayna was also the one who arrived in Tokyo at the time of the military *coup*. She gave us the story by telephone, the first call ever made between Tokyo and Paris.

We were responsible for the first news stories by such distinguished authors as Colette, Antoine de Saint-Exupéry, Jean Cocteau, Louis Gillet and Blaise Cendrars, who seemed furthest removed from this sort of writing. And then, of course, we published such veteran, internationally known specialists as Jérome and Jean Tharaud, Jules Sauerwein, Joseph Kessel, Paul Bringuier, Henri Danjou, Claude Blanchard, Bertrand de Jouvenel, Robert de Saint-Jean, Jacques Fransales (Raoul de Roussy de Sales), head of our United States office.

We did not, like the *Daily Express*, actually buy our readers. But we certainly did try to attract readers in all imaginable ways. One of our devices consisted in taking pictures on the street or in public places throughout France. A distinguished attorney would pick, at random, three of the many photographs and would select one person on each of the pictures. The three photographs would then appear in *Paris-Soir,* with a circle around the face of each of the chosen individuals; and then, if he could recognize himself as one of the three lucky ones, he was given 500 francs with the compliments of *Paris-Soir.* This little game, entitled "*Paris-Soir* has taken your picture without your knowledge," made such a big hit that thousands of readers wrote in, begging us to take their pictures "without their knowledge." Another one of our stunts worked like this: a five-franc note was put into circulation at a given place. Twenty-four hours later, we published the number of this banknote, and the lucky man who presented it at our office within a certain time limit was given 1,000 francs.

Paris-Soir had also achieved a reputation for benevolence. Through our Alexis Danan, we had undertaken an intensive campaign against conditions in the reformatories and in defense of unfortunate children. In the course of our investigations, we had uncovered veritable convict-prisons in which children—whose only crime, in most cases, consisted in having been abandoned by their parents—were being mercilessly exploited. These children, ill-fed, often cruelly beaten, were being forced to work as long as twelve hours a day, without pay. Our campaign resulted in a drastic reform of the entire system.

We also campaigned for elimination of city slums. And we organized numerous free excursions and parties for poor children.

Political events were soon to assume such dramatic importance that even the most outstanding individual contributions appeared trivial.

One night, at Jean Prouvost's hunting lodge in the Sologne, we hit upon the idea of transforming our sports weekly, *Match,* into a weekly picture magazine. Modelled along the lines of the American magazine, *Life,* it was to offer an explanation—by means of pictures and texts—of the events that were beginning to rock the world. We planned to approach our problem analytically: by identifying the trend of ideas leading to a given event, the men mainly responsible for these trends and the motives behind these men.

Match was to be an even greater success than any of our previous undertakings. Its circulation jumped from 80,000 to 1,000,000 in less than a year, and soon reached 2,000,000. The new *Match* made its appearance during those anxious days when the curtain-raisers to the Great Tragedy of Europe were being played. The magazine's great attraction lay undoubtedly in the fact that it was an unofficial and complete program, giving an explanation of the scenes and portraits of the principal actors.

Chapter Eighteen

From the Blood of Clichy to the Pretenders to the Throne of France

THE local section of the *Parti Social Français* (ex-*Croix de Feu*) of Clichy (the populous workingmen's suburb at the gates of Paris) had requested and obtained permission from the Ministry of the Interior to give a private benefit performance of a motion picture. Admission was to be restricted to members, and the proceeds were to go to their own Poor Relief Fund. But the *Front Populaire* organizations of Clichy protested against this reunion, and urged their followers to demonstrate against what they termed "a shameful Fascist provocation."

I had been told that the Minister of the Interior had been warned and that he would take the precaution of sending the *Garde Mobile.* Minister Marx Dormoy, successor to Roger Salengro, gave permission for the meeting on the grounds of freedom of assembly.

He insisted that the *Parti Social Français* was a regularly constituted party and had every legal right to show educational films to its members.

I sent a reporter to Clichy, with instructions to call me

at once if anything was brewing. I was summoned to the telephone while I was attending a performance in a Paris theater with Charles Gombault, my associate.

"Monsieur Lazareff? I'm calling from Clichy . . . They've been slaughtering each other for the past ten minutes. It's been horrible. There are many dead and wounded . . ."

Gombault and I started for Clichy.

In Paris everything was calm. No one seemed to know that anything was happening. Even in Clichy it was quiet. The shutters were all down. The houses were dark. Everybody seemed to be sleeping peacefully, unaware of what was going on just around the corner. But then, as we approached the City Hall, the picture changed: we heard shots, cries; we saw shadows moving, running; and the opaque, cottony darkness made everything seem nightmarish. A stray bullet whistled past my ears.

We had gotten out of the car, and were proceeding cautiously on foot. We came across a dozen or so young men who had taken their stand behind an overturned cart. They were busily reloading their revolvers. They mistook us for reinforcements.

"Get down, comrades. Duck," one of them said. "The *cognes* (cops) are coming up that street over there. You let them pass, and then let them have it—in the back."

They seemed immensely pleased at the prospect. But we went right on, without stopping to explain why we weren't taking part in their little game.

We walked right into a skirmish. It was so dark, we couldn't see which side was which. We were pushed around and punched, and just managed to escape a volley . . .

Finally, we arrived at the street corner where we were to meet our reporter. We could see him in the light of the street lamp.

"Ten seconds ago," he said, "they were firing from the windows up above this butcher store. The *flics* (cops) are up there right now, looking for them."

"How did all this start, anyway?" I asked.

"I can't figure it out. The counter-demonstration started peacefully enough. There were a lot of them, but there were even more policemen and *Gardes Mobiles.* But the partisans of the *Front Populaire,* faced by a solid cordon of guards, managed, somehow, to infiltrate behind the lines in small groups. In this way, they approached the building where the motion picture was to be shown. The police then commenced evacuating the hall, sending the audience out through a side door. All this was accomplished without any trouble. The P.S.F. members had left the hall and had gone home when, suddenly, the shooting started. From a small side street, someone had commenced shooting at the police; then, from another side, others began firing. Then the police fired back. It has been going on ever since."

We made our way to the City Hall. Léon Blum and Marx Dormoy arrived shortly after we did. They were wearing dinner jackets. They were greenish-pale, both of them. They had been at a concert together and had come out to Clichy directly on hearing the news.

Léon Blum wanted to know if there had been any casualties.

"Yes, unfortunately," a police *commissaire* told Blum. "Very many casualties."

The wildest stories were going around; the most fantastic figures were being mentioned. "Ten dead," somebody said. "No, 150," someone replied. "At least 150 dead."

Outside, on the street, the battle seemed to be dying down. By 2 A.M. everything was quiet.

We followed Marx Dormoy to the Ministry of the Interior. The newspapermen were waiting there.

"I'll be with you in five minutes," the Minister told the reporters. He went into his private office with his assistants. He permitted Charles Gombault and myself to come along.

Dormoy's first name is Marx, in honor of Karl Marx. His father was a militant Socialist. He, himself, is a militant Socialist, Mayor of the industrial city of Montluçon. He is very much of the old-time, militant Socialist, with his broad-brimmed hat (like Léon Blum's), his black beard and his ready flow of eloquence. He always impressed me as being a very decent, thoroughly honest man who tries to be fair and impartial and who attempts to perform his Ministerial functions with a maximum of broad-mindedness and energy. Now he was very much upset. But he tried hard not to show it.

He was consulting the last reports. "Six dead and 150 wounded," he said.

"What really happened?" Charles Gombault asked.

"A Communist *coup*," the Minister replied. "I had hoped that a strong police guard and the subsequent evacuation of the hall would prevent any trouble. But they wanted it. They were looking for trouble."

"But you said that you had been warned and that you had taken all necessary measures to prevent . . ."

"I did," the Minister said. "I spoke to Maurice Thorez [the head of the Communist Party in France]. He assured me that I had nothing to fear. But I should never have trusted him. The Communists suggested the counter-demonstration, but they made the Socialists seem responsible for the whole thing. For it was the Socialist Mayor of Clichy who signed the convocation, written—in most inflammatory language—by the friends of Thorez. And even worse than that, *Le Populaire,* our own Socialist newspaper, published a reproduction of the poster in which Léon Blum and myself are rebuked and insulted for having issued the permit authorizing forty harmless members of the P.S.F. to attend a motion-picture show in Clichy!"

"What are the Communists driving at?"

"Moscow," Dormoy said, "wants to be in a position to give orders, here in France. Moscow wants us to intervene in Spain. Furthermore, Moscow wants the Rome-Berlin Axis to focus its rage and its hatred on us, on France. But the Government of Léon Blum is not as easily led as all that. First and last, we are thinking of the welfare of France, not of Russia. Therefore, they want to stir up some scandal which will drive the Government of Léon Blum out of power and into oblivion. If people can say tomorrow morning: 'The Blum Government is red only with the blood of workers; Socialists and Communists have met their death because this Government permitted Fascists to provoke the workers'—if they can say that, the

Blum Government will have to step down, as the Daladier Government did after the Sixth of February. Then the Communists will demand their share of representation in the Cabinet—together with certain so-called Radicals and even certain Centrists, all devoted to Moscow (for electoral or other reasons)—and the trick will have been turned."

After a moment, Marx Dormoy went on: "But they won't get away with it. After what happened tonight, the militant Socialists understand what the Communists are driving at. And the *Fédérations Socialistes*—those of the Seine, for example—who consider Léon Blum to be too lukewarm, are even more opposed to Moscow than he is."

The Minister of the Interior then wrote out a brief statement and went into the outer office where the newspapermen were waiting. We followed him.

I hoped that he would publicly denounce the Communist intrigue as clearly and unequivocally as he did in his private office.

And there I heard Marx Dormoy make his official statement to the press. I heard him speak highly of the police. I heard him say something about *agents provocateurs* (meaning those of the *Croix de Feu*, no doubt). I heard him exonerate the Socialists and make a mild, extremely timid allusion to the Communists. Then he folded his sheet of paper, and slipped it into his coat pocket.

I was dumbfounded.

Marx Dormoy had thrown away a chance to achieve freedom for the Blum Government.

A new wave of strikes added to the embarrassment of the Blum Government.

Workers walked out without instructions from their unions or from the Confédération Générale du Travail. The strikes were led by young men who had recently joined the unions and who, in many instances, had just commenced working in the factories. The C.G.T., itself, became alarmed. The men who instigated the walkouts in the factories commenced by organizing small units in each workshop, and these minorities decided on a strike without consulting their comrades. Then the others were moved—by considerations of solidarity or of fear—to walk out, too.

These findings were confirmed by a *commissaire* of the *Sûreté*. He was detailed to keep an eye on foreigners. He told me that the ringleaders of these new strikes had plenty of money at their disposal. Furthermore, he said that it wasn't exclusively Russian money; that very many of the highly skilled laborers and craftsmen had spent some time in Germany and Italy. Were these men Fascist agents in France?

May 1 was the day of the official opening of the Exposition which was supposed to celebrate the triumph of the *Front Populaire* and of the democracies. On this festive day, three buildings had been completed: the German, the Russian and the Italian Buildings, representing the three Dictatorships.

The Russian Building, with the hammer and sickle on high, was just opposite the German Building with its swastika banner. On the roof of the Nazi building, Horcher, the celebrated Berlin *restaurateur*, opened a restaurant which became one of the smartest places in town.

I attended a gala *soirée* at the Russian Building, and an idea occurred to me. Something for *Paris-Soir*. The frescoes which decorate the Main Hall were likenesses of the Soviet regime's outstanding personalities. That is to say, these men *were* important figures when the frescoes were originally ordered. But by the time the Parisians were belatedly admitted to their Exposition, many changes had taken place in Moscow. Many of these distinguished personalities had disappeared from the scene. They were accused of treason. They confessed in detail to their alleged crimes, were condemned and, as a rule, executed.

My idea was to have these frescoes photographed, and to run the pictures with a brief commentary. But when my photographer arrived at the Russian Building a painter was trying to obliterate or to render unrecognizable the faces of the men who had been purged. He was adding a beard to the likeness of Marshal Toukhachevsky; he was supplying Radek with whiskers and hair to the bald head of Zinoviev.

Four men volunteered explanations of the Moscow trials, and in each case the explanation was the same. Not one of them would assume the responsibility of committing it to writing. The version of the Moscow trials which I shall give in detail has never been published.

My four men, who do not know one another and who got their information from different sources, were: *Paris-Soir's* correspondent in the U.S.S.R., Laville; Boris Souvarine, former delegate of the French Communist Party to Moscow; Georges Kessel, my friend and collaborator; and Nicolas Kossiakov, who has proven himself to be exceptionally well informed about Russia.

"There's nothing mysterious about the Russian trials," Kossiakov declared. "The German Ambassador asked to be received by Stalin, in person. He was advised to see Litvinoff. But he insisted that the message he had to convey was of the utmost gravity. Finally, Stalin granted him an audience.

" 'You are surrounded by traitors,' the German Ambassador said. 'The majority of your civil and military associates are in our pay. In case of war, you would find yourself in a most difficult position. The co-operation and help you have every right to count on will not only be lacking, but will be given to your enemies. Think it over. On the other hand, the Führer offers you—under conditions to be discussed—the possibility of an *entente*. If you do not agree to this, there will be war. And, in view of the present state of your General Staff, you will be heading for disaster.'

" 'What proof have you? I can't believe what you say unless you prove it.' Stalin said.

" 'I'll convince you.'

"Forty-eight hours later, Stalin was in possession of a series of thirteen very complete *dossiers* on thirteen outstanding Communists who were alleged to have been in touch with the Nazis. These *dossiers* contained full details as to the places and dates and even the exact hours of the interviews, together with the precise words in which agreements and promises had been made. Stalin was still skeptical, but somewhat alarmed. He ordered the arrest of the thirteen Communist chiefs. These men, faced with a mass of detailed accusations—which, they believed, had been the work of Stalin's agents—could do nothing but confess.

"The German Ambassador again went to see Stalin.

"'You see,' he said, 'you were wrong in doubting me. And now you probably feel secure in the thought that you have purged your regime of all dangerous elements. You'd be mistaken if you thought any such thing. You have no idea of the extent of our influence in Soviet Russia . . . Here, for example, are a few more *dossiers,* including an interesting one on Marshal Toukhachevsky, the Commander-in-Chief of your armies.'

"And then the same thing happened all over again . . . The men confessed, as the others had confessed.

"And the German Ambassador said to the Red Dictator:

"'This should be enough. But we have a few more. We'll just keep those to ourselves. What you have seen must have convinced you that your position in Russia is not precisely secure. Think it over at your leisure. There's no particular hurry. What the Führer asks of you cannot be decided in a few days nor even in a few months. In the meantime, however, we shall continue to take all necessary precautions.'"

Naturally, neither Kossiakov nor my other sources of information claimed to be quoting directly from the conversations between Stalin and Hitler's Ambassador. Two of them told me that Moscow and Berlin have been in increasingly close contact ever since the purges—despite the violent barrage of verbal artillery from both sides, which is nothing but a smoke screen.

While the attention of Europe was concentrated upon the Russian purges, the frequently preposterous but always dangerous plotting of the Royalists in France continued.

Bertrand de Jouvenel, who had recently joined Doriot's

pro-Fascist *Parti Populaire Français,* is a monarchist who believes that France will not regain her unity until she has a king. He insisted to me:

"There's only one king. Not the Duc de Guise, naturally, even if he is the official pretender to the throne of France. I mean his son—the Comte de Paris. He's intelligent and deeply interested in social problems—which are, after all, the only problems that really matter today. Furthermore, he's young and has a charming personality. I tell you, if he landed his plane in the Place de la Concorde some fine morning, the crowd would acclaim him and bring him to the Elysée."

He went on to tell me, with considerable relish, of the extraordinary predicament in which the Duc de Guise found himself following the Sixth of February. He thought that now his time had come. He issued an appropriate proclamation. But privately he confessed his concern to his friends. "This is terrible," the Duke said. "Things have happened so quickly. I'm quite unprepared. I have no Finance Minister."

Bertrand de Jouvenel went on: "But I assure you that the Comte de Paris is not at all like his father. After Clichy he did not imagine that the road to power had been cleared for him . . . The Duc de Guise, you know, was busily working on a profound treatise on the harmony of the hunting horn, when, as the result of a series of sudden deaths in the family, he suddenly became head of the House of Orléans. But his son, the Comte de Paris, has made a careful study of the political situation in France. Without actually breaking with them, he has intelligently disassociated himself from the more boisterous elements of *L'Action Française*. He counts numerous Centrists and Leftists among his friends. One of these days France will need a man who stands above and aloof from all parties, and this arbitrator can be the King and no one else."

Shortly afterward, during a visit to Brussels, I met the Comte de Paris. He was conforming with the law forbidding the Pretender to the throne and the members of his family to enter France.

The Comte de Paris was quite willing to propound his

views on questions concerning labor and the State. He was most unhappy, he said, to see that France was apparently abandoning her foreign policy of firmly maintaining her prestige. He admitted that he sometimes—secretly and incognito—came to France for a few hours, at the risk of being imprisoned.

"But, frankly," he said, laughing, "although the police organization of the Republic may leave much to be desired, I feel that they must know all about my little escapades. But they probably consider me to be utterly harmless—and just close their eyes to my occasional visits."

A few moments later, he told me that he was convinced that the hour of the Monarchy was approaching. What would bring its doom was the ringing of the church bells announcing the declaration of war.

A man entered the restaurant where we were having a late supper. He was gawky, awkward; his face was grayish-pale. He greeted the Comte de Paris with the barest sort of a nod. The Comte de Paris smiled back at him. A dark young man, who was leaving, first bowed to the Comte de Paris, then to the colorless gentleman.

"A funny thing just happened," the Comte de Paris said. "That gentleman over there—he's Prince Louis Napoleon, the Bonapartist Pretender. And the gentleman who just left is the Military Attaché of the Embassy of the French Republic. You can see that, even in exile, the three regimes are on fairly good terms."

The Comte de Paris was on excellent terms with King Leopold III and with the Courts of England and of Italy. The Nazis were making overtures to Prince Louis Napoleon. The name of Napoleon, evidently, rang sweetly in Herr Hitler's ears.

It is difficult to estimate the number of followers the Comte de Paris really has. According to the Ministry of the Interior, there are at the most 20,000 members of Royalist organizations, the great majority belonging to the *Action Française* and the *Camelots du Roi* groups. But the newspaper, *L'Action Française,* has a daily circulation of some 30,000.

Among the young intellectuals, the Royalist movement—or, rather, the movement for so-called *nationalisme intégral*—unquestionably was making headway. But this was due to the influence of Charles Maurras rather than to the Monarchist ideology itself.

As for the Bonapartists, there were 10,000, at the maximum, despite the fact that François Coty lavished his energies and no little part of his money upon the Cause.

There were other Pretenders to the throne of France. A certain Naundorff called himself Prince de Bourbon. His father, a photographer, claimed to have documents proving that he was a descendant of Louis XVII, the son of Louis XVI and of Marie Antoinette. This last of the Naundorffs, the Prince de Bourbon, was miserably poor, literally living off charity. But then he hit upon an excellent scheme: he legally recognized as his daughter Mlle. Cotillon, the adventuress who testified in the Councilor Prince Affair.

In the meantime, the Blum Government was beset by difficulties. Always in a precarious position from attacks on all sides, it finally toppled. The beginning of the end came when Paul Baudouin and Charles Rist, the two economists entrusted with floating the loan with a rate-of-exchange guarantee, resigned.

The C.G.T. attacked the *Front Populaire* Government for refusing to relieve the unemployment situation by instituting a broad program of rearmament and public works. The Communists, bitterly disappointed at having been prevented from exploiting the bloody Clichy incident, did their best to add to the confusion. The Right, of course, took every advantage of the opportunity to undermine Blum.

Blum asked for a free hand in financial matters. The Chamber agreed to give him these powers. But the Senate refused, following a speech by Joseph Caillaux in which an issue was made, not too subtly, of Blum's race.

Blum resigned. The demonstrations in the street outside the Senate were of minor proportions.

Camille Chautemps succeeded Léon Blum. Strange, but

those very men who plotted and incited the Sixth of February and who made the most of the Prince Affair—these same men now had confidence only in Camille Chautemps and Daladier, whom they had attacked so vehemently a little over a year ago. And the press was very amiable toward Camille Chautemps, who was taking Socialists into his Cabinet. As his Minister of Finance, he had chosen Georges Bonnet, whom Léon Blum had sent to Washington as Ambassador.

Chapter Nineteen

The Secret Dossier on the Cagoulards

ON THE EVENING of September 11, 1937, extremely violent explosions coming in rapid succession wrecked two buildings on the Rue de Presbourg. The buildings had been occupied by the *Confédération Générale du Patronat Français* and by the *Union Patronale des Enterprises Métallurgiques.*

An immense crowd was gathering. The President of the *Confédération Générale du Patronat Français,* C. J. Gignoux, drove up. Without troubling to wait for so much as a word of information on the subject, he jumped to his conclusion: "This means the Communists have gone over to direct action."

Camille Chautemps and Marx Dormoy soon arrived, together with the Prefect of Police and the Prefect of the Seine. The Premier listened attentively to the first reports.

It looked like a most unusual case. Whoever had planned it had set the bombs to explode on a Saturday night when the buildings would be empty. By a most fortunate coincidence, even the janitors in charge had left the buildings.

The following morning, the entire Rightist press and a number of the big newspapers demanded that the Communist Party be dissolved because it "was trying to create a reign of terror in France in order to bring on the Revolution." On the other hand, the Communist and the Socialist press spoke of "dastardly provocations."

That afternoon a young man presented himself at my office.

"I know who is responsible for those explosions in the Rue de Presbourg," he said. "The Cagoulards!"

The Cagoulards were a sort of federation of the secret societies of the extreme Right—united in their stand against Communism, and with ramifications throughout France, in every Government agency, even including the Army. The young man hastened to explain his association with this secret order. "I joined because I sensed the threat of revolution, and because I felt that the regular groups and organizations—such as the *Parti Social Français* and the *Camelots du Roi*—were no more adequately equipped to combat the Communist menace than was our Government itself. But just as soon as I became a Cagoulard, I began noticing things that soon dampened my enthusiasm. When I had definite proof that *la cagoule* was being sponsored by money from abroad, I realized that this organization was every bit as dangerous to France as the danger it was supposed to be combating. I was determined to denounce it. However, since the *cagoule* executes all those whom it considers traitors, and since it has its informers even among the police, I have decided to confide this dossier to *Paris-Soir*. I feel that *Paris-Soir* will keep my secret. Most of the other big papers are implicated themselves. . . ."

The youth sensed my skepticism.

"I believe that coming events will serve to convince you. In any event, I'll leave my dossier in your hands."

He left quite abruptly, as though he feared being followed.

I glanced through the dossier. Some of the things I read seemed actually funny, and not the slightest attempt had been made to prove any of the stories. I dismissed the whole thing with the remark: "Just another crank."

I had the dossier pigeonholed. However, I intended to

have certain points checked by members of our staff, especially material concerning the assassination of the Rosselli brothers. The bodies of these two anti-Fascist intellectuals—one of them had been Professor at the University of Turin—had been found, riddled with bullets, in a forest in Normandy, not far from Bagnoles de l'Orne.

Several days later Charles Gombault told me that the investigation of the crime of the Rue de Presbourg would produce sensational disclosures involving "numerous secret organizations of the extreme Right."

This reminded me of the dossier on the Cagoulards. I had photostatic copies made and put them aside. From the investigation of the Sûreté I learned that:

1) In the course of the inquiry following the disappearance of two munitions dealers in the employ of Italy—Baptiste and Juif by name—the authorities had found lists of names of individuals belonging to the greatest variety of professions and walks of life. These individuals had all been in touch with the Italian agents.

2) Somewhat later, the son of the famous French tire manufacturer, Pierre Michelin, had been in a terrible automobile accident, in which his wife was killed. In the course of the routine investigation of the accident, the gendarmes had been amazed to find, skilfully hidden away in specially built compartments in the body of the car, certain documents, which they had seized, copied and forwarded to the Sûreté. These documents consisted, essentially, of lists of names—and were the same names as those on the lists found among the papers of Baptiste and Juif.

3) For some time now, the authorities had been keeping an eye on the Michelins, who had transformed their factories at Clermont-Ferrand into a veritable general headquarters for groups preparing to take illegal, anti-democratic action. The Michelins were so powerful, however, that it seemed almost impossible to accuse them. They were in a position to exert considerable influence over most of the important newspapers; a number of members of the Parliament were Michelin hirelings; and the family had a powerful protector in Pierre Laval who considered

the Clermont-Ferrand district (where he was born) to be more or less his personal dominion.

The Sûreté had good reason to believe that the explosions of the Rue de Presbourg had been planned in the Michelin factories. But it was not in that direction that the authorities first acted. On November 10th, the Government announced that a vast conspiracy against the security of the State had been uncovered—but refrained from disclosing any of the known facts.

The people of Paris were therefore completely surprised when they heard that no fewer than 500 searches had been made, in the course of which 500 machine guns, fifty submachine guns, thirty anti-tank and anti-aircraft cannons, thousands of rifles as well as great supplies of ammunition and even some small forts had been found. Some of the materiel had been uncovered in the cellars of buildings belonging to certain Parisian dealers in antiquities; other caches were discovered in garages in the suburbs and in various châteaux in the provinces. It was also announced that numerous arrests had been made, including such prominent personalities as General Dusseigneur (one of the former heads of the military aviation), Duke Pozzo di Borgo (former associate of Colonel de la Rocque), Baron Moreau de la Meuse, Comte Hubert Pastré, Eugène Deloncle, Parent de Bernonville . . .

The Communist newspapers, *L'Humanité* and *Ce Soir*, exulted. "Here," they wrote triumphantly, "we see the results of the *Front Populaire's* spineless attitude toward the former *ligues*" (Fascist organizations). The big newspapers and the Rightist press waxed indignant, scoffed at the idea of any conspiracy; and claimed that the whole thing merely represented precautions taken in self-defense by groups which had reason to fear an imminent Communist *coup*. Apparently, these papers said, the Government was either unable or unwilling to do anything about this impending Communist action. And it was a disgrace, they said, to accuse and to imprison such war heroes as General Dusseigneur and the Duke Pozzo di Borgo. In their righteous indignation the newspapers went so far as to say that the arms and munitions found had, in fact, been originally seized by the alleged conspirators from hidden stores belonging to Communist cells.

The general public was confused by all these charges and counter-charges. Besides, the very name, Cagoulards, seemed to give a farcical note to the whole thing. There was no precise statement made of the Cagoulards' intentions, no denunciation of their methods.

There were some sensational developments, however. It was learned that the *cagoule* was composed, essentially, of two societies: the UCAD (*L'Union des Comités d'Action Défensive*) and the CSAR (*Comité Secret d'Action Révolutionnaire*). Members of the CSAR were accused of having assassinated the Rosselli brothers in the forest near Bagnoles de l'Orne, and members of the UCAD, who all happened to be engineers in Michelin's employ, were charged with having made and delivered the bombs which wrecked the buildings on the Rue de Presbourg.

Nevertheless, the public remained apathetic.

Those who had been arrested assumed a contemptuous attitude toward the whole thing, and, of course, found highly influential personalities to intervene on their behalf. The press, as a whole, systematically minimized the importance of the affair. The investigation dragged on. The Government seemed to be restraining the police and the magistrates. One after the other, cases were thrown out of court for lack of sufficient evidence. And other events were soon to divert attention from the Cagoulard conspiracy.

I recalled my mysterious visitor's dossier. I noticed that it mentioned the name of every one of the men in whose homes and places of business stores of arms had been found, of every one of the men whose estates had been transformed into veritable fortresses, of everyone who had been questioned and arrested in connection with the Rue de Presbourg affair. But the dossier contained more than a complete list of the men involved in the conspiracy. It contained, notably, a perfectly clear and simple explanation which sufficed to dispel the last clouds of mystery which still shrouded the Cagoulards.

Here is his explanation: A certain number of big industrialists and merchants, politicians and members of the *ligues* of the extreme Right (*Action Française, Parti Populaire Français, Croix de Feu, Jeunesses Patriotes,* etc.) responded to an invitation issued by one of their group, Eugène Deloncle, to unite "in order to preserve France from the Communist revolution which was about to break out." Eugène Deloncle, an industrial engineer, was a somewhat mysterious personage. He had funds of uncertain origin at his disposal and was known to have traveled constantly between Paris, Berlin and Rome. He said to the assembled group:

"I am in possession of the Communist plans. The very hour has been set at which definite action is to commence. The Communists have their accomplices and allies in every branch of our Government, in the Chamber of Deputies and in the Army as well. They are supplied with arms and munitions. Needless to say, the warnings of patriotic citizens were ignored. . . . If we want to deal with these Communists, we must act quickly. We must acquire subsidies. We must find friends and supporters among the military, the Deputies and the Senators. We must see to it that we are better armed than they are and that our troops are more resolute and more numerous than theirs. Like the Communists, we must operate secretly, surreptitiously. The *ligues* and the political parties to which we belong are full of spies. These *ligues* and these parties are not to know of our activities. Secrecy is imperative. No one must know of our plans. We must be prepared to make the greatest sacrifices. If any one of us is unable to keep his mouth shut, he must promptly be put out of the way."

This was the manner in which the UCAD and the CSAR were founded. As soon as the cadres had been constituted, they were instructed—by the hidden powers behind the UCAD and the CSAR—to busy themselves with converting others to the Cause. Important military and political figures were approached, and were told, in effect, the following: "The Communists are about to strike. The Revolution is imminent. And the Government refuses to take the necessary preventive measures. We, therefore, have organized groups which will meet force with force—which will crush the Red uprising and maintain Law and Order. Will you join us?"

Naturally, all the men approached, who were Rightists in the first place, sympathized enthusiastically with this viewpoint. Some of them hesitated to go so far as to become active members of the UCAD and the CSAR; but, by giving their approval, they became accomplices in and protectors of the movement. Their distinguished names, immediately inscribed on the lists of sympathizers, were to lend respectability. My mysterious dossier contained the names of these Platonic sympathizers.

The UCAD and the CSAR had, of course, solicited and obtained support from the most powerful monied interests. And these sums had been used to purchase, through various shady middlemen, arms and munitions—in Germany and Italy.

As a matter of fact, close contact with German and Italian agents was being maintained—without the knowledge of the rank and file of the UCAD and CSAR—by the real leaders of the *cagoule*: Eugène Deloncle and about a dozen confederates, including, notably, Dr. Henri Martin, who fled to Italy when the investigation was opened. Using the Communist bugaboo as a convenient pretext, their real intention was to create such a state of disorder and disunity in France that a new Government would come to power—a Government that would be friendly to the Rome-Berlin Axis.

The Cagoulard groups within the Army were under the direction of Major Loustaneau-Lacan, former orderly officer to Marshal Pétain, then attached to the Marshal's staff during his term as Minister of War in the Doumergue Government, and subsequently placed at the head of an important department in the *Deuxième Bureau* (Military Intelligence). Although Loustaneau-Lacan's involvement in the affair was not made public, he was relieved of his duties in the course of the inquiry. According to my dossier, he was a fanatical anti-Communist, and he was the man who had persuaded Marshal Pétain and General Weygand to lend their names in a drive for new members of the secret societies pledged "to the defense of Law and Order."

Since Big Business sponsored the UCAD and CSAR, it was not difficult to understand why the big newspapers were inclined to minimize the importance of the Cagoulard affair.

Ironically enough, the only newspaper to be officially implicated in the investigation was *Paris-Soir*. From time to time, Jean Prouvost and Béghin had been requested to donate funds to UCAD and CSAR. They had steadfastly refused. This information was given me, not by the two gentlemen, but by my dossier. And this point, no doubt, had moved my mysterious visitor to bring the dossier to *Paris-Soir* in the first place. But Major Oudard, director of our racing paper, *Paris-Soir Courses,* had been mentioned as a Cagoulard by the Communist paper, *Ce Soir*. His office was searched. Nothing was found. In all probability, Major Oudard never was a Cagoulard. It seemed likely that his former secretary, who had become the mistress of one of our men who had gone over to *Ce Soir*, had merely wanted to have her revenge (the Major had fired her). *L'Humanité* and *Ce Soir* had implicated an appreciable number of people for strictly personal reasons. The police, on the other hand, wanted to appear absolutely impartial, systematically investigated every name mentioned and thus found itself answering a considerable number of false alarms. All of which contributed, to no small degree, to the ultimate failure of the entire inquiry into the Cagoulard affair.

However, as a result of the precautionary measures taken, the UCAD and CSAR were, temporarily at least, prevented from doing any harm. And the conspiracy which could have led to a tragedy culminated in sheer burlesque.

The Duke Pozzo di Borgo, as soon as he was provisionally released from jail, publicly accused Colonel de la Rocque of having drawn from the Secret Funds of each successive Government since 1930, and of having employed a substantial part of these sums for his personal use. Colonel de la Rocque replied to this charge by suing the Duke for libel and slander.

In the course of the suit, André Tardieu stated, with considerable relish, that, as Premier, he had indeed given money to the famous Colonel. And he added that Pierre Laval had done the same.

When questioned, Pierre Laval refused to admit or to deny the fact. This tended, of course, to support Pozzo di Borgo's charge and André Tardieu's statement. I had frequently heard Ministers or their associates say that Colonel de la Rocque was not in the least dangerous because the "successive Governments of the Republic always had him well in hand."

Everyone assumed that the exposure of Colonel de la Rocque would induce many people to resign from his *Parti Social Français.* Strangely enough, however—and according to the Colonel's two right-hand men, Edouard Barrachin and Léonce Bonduelle (the latter connected with the business management of *Paris-Soir*)—there was a falling off of no more than one-half of one percent in the membership of the *Parti Social Français,* following the trial.

But why did Pozzo di Borgo and André Tardieu attack Colonel de la Rocque? Pozzo di Borgo felt that he had been denounced by the chief of the *Croix de Feu.* My apparently omniscient dossier, specifically mentioned that la Rocque had not only refused to join the *cagoule,* but had warned his followers against the dangers inherent in this organization, and that Pozzo di Borgo had then resigned from the *Parti Social Français.*

There was another reason. Some time previously, Colonel de la Rocque had bought Raymond Patenôtre's newspaper, *Le Petit Journal,* for the purpose of transforming it into his party organ. He had, in that manner, acquired an appreciable part of the following of the other Rightist newspapers. Bailby's *Le Jour,* notably, had lost many of its readers to this new competitor—and Léon Bailby was closely affiliated with Pozzo di Borgo and André Tardieu.

Le Jour, at that time, was practically dead on its feet. It was saved from utter collapse by the fact that another Rightist daily, *L'Echo de Paris,* suddenly suspended publication. At one time Henri de Kérillis was the political director and Pertinax was head of the department of foreign affairs. Henri de Kérillis, who had distinguished himself as an aviator (1914-18). Returning to civilian life after the War, he waged a fanatical, merciless campaign against Communism and against Germany. For Germany, he insisted, although defeated, had not abandoned her dream of world domination.

He had founded the *Parti Républicain National.* And in those days it was the Left that accused him of being a "war-monger." At a later date, the Right, in turn, was to attack him with the same epithet.

Before the elections of 1924, he put up placards throughout the country, bearing the inscription:

"France, having been invaded four times within the past hundred years, must not disarm until her security is assured. Vote against the men of the Left. They want to disarm France."

Then there was André Géraud, known as Pertinax, a man with amazing connections. Confidant of all the Chancelleries, of all the Ministries of Foreign Affairs, on the best of terms with all the chiefs of our General Staff, he would arrive at the office every afternoon, with a monocle in his eye, and, between some important luncheon and some big dinner, he would write his daily article. During his brief stay in his office, he would be called upon to answer innumerable telephone calls, and his replies would sound something like this: "Yes, Your Excellency . . . Very well, *Monsieur l'Ambassadeur* . . . Certainly, *Monsieur le Président* . . . Not really, *mon Général*?"

He always gave the impression that it would be physically impossible for him to have a conversation with anyone who did not have a resonant name or an impressive title. But in his articles, Pertinax tirelessly kept insisting that France must have a foreign policy entirely independent of all ideologies and transcending all questions of domestic politics. It was Pertinax who, at the time of the Ethiopian War, prematurely published the terms of the Pierre Laval-Samuel Hoare Accord, and thus effectively nipped the Accord in the bud.

Henri de Kérillis was pro-Italian at this time. Pertinax and de Kérillis, therefore, had a number of extremely stormy arguments on the subject; but they were always entirely sincere and moved only by patriotic considerations. Precisely because to them the welfare of France always came first, they were attacked by the Left and by the Right.

Their integrity, which did not, of course, prevent them from making mistakes, frequently puzzled their nationalistic readers. They could not understand, for example, how an outspoken Conservative like Pertinax could advocate the alliance with Soviet Russia. Nor could others understand how Henri de Kérillis could have been willing to bring a gift of a sword of honor to General Franco while pursuing his relentless campaign against Hitler.

Because the circulation of *L'Echo de Paris* was falling off steadily, it finally fell into the hands of the son of Edmond Blanc, founder of Monte Carlo. François Edmond Blanc sold the title of *L'Echo de Paris* to *Le Jour,* which was henceforth to use it as a sub-title.

Henri de Kérillis became associated with a new daily, *L'Epoque,* founded by Henri Simon, and Pertinax became editor-in-chief of a weekly, *L'Europe Nouvelle,* strongly in favor of the League of Nations . . . Europe was indeed to become *l'Europe Nouvelle* (the New Europe)—more so than even the far-sighted Pertinax had ever thought possible.

Chapter Twenty

The Royalist Program

After four years of domestic quarrels, after two years of the *Front Populaire,* after five years of Hitlerism—France suddenly woke up to the sound of the tempest raging at her door—the Sudeten question in Czechoslovakia.

Franco was now definitely winning in Spain; the Nazis and the Fascists were openly boasting of their responsibility for the glorious victory while the Communists were condemning Léon Blum for having permitted the Spanish Republic to be crushed.

The second Blum Ministry, formed immediately after the Austrian *Anschluss,* lasted barely a month. Léon Blum resigned when the Senate refused to grant him *pleins pouvoirs.* On April 13, 1938, Edouard Daladier formed the new Cabinet. Presenting his Ministry to the Chamber of Deputies, he made the following pronouncement:

"A great and free country can be preserved only through its own efforts. The Government of National Defense which stands before you is determined to personify our will to be saved."

Three years previously—after the Sixth of February—the press had called Daladier *le fusilleur* ("the executioner") and had declared that his career had come to its conclusion "in shame and in blood." And now these same newspapers were hailing him as a saviour, largely because they were so pleased to see the *Front Populaire* dead and buried.

As far as I was concerned, Daladier was still the man of February, 1936, who had shown himself to be so deplorably lacking in presence of mind when faced by the uprising, in courage during the rioting, and in good citizenship afterward. How then, could this man be expected to steer France through the infinitely greater difficulties looming on the horizon?

Edouard Daladier had chosen Georges Bonnet as his Minister of Foreign Affairs and Paul Reynaud as Minister of Justice.

In an interview Georges Bonnet told me what he thought of Daladier.

"He's not an easy man to understand. His popularity with the Army could be explained by the fact that he always permitted the General Staff to have its way in everything. And if he's accepted by both the Socialists and the Right, it may very well be because being without representation in the Cabinet, due to the nature of the present majority in the Parliament, they both hope to exert some power through the medium of this vacillating man. Furthermore, don't forget that Daladier is clever enough to give both sides reason to hope that he will govern the country with their collaboration. He gives the impression of being a strong man. And he'll be useful. He'll probably be very successful in helping France create the impression that she is strong again. But what I'm afraid of is not that our people may be fooled, but that Hitler knows the truth—namely, that we're weak."

Georges Bonnet explained his own theories to me. I must say that I was not surprised; but I was alarmed, nevertheless. I had known him a long time. As a very young newspaperman, I had worked under him on *Le Soir*, and there was something about him I always found disturbing. It must have been that I found him to be, paradoxically, both sharp and vague—physically and mentally. To go with his long nose and his sharp, tapering chin, and that prominent Adam's apple of his which jumped and quivered within the confines of a high, stiffly starched, impeccable collar as he spoke—to go with these features one would expect a different glance from the one that came from those pale-blue, shifty eyes of his. It seemed impossible for him to look you squarely in the eye. With his alleged predilection for Bergsonian clarity and purity of ideas, with his sincere ardor for pacifism, he should have been less cautious, somewhat less clever at coddling his various friends, somewhat less skillful at dodging ticklish questions and at avoiding a definite, clear-cut stand.

"Let's not go in for heroism," he said to me. "Britain won't stand by us. It's all very well to set yourself up as the gendarme of Europe, but in order to play the role successfully you have to have something better than a cap-pistol, handcuffs made of straw and jails made of cardboard. As Minister of Foreign Affairs, I am determined to go just as far as I can toward finding a solution—a timely solution which will obviate any move on the part of the Minister of War. France cannot afford another blood-letting. Our vital statistics are getting steadily worse. And in addition the *Front Populaire* has managed to put the country into such a state that what we need is a period of recuperation. Any hasty, imprudent move might very well prove fatal."

Then, after a moment, he went on: "Why do we want to be the last ones to recognize the *fait accompli* in Ethiopia and in Spain? England has just come to a gentleman's agreement with Italy. Even Prague has recognized the Italian Empire."

That gave me an opening to ask him about the burning question of the day—Czechoslovakia.

"On March 14th," he said, "two days after the *Anschluss,* with the famous Czech Maginot Line flanked, Léon Blum formally assured the Czech Minister that 'France will fulfill her obligations in accordance with her Treaty with Prague.' Ten days later, however, Neville Chamberlain publicly declared that Great Britain could not promise to intervene in the event of aggression against Czechoslovakia."

I reminded him that England had no official obligation toward that country and that Neville Chamberlain clearly stated that legal obligations were not the only ones to be considered in the matter of war and peace.

"Very true," Georges Bonnet replied. "But when you say that you're not sure whether or not you'll fight, but that you may, possibly, fight, a man like Hitler draws the conclusion that you're merely trying to behave in such a manner that you won't be forced to fight him. Incidentally, I consider the English attitude to be intelligent and very sensible."

Early the following morning, I saw Paul Reynaud. He had gotten up at 6 A.M. to take a bicycle ride in the Bois de Boulogne. He was always careful about keeping in good physical condition.

In his dry, incisive manner he said: "Georges Bonnet is pursuing a very dangerous line. I think he'd be willing to sacrifice everything to appease Hitler. Hitler, of course, will take advantage of each new concession. If we want to be totally ruined, the policy of appeasement is just the thing. The only really weak ones are those who admit their weakness and who thus discourage their potential friends and allies. If we allow Hitler to take one more step, we shall lose the rampart of Czechoslovakia, then the Polish alliance as well as the possibility of taking concerted action with Russia. We shall definitely discourage the Little Entente and the Balkan States. England, who has already manifested a tendency in this unfortunate direction, will allow herself to go all out for appeasement. We must show that we are resolute. If we don't, if Paris flirts with Gretchen—why, London will probably go even farther and pinch her lovingly on the buttocks."

The situation must have been very serious indeed, for ordinarily, Monsieur Paul Reynaud never permitted himself to use such language.

At Fouquet's, the big café on the Champs-Elysées, I saw Otto Abetz. He was accompanied by the daughter of his friend, Jean Luchaire—Corinne Luchaire, who had become a popular movie star.

"Come on over and have a drink with us," he said.

"What do you think of the situation?" I asked.

"Everything will be all right. I not only hope so from the bottom of my heart, but I'm sure of it. After all our efforts, we're not going to fight now on account of three and a half million Germans who want to remain Germans. Czechoslovakia was created according to the principle of self-determination of nationalities. Hitler is basing his claim on precisely this principle. And President Benes will not be able to ignore this point. . . . Russia is behind all this. Russia wants the others to fight—to her ultimate advantage."

"Tell me, Abetz, frankly," I said. "After the Sudetenland has been settled, how long do you think it'll be before Hitler lays claim to all of Czechoslovakia?"

He looked sad. "It hurts me to hear you say a thing like that."

They were working together very smoothly, Herr Otto Abetz and his accomplices, Dr. Schmoll and the writer, Frederick Siebourg. Anything any one of them ever said in the course of any conversation reminded you of something you'd read in any one of the numerous articles appearing in the magazines and in the newspapers—written by them. They certainly knew their stuff by heart.

On the all-important question, as to whether or not Hitler should be appeased, all the political parties were split wide open, with the exception of the Communist Party, which was united.

As for the Socialists, Léon Blum was proclaiming the necessity for strengthening national defense. On the other hand, Paul Faure and Charles Spinasse, Léon Blum's principal collaborators, declared themselves to be "faithful to the principles of Socialism—peace above all." The *syndicalistes* shared Paul Faure's views, in opposition to the Communists.

A growing number of liberals subscribed to the theories of Jean Giono, the novelist—theories which he had condensed into the phrase: "There is no such thing as a shameful peace; there are only shameful wars." Schoolteachers drilled these sentiments into their pupils.

And the General Secretary of the *Syndicat des Instituteurs* (Teachers' Union) was not removed from his post after making the following pronouncements in the course of a speech at a general assembly of his Union:

"Better to live as a German than die as a Frenchman. Slavery is better than death."

Le Populaire, the daily organ of the Socialist Party, published opinions of the "hard" and the "soft"—meaning, of course, of those who believed in a firm attitude toward Germany and of those who favored a policy of appeasement. The appeasement group, however, was obviously allotted considerably more than half of the available space.

The *Parti d'Union Socialiste Républicaine* (USR), composed of refugees from the Socialist Party, was also divided into two factions: one, headed by J. Paul-Boncour, insisted that treaties be respected; the other, headed by Marcel Déat and Adrien Marquet, was of the opinion that "a bad settlement was better than a good war."

Marcel Déat, a former professor, was the man who had been most flagrantly responsible for France's failure to act at the time of the German remilitarization of the Rhineland. And he boasted of his accomplishment. After the unsuccessful *coup* of the Sixth of February (1934), Déat had taken part in a series of questionable activities, in which were involved the shady elements of all political parties in France, as well as the ever-present Otto Abetz and other Nazi agents.

The powerful Radical Party was also divided. Proudly wearing the mantle of the old revolutionary Jacobins, Edouard Herriot believed that France should pursue a resolute foreign policy based on the support of Britain and of Russia, regardless of the domestic politics of these countries. To his Left, however, there was Pierre Cot, former Minister of Aviation, who had failed to straighten out the chaotic condition which prevailed in our aviation and who was blindly pro-Russian. To Herriot's Right, Joseph Caillaux and his followers were inclined to favor a policy of *repliement colonial* (withdrawal to the Colonies) —a theory which I had heard Otto Abetz recommend.

Pierre Etienne Flandin, President of the *Parti de l'Alli-*

ance Démocratique, also advocated a policy of withdrawal —withdrawal behind the Maginot Line. Whereas the Vice-President of this group, Paul Reynaud, insisted that Hitler be stopped before it was too late.

"The Germans," Paul Reynaud said, "will play Poland against Czechoslovakia before swallowing Poland themselves. Then they'll play Russia against Poland before devouring Russia. Then, if they can manage it, they'll play England against France, preliminary to feasting on both of us, one by one. They are attempting to create an atmosphere in every country of Europe—an atmosphere of meekness, of cowardice—which is to make an easy matter of the ultimate *coup de grace*."

The French Catholics, on the whole, were extremely mistrustful of Hitler because of the pagan character of National Socialism and because of his religious intolerance. The high clergy, however, considered Soviet Russia to be the real enemy and threw its support to anyone who might combat Communism. The less exalted members of the Hierarchy and the Dominicans, the members of the *Parti Démocrate Populaire Chrétien*, the workers' religious organizations and numerous Catholic writers—including the ex-Ambassador and poet, Paul Claudel, and the novelist, François Mauriac—recognized the imperative necessity for combating the advance of Nazi barbarism.

Among the Nationalists and Conservatives, the older men advocated stemming the Nazi torrent. But the younger Rightists, the former members of the pro-Fascist *ligues*, considered Hitler the champion of the anti-Communist cause. Fundamentally, these young reactionaries hoped that a pro-Nazi policy would result in the death of democracy in France.

As for the Royalists, their foreign policy was consistently anti-German. Their authority on international affairs, Jacques Bainville, the historian, was an avowed member of the school of thought recommending that Germany be split up into numerous fragments—the sort of Germany that had existed until the eighteenth century, thanks to the vigilance of the Kings of France. In his last books, published shortly before the present war, Jacques Bainville had proved himself to be a merciless critic of Hitlerism. However, *L'Action Française,* the principal Royalist organ —in a series of articles by the Party leader, Charles Maurras, the philosopher—had begun to expand a conflicting viewpoint. While approving, generally, of Bainville's theories, Charles Maurras announced the opinion that France should go to war only if and when directly attacked.

A member of *L'Action Française* explained the new position of his militant organization in this way:

"We approved of the last war, we supported the war effort to the utmost, and we were actually the leaders of the militantly patriotic policy from 1914 to 1918—and do you want to know why? Because we hoped—as Charles Maurras has openly admitted—that the post-war situation would give us an opportunity to enhance our influence in the country. At the expense of the Republic, of course. But we soon discovered that we had miscalculated, that the Republic was reaping all the benefits and all the glory of victory, and that it was the democratic principle that had triumphed in Europe on November 11, 1918. Nevertheless, *L'Action Française* adhered to the anti-German line after the war, and violently criticized Briand for his spineless attitude toward the Weimar Republic. . . . But then Italy went Fascist. Hitler came to power in Germany. We knew what to do now. Secretly, we changed our plans. If the Republic won another war, the regime would be strengthened. Therefore war was to be avoided at any cost; that is to say, a war in which the French Republic would be victorious. Any other outcome would, inevitably, be favorable to the principles which we cherished. If France refused to fight, she would have to live under the domination of an immense anti-democratic Power, and France would have to set up a reactionary regime to appease that Power. But if France did choose to fight, we should want her to be defeated. Then, at last, the Republic would perish."

The Party sponsoring this outrageous policy was composed of Army officers, higher officials and young intellectuals. The situation was so appalling and so dangerous that I decided to discuss it with some Monarchists. To my amazement, I learned that nine out of ten of them endorsed the secret policy of *L'Action Française*. They preferred the prospect of France reduced to virtual slavery—either as the result of Hitler's domination over Europe, or of a military defeat—to a continuation of a democratic regime.

As the general outlook grew darker and darker, the attitude of *L'Action Française* became increasingly firm. Because the majority of the active Army officers looked upon *L'Action Française* as gospel, and many reserve officers were under its influence, this sheet constituted the gravest menace to the country.

I was appalled by the attitude of many Deputies, who dismissed the whole thing, saying, with a smile: "Come, come, now. *L'Action Française* doesn't amount to a thing. They have one Senator and one Deputy. And they are of absolutely no importance and never open their mouths."

That was all they cared about: the performance in Parliament.

Chapter Twenty-one

The Road to Munich

(From my Notebook)

MAY 10, 1938.

My secretary, pale and trembling, showed me a copy of the weekly, *Je Suis Partout* ("I Am Everywhere"), commonly known in the trade as *Je Suis Nulle Part* ("I Am Nowhere") because of its miserable circulation.

There, under the title "To Be Shot," *Je Suis Partout* was demanding the immediate execution of Léon Blum, Paul Reynaud, Georges Mandel and Pierre Lazareff.

"I'm in excellent company," I said to my secretary.

Reading the article, I learned that I was "bloodthirsty" and that I was dragging *Paris-Soir* into a course of the most unbridled *bellicisme* (war-mongering).

Belliciste! That was the word *Je Suis Partout* had hit upon as the slogan to be used over and over again by those who could not conceal their pro-Hitler sentiments and who wanted to see France give in to Germany. The men who now most eagerly employed the term *belliciste* were the ones who had regularly hurled the epithet *"pacifistes bêlants"* ("bleating pacifists") at those Frenchmen, who—prior to the advent of Hitler—had endeavored to create a system of European collaboration within the framework of the League of Nations.

The leading contributors to *Je Suis Partout* were young Monarchists of *L'Action Française* group. The weekly belonged to a certain Monsieur Charles Lecca, who had made a fortune in Argentina. *Je Suis Partout* declared in every issue that—together with *L'Action Française,* of course—it had a monopoly on all genuine patriotism, and it declared, simultaneously, that it was all for Hitler, for Mussolini, for Franco, for Léon Degrelle (the Belgian Fascist who had just attacked France in the bitterest language) and even for Codreanu, the chief of the Rumanian Iron Guard, who, in a famous speech, had recommended the annihilation of France.

Lucien Rebattet and Alain Laubreaux were among the principal editors of *Je Suis Partout.* Lucien Rebattet was often seen in the company of Otto Abetz. Alain Laubreaux was a journalist who was sued and found guilty of plagiarism when he published his first and only novel. *Je Suis Partout* endorsed all the Nazi theories and was, of course, violently anti-Semitic.

Incidentally, anti-Semitic publications were increasing. A member of the Municipal Council of Paris, Darquier, who preferred to be known as "Darquier de Pellepoix," directed one of these publications, *La France Enchainée,* which was handed out on the streets and delivered free of charge. Where did the money come from? Perhaps Monsieur Darquier de Pellepoix hoped to be able to reimburse his generous sponsors when his program was put into effect. He did not hesitate to write: *"Hitler has revived the grand tradition of the French Monarchy which consisted in permitting the Jews to fatten themselves for just so long—then to banish them and take over their property."* Naturally, he declared that war was imminent and that it would be "a Jewish war."

The same slogans were to be found in *Le Défi,* a sheet belonging to a lawyer, Jean Charles Legrand, and in *Choc,* published by Colonel Guillaume and Duc Pozzo di Borgo, Colonel de la Rocque's opponents.

These sheets were constantly fighting each other, although they advocated the same vicious ideas. *La France Enchainée* announced that *Choc's* anti-Semitism was fraudulent and that the paper belonged, in effect, to a certain Monsieur Jacques Kahn, one of the leaders of the *Parti Républicain National.* The President of this Party, the Rightist Deputy, Pierre Taittinger, met Darquier de Pellepoix and tried to defend Jacques Kahn.

"How can you call a man who received five citations in the last War a dirty Jew?" Pierre Taittinger asked.

Darquier de Pellepoix replied: "If you had a bulldog who won five first prizes, that wouldn't make him a greyhound, would it?"

"A Jewish war," "The Jewish Maffia," "The War into which the kikes are pushing the goys to wreak revenge on Hitler . . ." Those were the slogans from Berlin which the Nazi agents were trying to spread in France.

Gringoire fired a salvo of anti-Semitic articles from its heavy gun, Henri Béraud, with the result that one of the weekly's leading contributors, Joseph Kessel, resigned and published a scorching reply to Henri Béraud.

May 22, 1938.

Hitler has gone to see Mussolini in Italy.

Georges Bonnet asserts that negotiations were proceeding actively, and that England and France were exerting pressure on Prague, urging Czechoslovakia to be patient and "generous."

The English Ambassador to Berlin has made overtures to the Wilhelmstrasse—on May 7th and 11th. César Campinchi said that the Chamberlain Government has been making glittering promises to Hitler on the condition that he behave himself, and threats in case he's a bad boy.

Campinchi, the Minister of the Navy, added: "The attitude of the French Ministers—despite Georges Bonnet—is firm. Reynaud, Mandel, Jean Zay, Champetier de Ribes and myself—all of us have threatened to resign in the event that France does not keep her solemn promises to Czechoslovakia." He also stated that Daladier and even President Lebrun were taking a resolute stand.

Henlein has been to London (May 12th to 14th). It looks as though Hitler were afraid to start a war right now. A state of siege has been proclaimed in the Sudetenland.

Léon Herman, our Vienna correspondent, has been transferred to Prague. He reports that there have been incidents which both the Czechs and the Germans have refrained from announcing. Nevertheless, there are persistent rumors that German troops have been concentrated near the frontiers of Bohemia, rumors which have been elaborately embroidered upon by *L'Humanité* and *Ce Soir*.

In any event, the English Ambassador to Germany has asked for an explanation of the presence of Nazi troops at the Czech frontier, and Ribbentrop has categorically denied any such troop movement. Yesterday, however, two Sudetenlanders—named Hoffmann and Bohm—were shot and killed by the police on the road from Cheb to Goldberg. They had refused to stop their motorcycles when ordered. These two deaths may well bring on a series of incidents.

At Tabor, President Benes, in a ringing speech, called on his compatriots "not to be afraid of what the coming days might bring, not to be afraid of anything, but to be prepared for every eventuality."

Prague has mobilized two classes of reservists and a large number of specialists.

This morning our Berlin correspondent telephoned that the English Embassy's special train—which was to evacuate the women and children of diplomatic personnel—had been cancelled, quite suddenly. He added that, in view of the firmness displayed by Prague, Paris and London, Hitler seemed to be backing down—for the first time.

July 15th.

Daladier seems to be holding firm. On July 12th, Edouard Daladier stated: "The solemn pledges made by France to Czechoslovakia are unequivocal and sacred." The Germans have mobilized behind their Siegfried Line, but on the Allies' side there's nothing but talk of concessions. In the meantime, negotiations are proceeding. Henlein has conferred with the Czech Minister of Foreign Affairs, Hodza. The Foreign Office has sent William Strang to Prague and to Berlin. The Führer has sent his right-hand man, Captain Wiedemann, to London. Wiedemann and Lord Halifax had a mysterious interview, about which I managed to get some information, concerning the delicate problem of getting Prague to consent, as promptly as possible, to the annexation of the Sudetenland by Germany. The City is trying hard to effect a compromise. On July 1st London concluded a financial accord with Berlin concerning the Austrian debt as well as a new commercial agreement.

August 30th.

The news out of Germany is bad, very bad. Reynaud is most pessimistic. A million and a half men are under arms.

Mussolini has inspected the fortified Island of Pantellaria. Hitler, accompanied by his Generals, has taken a stroll on the bridge of Kehl, opposite Strasbourg, to within a few centimetres of the French frontier. The mission of Lord Runciman, who was sent by London to mediate in Prague, seems to have failed.

"We weren't told anything about this mission until the day before Chamberlain publicly announced the departure of his envoy," Paul Reynaud said to me, angrily. "Georges Bonnet carries on his personal negotiations without troubling to keep Daladier or the Council of Ministers informed. Daladier, himself, is pretty chummy with the Hitlerite gang. Hitler secretly sends him personal messages. Hitler has always felt he could count on Daladier, it seems to me. In 1933, shortly after coming to power, the Führer invited Daladier to a very Wagnerian conference in the Black Forest. They were to discuss the plan of offering the world 'a veterans' peace.' At the last moment, and after considerable hesitation, Daladier finally decided not to reply to the invitation. But nowadays our Premier makes use of men like Edouard Pfeiffer, Joseph Caillaux's flunky, and Fernand de Brinon, a salesman of Nazism, to shuttle back and forth between Paris and Berlin on secret and very private missions.

"We hardly know what's going on! Who is going to

have the courage to tell the people that if we avoid war today—at the price of our honor—we'll lose the war tomorrow? The Nazis and their accomplices have softened up the country to such an extent that many of our fellow citizens now think that it's courageous to confess to cowardice, and that to be resolute and courageous is, in fact, a cowardly thing."

September 14th.

Neville Chamberlain was flying to Berchtesgaden. We put out a special edition. Jean Prouvost was amazed because he'd seen Georges Bonnet, who, apparently, hadn't even been informed of the English Premier's plans!

The news was spreading.

Jules Sauerwein had just seen Benes. The President of the Czechoslovak State, speaking as an old friend, had said: "Peace is still possible. It all depends on the price we and the English are willing to pay."

And he had also said: "Poland and Hungary are just waiting to pounce on us. As for Stalin, he won't move until he is convinced that the Democracies aren't scheming to have the U.S.S.R. face Hitler alone. That's what he's afraid of."

September 20th.

Edouard Daladier and Guy la Chambre spent two days —the 18th and 19th—in London. Chamberlain told them the details of the Berchtesgaden conference.

Georges Bonnet told me that the Führer had commenced by announcing to the English Premier that . . . he wanted the Sudetenlanders to have the right to decide for themselves and to return to the Reich if that was what they wanted . . . and that he, Hitler, was unwilling to wait much longer, and that he was prepared to risk a world war.

However, Bonnet said, Daladier had won Chamberlain's and Halifax's approval of the following procedure: to ask Prague to cede to Germany those zones which, in the last municipal elections, had shown more than a 50 percent German vote. Furthermore, and despite England's traditional disinclination to assume formal obligations, Daladier had persuaded London to join in an international agreement intended to serve as compensation to Prague. Thus one more country was solemnly to guarantee the frontiers of Czechoslovakia after the Sudetenland had been ceded to Germany.

There was a Council of Ministers this morning. Georges Bonnet reported to his colleagues on the conversations that had been held in London. No one protested against the planned procedure. Only Mandel and Reynaud expressed some sort of displeasure by their manner. The suggestions were duly transmitted to Prague—where they were promptly rejected.

Later, during the evening, Georges Bonnet received a telegram from our Minister at Prague, Monsieur V. de Lacroix. This telegram, which has never been published among the official documents, read as follows:

September 20, 1938.
(*Télégramme réservé* No. 2219-2220)

The President of the Council of Ministers summoned me. He said that, in accord with the President of the Republic, he has to inform me that if I were to notify him during this night that, in the event of war between Czechoslovakia and Germany because of the Sudeten Germans, France—in view of her engagements entered into with Britain—would not act, the President of the Republic would take note of this declaration, the President of the Council would immediately convoke the Cabinet, all members of which are in accord with the President and with the Premier, *pour s'incliner* (to yield, to submit).

"The members of the Czechoslovak Government require this specific statement to enable them to accept the Franco-British proposal. They are sure of the Army, for its leaders have declared that it would be suicidal to face Germany alone. Monsieur Hodza states that this step, suggested by him, is the only way to preserve peace. He wishes to have everything decided before midnight, if possible, or, in any case, during this night. The President of the Council is addressing an identical communication to the British Minister.

"LACROIX."

Georges Bonnet immediately advised Edouard Daladier

and Albert Lebrun. Daladier took the position that he could do nothing unless he knew London's attitude.

"It's a quarter past eleven," Georges Bonnet said, "and London has nothing to do with it. Besides, you know England's line perfectly well. Prague must have our reply by midnight. The peace of Europe is at stake right now, at this very moment."

Daladier accused Bonnet of having suggested this move in the first place, of having instructed our Monsieur de Lacroix to suggest the idea to Monsieur Hodza, subsequent to Benes' rejection of the Franco-British proposals.

Georges Bonnet denied this. Then he adhered to his line. "If you want to destroy Czechoslovakia," he said to Daladier, "if you want to assume the responsibility for war, all you need do is let this fateful hour pass."

At 11:45 P.M., Edouard Daladier and Albert Lebrun authorized Georges Bonnet, *on his own responsibility,* to send Monsieur de Lacroix the statement, as requested.

September 22nd. Midnight.

Chamberlain has left for Godesberg on the Rhine, after having addressed a solemn appeal to Berlin and to Prague to be calm during the impending conversations.

Tension in Paris is at its height. It's being rumored that Georges Bonnet is about to leave the Quai d'Orsay. The *Délégation des Gauches,* comprising members of the Parliamentary Majority, has issued a statement demanding a firm foreign policy.

The Czech Minister, Osusky, is saying that Hodza has been misinformed by M. de Lacroix as to France's real stand—misinformed, deliberately, at Georges Bonnet's instigation—and that Prague will not consent to being bullied into submitting, and that, furthermore, Benes has already requested a written confirmation of the note he received verbally from Monsieur V. de Lacroix.

Georges Bonnet states that he will send this signed confirmation, and, taking the offensive, accuses Reynaud and Mandel of having undermined the effectiveness of his communication by spreading the rumor in Prague—either by telephoning directly or by having someone telephone—that he, Georges Bonnet, was on his way out.

The English Ambassador is very uneasy because Prague has not replied. At 4 P.M. he tells Georges Bonnet that he is deeply concerned, and informs Osusky that England might be moved to recall her Minister to Prague, if Monsieur Benes should continue to procrastinate.

At 5 P.M. we get the news that Prague has finally replied—in the affirmative. Immediately, Paul Reynaud, Georges Mandel and their colleague, Champetier de Ribes, in a body, go to the office of the President of the Council of Ministers and threaten to resign in the event it can be proved that Georges Bonnet, personally, without authorization of the Cabinet, has exerted pressure on Prague. Paul Reynaud is furious. To quiet him, Daladier promises to convene a Cabinet Meeting the day after tomorrow, as soon as the results of the Godesberg conversations will have become known.

Jules Sauerwein has just telephoned me from Godesberg. He tells me that Hitler and Chamberlain don't seem to be reaching any sort of an accord. He has spoken to Sir Horace Wilson, who accompanied the English Prime Minister. It seems that Hitler intends to move immediately, without awaiting the outcome of the conference; that he wants to send in the Nazi Army to occupy all the Sudetenland zones showing a German majority.

September 23rd.

Very early this morning, I informed Paul Reynaud as to what had happened in Godesberg last night.

I've been sticking close to the telephone, hoping to hear Sauerwein's voice. When his call did come, it was a disappointment. Chamberlain, he tells me, is drawing up a memorandum, is sending it to Hitler, who is expected to give his answer during the afternoon. We won't know a thing before tomorrow.

September 24th.

The Cabinet has met. To exonerate himself, Bonnet read the telegram from Monsieur de Lacroix. The meeting was calm enough. In view of the critical situation, Reynaud and Mandel are refraining from provoking a Cabinet crisis. Besides, their interview with Daladier has convinced them of the Premier's fundamental intentions. Furthermore, the situation has taken a new turn: after having notified Paris and London, Prague has issued the order for General Mobilization. Neither the Foreign Office nor the Quai d'Orsay dared to advise against this precautionary measure. Hitler and Chamberlain learned of Czechoslovakia's decision at the very moment when the Führer was pointing out on a map the districts he intended occupying. The zones had been colored red, and Hitler was telling the English Prime Minister that, if these territories were not within the Reich by October 1st, the Reich would take them over.

Chamberlain is not pleased. He has promised, however, to forward Hitler's memorandum to Prague—to forward the terms, but not to recommend their acceptance.

September 26th.

We are at the brink. Mobilization has begun. Prague has rejected the Godesberg memorandum. Daladier and Georges Bonnet have gone to London.

In London, Daladier had stressed the point that the honor and security of France were at stake. Constantly, however, Georges Bonnet had tried to interrupt him, but Daladier had not permitted him to do so. As for the English Ministers, they were consistently unreceptive. Sir John Simon and Sir Samuel Hoare had distinguished themselves by their efforts to discourage all resistance to Hitler.

Daladier had gone to London armed with the solemn assurances of General Gamelin and Admiral Darlan that the French Army and Navy were ready for action. General Gamelin had added, however, that, in the event of war, England should immediately decree conscription.

Then Neville Chamberlain had cried: "But we have most discouraging news on the state of your aviation."

He was referring to the truly terrifying report made by Lindbergh to Mr. Joseph Kennedy, the U. S. Ambassador to London.

The conference of the French and English Ministers had

broken up at 2 A.M. They had not arrived at any accord as to the stand that was to be taken.

After their return to Paris, Georges Bonnet brought Daladier a letter, dated September 24th, in which he begged the Premier not to order General Mobilization, stating that France would find herself isolated, since neither Britain nor Russia would move to support her.

"I shall mobilize at least ten classes," Daladier replied.

September 27th.

Cabinet meeting this morning.

Daladier sat across the table from President Lebrun. Georges Bonnet, at his right. Albert Sarraut, Minister of the Interior, at his left.

Daladier opened the discussion by announcing: "Gentlemen, I have decided on General Mobilization."

Georges Bonnet promptly rose.

"Three weeks ago," he said, "General Vuillemin, Chief of Staff of our Air Corps, paid a visit to Germany. On his return, I asked him what he thought. He replied: 'Within a fortnight, at the outside, our Air Corps would be destroyed.'"

"That's very serious, very grave," Paul Reynaud replied. "But it's either too early or too late. If Hitler got wind of your remarks, he wouldn't hesitate to attack Czechoslovakia at once."

"I don't imagine," said Georges Bonnet, drily, "that any one of us is going to oblige Monsieur Hitler with a report on the confidential information I'm giving my colleagues."

(In view of the fact that, within an hour after the Cabinet meeting's adjournment, and thanks to two Ministers, I was in possession of what amounted to a verbatim report of the proceeding—it seemed likely that Hitler, thanks to his innumerable agents, must have been supplied with the same information, quite as promptly and as completely. Incidentally, I understand that Otto Abetz has been in Paris since yesterday.)

César Campinchi and de Chapdelaine supported Paul Reynaud's stand, and declared themselves opposed to "a weak and panicky foreign policy."

Daladier took out his pen and wrote on a piece of paper: "*Monsieur le Président de la République:* I have the honor to tender you the resignation of my Cabinet."

Georges Bonnet, looking over Daladier's shoulder, saw what was going on and wanted to intervene. Albert Sarraut, on the other side of Daladier, had also read the note, and whispered: "No, not yet. You can't do that. We must wait."

Camille Chautemps had hitherto been one of the principal supporters of Georges Bonnet and of Bonnet's policies. He now got up and made a long speech that did not succeed in saying much of anything.

Thereupon, amidst considerable confusion, the meeting was adjourned.

September 28th, 10 A.M.

Sauerwein tells me the German troops are going to march into Czechoslovakia today.

Lord Halifax and Georges Bonnet have had a lengthy telephone conversation. Immediately thereafter Georges Bonnet saw Daladier and gave him a message from the English Foreign Secretary, a message containing some very bad news with regard to the state of the Czechoslovak Army.

Georges Bonnet, on his own responsibility, asked our Ambassador, François-Poncet—by telephone—to persuade Hitler to postpone the invasion of Czechoslovakia until February 1st. "Tell him that by that time," Georges Bonnet said, "I shall have done everything possible to arrange a peaceful settlement of the problem."

Our London correspondent tells me that Chamberlain has sent Benes the following telegram:

> I have to inform you that advices reaching me indicate that German troops will march into Bohemia tomorrow at 2 P.M. I do not believe that any action undertaken by any Power can prevent this. I believe that Bohemia will be overwhelmed within forty-eight hours. I feel that I should apprise you of this situation and permit you to decide upon the attitude to be adopted.

1:30 P.M.

François-Poncet telephoned Georges Bonnet. He has spoken to Hitler. The Führer, it seems, is "perfectly calm." He has had a long telephone conversation with Mussolini.

2 P.M.

Paris-Soir has been authorized to make much of this Hitler-Mussolini phone call. We are publishing Mussolini's announcement that he has succeeded in obtaining Hitler's promise to wait another twenty-four hours. Nice of him.

4 P.M.

Coup de théâtre! Chamberlain has just announced that Hitler has called a conference of four at Munich for tomorrow. Mussolini, Daladier and Chamberlain have accepted the invitation. The fate of Czechoslovakia will be decided without the presence of a Czechoslovak representative. Nor will Russia, co-guarantor with France of Czechoslovakia, be represented.

September 30th.

Daladier and Georges Bonnet were hailed and cheered as heroes on their return from Munich by plane. The performance was extraordinary. As Daladier was about to step out of the plane, he looked around, saw the vast crowd at the airdrome—and hesitated for a moment. Later, Guy la Chambre, one of the few Ministers who had come to call for Daladier, told me that the Premier had confessed that he had been frightened. "I was afraid," Daladier said, "that the crowd was going to give me a bad reception." He soon discovered, to his great surprise, that the crowd was giving him a wildly enthusiastic welcome. And he was unable to prevent himself from muttering: "The fools, they don't realize what they're applauding!"

It's a strange situation. The crowd was acclaiming Daladier—and only Daladier. The public was sullen and downright hostile toward Georges Bonnet. Instinctively, they mistrust him.

The people, for the moment, are celebrating their regained "security." There won't be any war. The *mobilisés* are coming home!

Paris-Soir has opened a public subscription. The funds are to be used to present Neville Chamberlain with a little house in the country, on French soil and to be named *La Maison de la Paix*.

October 1st.

On the evening of September 27th, I had run into Otto Abetz again. On the 29th, he was in Munich, radiant with joy. His job was to welcome and entertain the French newspapermen.

He told our Paul Bringuier—who, together with Sauerwein, represented *Paris-Soir* at Munich—that, after the Agreement had been signed, Hitler stood at the window and watched Chamberlain and Daladier drive away in their cars. He turned to von Ribbentrop and said disdainfully:

"It's terrible. I always have to deal with nonentities."

Chapter Twenty-two

During the Intermission

I FEEL torn between a feeling of cowardly relief and one of shame." These words, written by Léon Blum on the day following Munich, seemed to express the sentiments of the average Frenchman.

Insofar as the great mass of public opinion was concerned, the moment of "cowardly relief" soon passed, but the feeling of profound shame remained. The Chamber of Deputies ratified the Munich Agreement unanimously —with the exception of the Communist votes and the vote of Henri de Kérillis and one obscure Socialist deputy.

The Munich crowd was strengthened by all the elements which, for one reason or another, were furthering German propaganda. This propaganda became bolder and bolder. Books appeared, published *à comptes d'auteur* (at the authors' expense), describing Hitler as "the creator of a New European Order," as the leader of the "Crusade against Bolshevism." They accused Czechoslovakia of having imperiled the peace of the world. And they announced that "the Capitalists, the Jews and the Communists" had come to a secret agreement—a sort of Holy Alliance—with the object of plunging all of Europe into war.

Paul Ferdonnet had produced a number of those books in praise of Hitler, each one enthusiastically acclaimed by

Je Suis Partout. He offered to supply me, free of charge, with news from Berlin. He assured me that he enjoyed the friendship of many highly placed Nazis, and that he was already serving as correspondent for a number of Paris newspapers. I declined his offer with thanks.

The name of Ferdonnet again came to my attention in connection with a rather mysterious news agency that had been launched in Paris under the name of "Prima Presse." This organization distributed—either free of charge or for a nominal sum—news items as well as photographs to newspapers, notably to the provincial press. As an added attraction, the Prima Presse agency promised its subscribers the benefits of a newly perfected, improved process for stereotyping photographs. This process had been patented in Berlin early in 1933, prior to the advent of Hitler, by its two inventors, Jews, who had been sent to a concentration camp after their blueprints and machinery had been confiscated. Paul Winkler, President of the *Syndicat des Agences de Presse,* told me that he had heard various rumors concerning the mysterious doings of Prima Presse, and that it was being run by Monsieur Paul Ferdonnet and a certain Pierre Mouthon. He also showed me a number of the so-called "dispatches" that had been released by Prima Presse. Regardless of their date lines, all these bulletins were definitely and without exception of Nazi origin. I soon learned that Paul Ferdonnet was in the employ of the famous Dr. Schmoll (of the German Embassy) and Otto Abetz.

Ferdonnet's political theories were identical with those held by the *Parti Franciste.* The President of this Party, Marcel Bucard, and all the members distinguished themselves by wearing blue shirts. The Vice President of this group was a lawyer by the name of André Herman Grégoire. Monsieur Grégoire, born in Alsace of German parents, had fought in the last war on the side of the Kaiser. He had become a Frenchman and had been admitted to the Bar in Paris. He strutted up and down the corridors of the Palais de Justice, proudly displaying the ornamental scars acquired during his university days. Besides these unmistakably Germanic *Schmisse,* he wore a ribbon on his barrister's robe, a broad ribbon unlike any of those worn by his colleagues.

"This," he would boast, "is the Iron Cross. I won it on the battlefield. On the other side."

Grégoire, after the Nazis' accession to power, had been appointed official attorney for the German Embassy in Paris. Incidentally, he was also chosen to serve as counsel for the Duchess of Windsor, ex-Wallis Simpson, when she sued *Paris-Soir* for having published a series of articles about her, written by her cousin, Newbold Noyes, an American newspaperman.

Grégoire was in the habit of taking rather frequent trips to Germany. He was the moving spirit behind the anti-Democratic and anti-Semitic party nominally headed by Marcel Bucard. The Francists, with their direct pipeline to the offices of Herr Doktor Goebbels, had naturally chosen as their motto: *"France d'abord"* (France First).

No one was in the least surprised that *Le Matin* expounded the German viewpoint. Monsieur Bunau-Varilla had, of course, been duly rewarded. For one thing, the Germans had "recognized" the true value of his incomparable and unfailing cure-all, *Synthol,* and had promised to promote this product on a huge scale. Later, Otto Abetz, laughing to the point of tears, told how one of his colleagues, representing German chemical interests, had solemnly signed the contract and had flattered the old man by saying: "I should like you to know, Monsieur, that our chemists, vastly experienced as they are, have been amazed by *Synthol.* They have succeeded in analyzing it, but they have found it utterly impossible to reproduce the compound synthetically." Maurice Bunau-Varilla's admiration for Germany and for things German mounted. He had, up to that time, played a rather cautious, subtle game. Shrewdly enough, he had screened his true sentiments by appointing as his Berlin correspondent and then as editor-in-chief a man who was a French patriot in the best sense of the word—Philippe Barrès, a veteran of the last war (his father was the celebrated nationalist author). Philippe Barrès, far-sighted and fearless, had consistently denounced Germany's preparations for aggression and imperialism. *Le Matin* had regularly featured his contributions. But one fine day Philippe Barrès observed that *Le Matin* was exploiting his stories about Germany's prodigious rearmament, not—as he had intended—to warn France to see to her own defenses, but to preach the futility of attempting to offer any resistance. He resigned, at once. It was *Paris-Soir's* gain, for he joined our staff.

Le Temps had been *munichois* long before Munich, and had even published an article by the eminent jurist, Joseph Barthelemy in which he attempted to demonstrate that "the Franco-Czech Treaty had become null and void as a result of the collapse of the Locarno Accord." After Munich, *Le Temps* became even more *munichois.*

And the Trotskyite, the Anarchist and the Syndicalist newspapers assumed the same attitude as the Rightist press, represented by Pierre Guimier's *Le Journal,* Léon Bailby's *Le Jour,* and *Candide, Gringoire* and *L'Action Française.*

On September 21st, *Le Journal* had run a rather strange article by Gabriel Hanotaux, in which the learned ex-Minister of Foreign Affairs and Member of the French Academy referred to the Czechoslovakian question as a strictly *Balkan* problem. It was in *Le Journal* that the ex-Premier, Pierre Etienne Flandin, had conducted his campaign on behalf of France's withdrawal from all action on the European continent. On the day the Munich pact was signed, Flandin sent telegrams of congratulation to all the signatories, including Hitler.

Monsieur Léon Bailby revealed his innermost thoughts when he wrote: "We do not want any war now. What we hope for is a reprieve which will give us time to rid ourselves of our present leaders."

And *L'Action Française,* of course, kept repeating, day after day, that war would open the doors wide to Communism. On September 29th, *L'Action Française* was seized and indicted for incitement to murder, after having published the following parody on "*L'Internationale*":

S'ils s'obstinent ces cannibals
A faire de nous des héros
Il faut que nos premières balles
Soient pour Mandel, Blum et Reynaud.
(Literally: If they insist, those cannibals
On making heroes out of us,
Our first bullets
Must be for Mandel, Blum and Reynaud.)

Those who opposed a policy of submission to Hitler were branded by the *munichois* press as "Soviet agents," or as "members of the Franco-Russian Party," as "Jews," or as "flunkeys of capitalism."

Let us look at some of these so-called Franco-Russians. Henri de Kérillis, in his newspaper, *L'Epoque,* was the first to denounce Otto Abetz and the crowd that had fallen under his influence. Both in his writings and in his speeches before the Chamber of Deputies, Henri de Kérillis distinguished himself by his forthrightness and courage. After Munich, in the course of the session that was to ratify the Treaty, he shot the following unanswerable remark at Daladier:

"It has been said, in certain quarters, that this political disaster is to be blamed on the state of our Army. Let us not be told anything like that now. Or I shall reply that the President of the Council of Ministers—who, throughout two and a half years, has been the Minister entrusted with our Army—was well aware of its state when, with the whole world listening, he repeatedly made these well-known promises."

Indeed, as late as July 12th, Daladier had made a speech in which he reaffirmed "the solemn, unequivocal and sacred promises made by France to Czechoslovakia."

Henri de Kérillis' ex-colleague on the *Echo de Paris,* André Géraud—known as Pertinax—had achieved a reputation for being extraordinarily well informed. Nevertheless, his far-sighted and trenchant articles now appeared only in publications with very restricted circulation—the weekly, *L'Europe Nouvelle,* and the newspaper, *L'Ordre,* directed by Emile Buré. Both of these publications, however, were read by the country's leading citizens. Tirelessly, Pertinax pointed out that history had conclusively proved that Sadowa led, inescapably, to Sedan. He was the only one to express surprise at the spectacle of General Vuillemin, the commander of our Air Corps, going to Germany at the very moment of the Czechoslovakian crisis, allowing himself to be hailed and cheered there, and then returning with the statement that it would be "folly, before many years of preparation, to attempt to oppose the German *Luftwaffe*." And Pertinax did not fail to point out that it had been precisely the military head of our aviation who had most consistently stood in the way of the expansion and development of our aeronautical industry.

Another personality designated by the *munichois* as Franco-Russian was Madame Genevieve Tabouis—a gracious, white-haired lady. As a grand-niece of Ambassador Cambon, she had an entrée into all political and diplomatic circles. She had the journalist's insatiable thirst for information and was endowed with prodigious vitality. She created a new *genre* of diplomatic reporting. It was far more than mere reporting: she undertook to write up a daily story on what was going on in the chancelleries, to show what was really going on behind the scenes and, furthermore, to predict what was going to happen next. Her name became known internationally when, in one of his speeches, Hitler said something to the effect that Madame Tabouis knew, better than he did, what he was doing and what he was about to do.

Genevieve Tabouis' articles appeared in *L'Oeuvre*, the outstanding Leftist daily. Under Havas Agency control, *L'Oeuvre* went through a series of strange ups and downs when it was under the actual, although secret, direction of such men as Ferdinand Buisson, ex-President of the Chamber of Deputies, President of the Council of Ministers for *one* day, and the friend and right-hand man of Pierre Laval; and Jean Hennessy, the big *cognac* man, who had been *Le Quotidien's* grave-digger as well as the founder of the first French National Socialist Party. The public, of course, was blissfully ignorant of this, and continued to take *L'Oeuvre* at its face value—namely, as a Radical-Socialist newspaper.

Side by side with Madame Genevieve Tabouis' articles,

L'Oeuvre published the ultra-pacifist writings of Marcel Déat and of Georges de la Fouchardière. The latter's contribution of September 1, 1938, read, in part, as follows:

"A year ago, no one even dreamt of the existence of the Sudetenlanders, and today there is talk of war because Monsieur Hitler insists that they are entitled to wear white socks if they so desire, and we are told that it is our sacred duty to support our friends, the Czechs, who want to force the Sudetenlanders to wear colored socks. Men, it seems, have become even more stupid than swine, for it is normal to make sausage-meat out of swine."

Monsieur de la Fouchardière did not hesitate to take savage pokes at Madame Genevieve Tabouis, whose articles regularly appeared on the same page as his own. "Mademoiselle de Thèbes (the name of a famous fortune-teller) has a key," he wrote, "a key which opens all the diplomatic pouches. The chancelleries address their code messages to her and not to those stupid diplomats. Her double, triple and even quadruple sight functions from London to Prague, via Moscow and Tokio, and she sits on her tripod, foaming at the mouth with prophetic frenzy. But let us be fair; occasionally, in harmony with the law of averages, her predictions do come true—in just about the same proportion as do those of tipsters at the race track who offer you a sure thing."

As a matter of fact, the predictions of Madame Genevieve Tabouis came true often enough to enrage the pro-Nazis and to assure her of a large and faithful following, and practically to compel the management of *L'Oeuvre* to continue running her column.

Emile Buré, Pertinax, Henri de Kérillis and Madame Genevieve Tabouis were, all of them, *bourgeois,* a bit on the conservative side and strongly anti-Communist. But they were constantly accused of being in the pay of the Soviets because they advocated the military alliance with Russia.

Naturally, the Jews were also accused of wanting to precipitate the conflict, and there was talk of punishing them cruelly for this. Lucien Rebattet, writing in *Je Suis Partout*, embroidered on the theme, and described with relish a pogrom he had witnessed in Austria. This performance had impressed him so favorably that he recommended the procedure to his fellow-citizens in the following terms:

> In all those streets, in all those alleys, which I had formerly seen swarming with these grimacing and feverish people—the Glockengasse, the Tempelgasse, the Ferdinandstrasse, the Taborstrasse—there was nothing but silence, the frightened silence which follows disaster. Here, the anti-Jews had had their way. . . . Students, laborers, craftsmen—each one according to the dictates of his imagination and to his heart's content.
>
> Every sign board, every shop window, horribly smeared and besmirched with ink, with grease, with tar and even with—yes, you've guessed it, and serves them right, too. And, all over, in big letters, "*Sau Jude* . . . Jewish Pig," and the two crossed triangles and Talmudic caricatures crudely daubed, and everywhere the words: "Jewish house, don't buy." On the walls along the corridors, there was this inscription: "This house infested on every floor with the Jewish pestilence. To be fumigated without delay."
>
> In short, a pogrom. German anti-Semitism has, at last, broken into and smashed the ghetto. And rightfully. We have dealt far too gently with the Jewish people. I wonder what could prevent us from saying that German anti-Semitism stands as a splendid example of distributive justice, from which the Jew-ridden countries should take a lesson rather than hide their faces and complain of barbarism.

Simultaneously, the writer, Louis-Ferdinand Céline—who had made a name for himself with his book, *Voyage au Bout de la Nuit*—also demanded pogroms, in a new book entitled, quite simply, *Bagatelle pour un Massacre*.

However, a great number of Jews were to be found in the ranks of the most ardent *munichois*. There was, for example, Emmanuel Berl, the first director of *Marianne*, who, in the spring of 1938, had founded a pamphlet, *Le Pavé de Paris*, demanding an *entente* with Germany. There was Michel Alexandre, delegate of the *Comité Syndicaliste* for action on behalf of peace. And there were Mesdames Jeanette Alexandre, Betty Brunschwigg, Yvonne Hagenauer, Madeleine Paz, Sarah Weil-Raynal, who signed a women's petition against war, entitled, "War Never: Negotiation Always." And then there were numerous Jews who belonged to *L'Action Française* and to the various Rightist parties; a great number belonged to the *Parti Social Français,* ex-*Croix de Feu* as well as to the sundry pacifist organizations.

In short, the French Jews were just as much divided on the question of the policy to be pursued toward Germany as were all other Frenchmen. Very many of them were openly opposed to Léon Blum, not only because they were opposed to the *Front Populaire,* but also because they feared that their co-religionist's political line might give rise to anti-Semitism in France. In 1937, the Grand Rabbi of Paris suggested to Léon Blum that he resign.

In order to make the French masses believe that the Jews were trying to drive the country into war, the Nazi agents in France made a systematic scandal about the policies of the two Jewish Cabinet Members—Georges Mandel and Jean Zay. Georges Mandel was simply adhering to the line of his former *patron,* Georges Clemenceau. As for Jean Zay, who received the lion's share of the insults, his father was Jewish and his mother was Protestant; Zay, himself, had been brought up as a Protestant, had married a Protestant, and was bringing up his children as Protestants. This was known only to his friends, however, and he had requested them not to reveal these facts now, for Jean Zay did not want to appear to be disavowing, in cowardly fashion, the ancestors of his father.

But, on the Right, Paul Lévy, the director of the weekly, *Aux Ecoutes*; in the Center, the philosopher, Julien Benda; to the Left, Georges Boris, the Socialists, Solomon Grumbach, Louis Lévy, Georges Gombault—all were demanding the same foreign policy as were the Catholics and the Protestants of all parties who were denouncing Hitler as a menace to the nation and to the world.

The International League against Anti-Semitism, to which the young polemic writer, Bernard Lecache, devoted himself almost fanatically, burned with indignation at the fate of the unfortunate Jews in Germany. One of the League's great achievements was that it denounced, in no uncertain terms, those Jews "who howled with the wolves and who were, themselves, being fattened for the kill."

And now, as to the role of the "capitalists."

The financial oligarchies—in London as well as in Paris —unsparingly supported the policy of surrender to Hitler. Just before Munich, Albert Sarraut, the Minister of the Interior, was given the recording of a telephone conversation obtained by his wire-tapping department. The record revealed that a very big Franco-British bank—the bank which regularly executed international exchange operations for the account of the French Government—had telephoned from Paris to London to purchase enormous blocks of stock on the London Exchange, and that, in the course of this conversation, the most minute details had been given concerning the negotiations and the plans of the French Minister of Foreign Affairs—details which Sarraut, himself, did not know about. He promptly brought the record to Daladier, who flew into a violent rage and summoned Georges Bonnet. But then it was decided that it would be imprudent, in view of the acute crisis, to make an issue of the affair. In other words, the matter was dropped.

The Banque Lazard Frères, the Comité des Forges (the steel cartel), the Royal Dutch and its subsidiary companies, the Rothschild and the Mendelsohn Banks, the big chemical corporations, the utilities, the Comité des Houillères (the coal cartel), the big insurance companies—all energetically and lavishly supported Monsieur Georges Bonnet and his foreign policy.

Why? Well, because the munitions makers wanted the rearmament race to continue for many years, because they fondly hoped that Hitler would attack Russia and destroy Communism, or, quite simply, because they believed in the two-century-old theory of the Rothschilds—namely, that war does not pay.

Monsieur Schneider, the owner of the vast Creusot mills, was also interested in Skoda, in Czechoslovakia, and in numerous Central European enterprises, including Asap (automobiles), Avia (airplanes), Konstructiva (public works), the mines and iron-works of Banska, the Banque de l'Union Européenne; and it was claimed that he had sold out his shares in these concerns during the months preceding September, 1938. What conclusions were to be drawn from that? Did it mean—as some said—that this was the decisive round in the struggle between Imperial Chemicals (British) and the I. G. Farbengesellschafft (German), on the one hand, and Kuhlmann (French), and the Czechoslovak chemical consortium of Aussig (in the Sudetenland) with the support of the American Dupont de Nemours Corporation, on the other? Or was this move to be construed as evidence of a struggle between Vickers (British, munitions, associated with Krupp) and the Skoda-Schneider group?

In any event, the negotiations preceding the Munich accord had led to the transfer of the majority of the Franco-British holdings in Central Europe to German capitalists.

The economic situation in France was growing steadily worse. On November 1st, Paul Reynaud succeeded Monsieur Marchandeau as Minister of Finance. On November 7th, a young Pole by the name of Grynszpan, whose parents had been tormented and tortured by the Nazis in concentration camps, shot and fatally wounded Councilor Vom Rath at the German Embassy. Using this incident as an excuse, Germany immediately organized a vast and fearful pogrom throughout the Reich.

The entire civilized world protested indignantly. To show its disapproval, the United States recalled its Ambassador from Berlin "for consultations."

At the Council of Ministers on November 23rd, Georges Bonnet announced that the Reich had expressed its willingness to sign a nonaggression treaty with France, similar to the document signed by Chamberlain and Hitler immediately following the Munich accord. Bonnet announced that von Ribbentrop would come to Paris to be present at the solemn, epoch-making, etc. inauguration of this new era in Franco-German relations. The Ministers were, to say the least, surprised; they had never been told that any such negotiations were under way. Some of them protested, saying that the moment was surely not opportune. Daladier admitted that public opinion should have been prepared, that the public should have been informed of these negotiations, and that the arrival of von Ribbentrop in Paris at this moment might create an unfavorable impression, both in France and abroad. President Albert Lebrun, who rarely took sides, spoke up, however, and declared himself in agreement with the Premier's viewpoint. Jean Zay and Campinchi stated that they feared demonstrations and disorder. Another Minister, Monsieur Anatole de Monzie, suggested that the meeting take place in Strasbourg.

Finally, Paul Reynaud declared: "The signing of this Treaty must be postponed, for, even though the Treaty may be to our advantage, the trip is surely to theirs. They need something like this to regain their prestige."

But Georges Bonnet stubbornly insisted that the trip could not be postponed. "Germany would consider it an unfriendly gesture," he said. "She does not see that she is to derive any benefit from the accord. She has consented to it *merely to be agreeable to France*. Shall we now bring up again all the problems that were resolved at Munich?"

Supported by Camille Chautemps, Guy la Chambre and by the Minister of Agriculture, Queuille, Georges Bonnet had his way.

Moscow then began to realize that she was about to lose the game she had been playing. According to custom, therefore, the U.S.S.R. went into action through the medium of the Communist Party. The Party persuaded the *Confédération Générale du Travail* to call a General Strike. But the public had been through a lot of excitement recently, and wanted nothing but peace and quiet. The strike, scheduled to take place on November 30th, was highly unpopular, even among the workers. Daladier was well aware of the trend. He opposed the strike energetically, declaring that very severe penalties would be imposed upon whoever failed to report for duty, and that laborers and employees who remained absent from work could be discharged by their employers. The strike was a complete failure. Whereupon at least a million workers left the *Confédération Générale du Travail*—and Daladier's prestige was considerably enhanced.

On November 30th, *Le Petit Parisien* ran the following dispatch, datelined London: "The opinion in Berlin is that Monsieur Daladier will get the better of it in his struggle with the labor unions. Moreover, the Reich would certainly not be inclined to sign an accord with a Leftist Government."

Very much along the same lines was Hitler's speech, held a few days previously, in which he had blackballed, so to speak, certain English statesmen (notably, Winston Churchill and Anthony Eden) and had specifically mentioned those with whom he would be willing to negotiate.

On November 30th, the day of the strike—but before its dismal failure became known—Italian Deputies, meeting in Rome, for the first time clamored for Nice, Corsica, Savoy and Tunisia.

Otto Abetz had come to Paris with von Ribbentrop for the formal and solemn signing of the Franco-German accord. During von Ribbentrop's stay, there was not the slightest ripple of public displeasure. There was, in fact, nothing but profound indifference. Georges Bonnet gave a big dinner in honor of the German Minister of Foreign Affairs—a dinner which was attended by a number of distinguished personalities, including representatives of all the big financial institutions and industrial enterprises. Great care was taken, of course, not to disturb the serene atmosphere by the presence of any Jews (the Banque Lazard Frères was represented, however, by its Aryan attorney, Monsieur Daniel Serruys). There was also an elaborate reception at the German Embassy, and, contrary to established custom, the invitations to this reception were written in the German language. There were some few Frenchmen, at least, who had enough self-respect to return their invitations to Ambassador von Welzcheck.

Two days after von Ribbentrop had returned to Berlin, I ran into Paul Reynaud and the Polish Ambassador, Lucasiewics, at Minou de Montgomery's.

"You celebrated Czechoslovakia's misfortunes too

hastily," Paul Reynaud said to Lucasiewics. "It won't be long before the Germans get after you."

Lucasiewics was intelligent, but quick-tempered and stubborn. "Never," he exclaimed. "Germany will never dare. We're stronger and more intelligent than those Czechs. And, besides, you see that they're leaving Czechoslovakia alone now."

"By March," said Reynaud, "Germany will have devoured Czechoslovakia. And in August she'll attack Poland."

Chapter Twenty-three

Cherchez la Femme

HÉLÈNE REBUFFEL was ambitious. She was wealthy and had valuable connections. One of her father's best friends, André Tardieu, introduced her to Paul Reynaud, who was at the time beginning to attract attention.

Reynaud had distinguished himself at the Palais de Justice by his originality, his clarity of mind and his gift for coining telling phrases. His political career was ascending. He had been elected Deputy from the Basses-Alpes immediately after the War. He had married the daughter of his *patron*, Maître Henri-Robert, President of the Order of French Advocates. A daughter, Odette, had been born to Paul and Jeanne Reynaud.

A romance developed between young Hélène Rebuffel and Paul Reynaud, who was twice her age. Strangely enough, Hélène and Madame Reynaud became devoted friends. Hélène was proud and would not play a secondary role. She met young Jean de Portes, and in marrying him acquired the title of Countess.

As Hélène de Portes she entertained lavishly. Her home became a salon at which political celebrities were frequent visitors. When André Tardieu was in power, he was the star attraction. It was Hélène who introduced him to Colonel de la Rocque, the head of the *Croix de Feu* and her husband's cousin. She also managed to attract such prominent guests as Pierre Etienne Flandin, Pierre Laval and Georges Bonnet.

In 1930 Paul Reynaud had been chosen Minister of Finance. Shortly afterwards, he was named Minister of Colonies and went to Indo-China. He was a conspicuous success as an administrator.

In the meantime Hélène de Portes suffered an attack of nervous depression and spent several months in a sanatorium in Switzerland. On her return to Paris she saw a great deal of Thierry de Ludre. Since Berlin must have known of the influence she exerted over Paul Reynaud, it is safe to assume that Thierry de Ludre was acting under instructions to reach through her one of the most uncompromising foes of Nazism.

Hélène de Portes knew that Paul Reynaud was far removed from sharing her fondness of Fascism. But she reasoned that this energetic man, who loathed Communism, might become Dictator some day. Reynaud was becoming more deeply infatuated with her, and was falling more and more under her domination.

She had gone to Vienna to see a specialist about her nervous condition. There, thanks to Thierry de Ludre, she had met the Austrian and German leaders of the Nazi Party. On her return to Paris, however, she established herself as Otto von Hapsburg's manager! Subsequently she paid several visits to the Comte de Paris, put herself at the Royal Pretender's command, and even went so far as to promise him the support of Paul Reynaud, an ardent Republican.

The more Paul Reynaud drifted toward the Left, the more Hélène de Portes kept pulling toward the Right. But it was Hélène de Portes who persuaded Paul Reynaud to visit Nazi Germany. On his return to Paris he made his famous statement, to the effect that the "bloodless period of the war" had already commenced.

Such pronouncements antagonized a good part of Paul Reynaud's Rightist following. But Hélène de Portes—whose affair with Paul Reynaud was now an open secret—tried hard to placate this element. She promised them that, sooner or later, she would succeed in getting Paul Reynaud to change his mind.

The Marquise de Crussol was less ambitious for political power than Hélène de Portes. When she met Edouard Daladier, he was a widower with two sons. The son of a small-town baker, he had taught history, had taken an active part on a local political committee, and, since his arrival in Paris, had been living modestly in a little apartment on the Avenue Victor Hugo.

This unsophisticated provincial was flattered by the attention of the charming Marquise de Crussol. Before long Daladier came to depend upon her for plans of strategy which he would put into effect in the Chamber of Deputies.

Daladier appeared to be the man ideally suited to appeal to the French people. They were convinced that he was honest and patriotic, "uncompromisingly devoted to the immortal principles of 1789." They believed him to be firm and resolute because he could shout and bellow from the rostrum, when necessary, and pound his desk with an immense show of strength. The Left appreciated Daladier, for he had, after all, nipped the Fascist conspiracy of February 6, 1934. The Right gratefully remembered how he had checkmated the General Strike of November 30, 1938.

Two men as dissimilar as Daladier and Reynaud could not be expected to get on well together. It was not due to this clash of personalities, however, but to their respective "patronesses" that an open conflict flared up between the two men—a struggle which was to add, if possible, to the general confusion and disunity.

Each one of the ladies—the Countess and the Marquise—wanted to see "her man" in first place. For the moment, Daladier held the lead. But Paul Reynaud was coming up.

The Marquise de Crussol was steering and pushing Daladier in the direction of the Elysée (the Presidency). And Hélène de Portes was advising Paul Reynaud to support Daladier's candidacy, for, with Daladier out of the way as President, the office of Premier would be open, she reasoned.

It was at this stage of the game that Hacha, who had succeeded Benes as President of Czechoslovakia, was abruptly summoned to Berchtesgaden. There Hitler put him in the dreadful dilemma of having to choose between total surrender and total destruction. Then, immediately afterward, came the march of the German troops into Bohemia and Moravia, not to mention the collapse of the last fond illusions entertained by the *munichois*. They well remembered how Hitler had solemnly assured the signatories of the Munich Accord that "the Sudetenland represented his last territorial ambition in Europe, and that he had no desire to incorporate within the Reich people who were not of the German race."

Daladier flew into a terrible rage when he heard of Hitler's new *coup de force*. He summoned his colleagues and told them: "This is the end. We must be prepared now to make it impossible for this perjurer to commit another felony, or it means that France, too, is finished."

Our London correspondent telephoned to say that Lord Halifax and Neville Chamberlain were depressed. Hitler had not behaved like a gentleman. He had humiliated England. England would never be able to forgive him for that.

Daladier was now out of the question as President. Under the circumstances, he could not leave his position. There was talk of the possible candidacy of the former President of the Chamber, Fernand Buisson, supported by Pierre Laval; and of the incumbent Radical Minister of Agriculture, Queuille, who had consistently seconded Georges Bonnet's policies within the Cabinet.

Bonnet was still adhering tenaciously to the line of appeasement. As a result he was rather coolly received when he went to London, together with President Albert Lebrun, to return the visit of the King and Queen. Albert Lebrun, however, was enthusiastically acclaimed in England, and, shortly afterward was called upon to succeed himself.

Just before the Deputies and the Senators formally

confirmed their choice of Albert Lebrun, I was in Versailles with no fewer than two Ambassadors, William Bullitt (U. S.) and his inseparable friend, Lucasiewics (Poland), two Cabinet Members, Anatole de Monzie (Public Works) and Charles Pomaret (Labor), two distinguished writers, Colette and the Princess Marthe Bibesco, Hervé Alphand, the young expert on financial accords, the Duke and the Duchess d'Ayen, the banker, Raymond Philippe, the Countess Madeleine de Montgomery—and the Countess Hélène de Portes, who, at Paul Reynaud's specific request, had not been invited until the very last moment (most probably because he didn't want to show himself in her company at Versailles). Among my other guests, there was Paul Reynaud's *Directeur de Cabinet* and my personal friend, Georges Palewski. Hélène de Portes was manifestly jealous of him because of the influence he had over Paul Reynaud, an influence which was counteracting hers.

Hélène de Portes arrived very late, refused to greet her friend's associate, and created no little disturbance by asking people to move so that she might sit next to Minister Anatole de Monzie—who, incidentally, had not been on speaking terms with Paul Reynaud for some years. At the next table, Georges Bonnet, more ghastly green than ever, was lunching with his wife and a few friends. Maurice Chevalier walked into the restaurant with his partner, Nita Raya. They stood there for a moment, looking about for a table. The Minister of Foreign Affairs and his wife asked the celebrated comedian and his companion to join them. And then, after a few moments, Odette Bonnet suddenly saw Raymond Philippe, the financial backer of *L'Europe Nouvelle*, the review for which Pertinax was writing. She became deathly pale and, losing all self-control, almost shouted: "What's he doing here, that dirty Jew who criticizes my husband because he won't declare war?"

Georges Bonnet just barely managed to quiet his wife in time. Fortunately, Raymond Philippe had not heard her outburst.

To my great surprise, Hélène de Portes leaned slightly

toward Anatole de Monzie and said: "Odette is perfectly right. Something ought to be done about those war-mongering campaigns. If Hitler is stronger than we are—why, the only thing to do is to give in to him."

"What would Paul Reynaud think if he heard you saying things like that?" Anatole de Monzie asked.

Hélène de Portes replied: "I keep telling him things like that every day. And I'll end up by convincing him. You'll see."

From somewhere near the other end of the table, Colette spoke up in her good, strong Burgundian accent: "Since we're all going in for predictions today, I'd like to know whether or not there's going to be war."

"No, Madame," Ambassador Lucasiewics replied. "There's not going to be any war. Hitler attacks only the weak. And my country and yours are too strong."

Mr. William Bullitt nodded agreement.

But then Anatole de Monzie said: "I think the question is a bit more complicated than that. I feel confident, however, that the universal desire for peace will prevail."

At a table behind us, a man was listening and taking copious notes. He was a correspondent of the D.N.B., the official German news agency.

The conversation veered around to the subject of Daladier. The general opinion seemed to be that he was completely dominated by the Marquise de Crussol, who dictated her instructions to his associates, Clapier, Roger Génébrier, Jacques Kayser and the writer, André Chamson, who prepared Daladier's speeches.

"He doesn't see anybody any more," said Anatole de Monzie. "He especially avoids his Ministers and he isn't even in contact with Parliament."

"Does he see the military leaders?" asked Princess Bibesco.

"Yes, I think so," Charles Pomaret said.

In unison, everyone said: "Well, that's what counts."

On his return from Morocco, Jean Prouvost told me to go to America. I booked passage on the *Paris*. I was disturbed at the time by a letter from Robert Lorette, one of our Berlin correspondents, saying that: The Nazis had sent a new wave of agents into France. Furthermore, in order to impress public opinion in France and in the United States, these agents were to perform a number of sensational, terroristic acts. One of the first things to be attempted was to be the burning of a big transatlantic liner at le Havre, preferably the *Normandie,* but if this ship was too well guarded, the *Paris* would do.

I immediately sent this letter over to Albert Sarraut, who, in turn, advised Monsieur Bussières, the director of the *Sûreté Nationale.*

"I shall give specific instructions to le Havre," he said. "But, frankly, *entre nous,* I don't for a minute believe in this story. The Germans are being suspected of anything and everything, nowadays. Besides, all this sounds much too romantic—beautiful spies, crack transatlantic liners and all that. . . . But we'll see."

A few days later I received another such communication from Robert Lorette, confirming his first letter. I again went to the Ministry of the Interior. In my presence, Albert Sarraut telephoned to the *Sûreté Nationale* and asked whether their investigations had revealed anything. All of a sudden, I saw his face redden. Then he turned pale. And he shouted into the telephone: "But that isn't the point at all. . . . What have you done at le Havre? Have the hotels been watched? Let me have the complete *dossier* right away." He hung up the receiver. Then he turned to me. "I asked them how their investigations were getting along. And what do you think they said? 'Everything's getting along very well,' they replied. 'We've already made inquiries about Monsieur Lazareff's Berlin correspondents, and the reports are all highly satisfactory.' "

The following morning we received the news that the steamship *Paris* had caught fire at its dock in le Havre and had been entirely destroyed. To this day it is not known how this feat was accomplished, nor by whom.

As he had already done on the occasion of the Führer's previous speeches, Daladier summoned the representatives of the big newspapers before the speech of April 27th was to be delivered and requested them to refrain from playing up Hitler's remarks. "With your big headlines every time the German Chancellor opens his mouth, you're unwittingly playing his game," Daladier said. "Treat Hitler as you treat any other Chief of State—Mr. Roosevelt, Mr. Chamberlain or myself." And he couldn't help smiling, for the truth was that Daladier's speeches had never received as much publicity in the newspapers of his own country as had Hitler's pronouncements—a fact which displeased Daladier considerably.

My visit to New York was brief. On my previous return from America, I had found *Paris-Soir* under heavy attack by the Communists and their organ, *L'Humanité*. This time—early in July, 1939—I found *Paris-Soir* in a dogfight with the Royalists and their newspaper, *L'Action Française*. Their leader, Charles Maurras—paced by the weekly, *Je Suis Partout*—had undertaken a systematic campaign against our newspaper, accusing us of warmongering as well as of immorality. Jean Prouvost, personally, was under heavy fire. He and Charles Maurras named seconds to arrange a duel. It never came off.

The first thing my boss said to me was: "Those people are all more or less in the pay of the Nazis. And they resent us because we write as we please. The Germans can't buy us, and they know it."

He was indignant. So I tried to take advantage of this moment by proposing that he publish the real reasons for these attacks against him. In other words, I suggested that we expose everything we knew about the venality of the French press.

Jean Prouvost simply didn't have the courage to undertake such a daring and dangerous crusade.

"We have enough enemies as it is," he said, lamely. "And, besides, we mustn't demoralize the country at a time like this."

Later that year, when Mr. Henry R. Luce, the American publisher, came to France, he was received by what is conventionally known as *"la grande presse"* with a storm of indignant protests. Nothing less than his immediate deportation was demanded. Why? Because his magazine, *Time,* had dared to say that French newspapers frequently sold their editorial policies to the highest bidder.

Le Matin, Le Journal, Le Temps and their associates were among the most vociferous in their righteous indignation. The *Fédération de la Presse* actually filed suit against Mr. Luce for libel. Amazed and shocked at this display of utter cynicism on the part of my colleagues, I immediately tried to get in touch with Mr. Luce. But I couldn't reach him. I received a phone call, however, from his Paris lawyer—René de Chambrun, Pierre Laval's son-in-law, and the *protégé* of Bunau-Varilla of *Le Matin* and of Pierre Guimier of *Le Journal.*

I said to René de Chambrun: "I have a *dossier* on the venality of the press. I can let you have it. It will permit Mr. Luce to confound his opponents. Besides, the revelations will tend to clear the atmosphere, generally."

"Thanks very much, *mon cher,*" René de Chambrun replied. "But matters are being straightened out very nicely. . . . I feel that it would be better for France—especially in view of Mr. Luce's importance—not to engage in any controversy at the moment. Everything is being arranged quite satisfactorily. Mr. Luce is writing me a little note, calling my attention to the fact that the article in question appeared in *Time* during his absence. The newspapers are going to reproduce this little letter, together with a few kind words about Mr. Luce. In this manner, you see, the incident will come to a perfectly happy ending."

Chapter Twenty-four

Abetz Departs

LATE in June, 1939, a reception was held in the gardens of the de Sagan mansion, which had quite recently been acquired by the Polish Government to serve as the Embassy in Paris. The guests stood in a large circle in the center of which was S. E. M. Lucasiewics, the Polish Ambassador to France. Earlier in the evening he had discussed politics and had given his opinion of the European situation.

"Hitler now knows," he said, "that he can't have his war against us alone. The guarantees which England spontaneously offered Poland after the march into Prague must have convinced the master of Germany that Great Britain will not subscribe to another Munich. . . . As to our relations with France, the situation is, momentarily, somewhat more delicate. Our two countries are bound by solemn engagements. The military alliance of February 21, 1921, signed for France by Marshal Foch and General Buat, is unequivocally clear and precise. There is no time limit and no provision for repudiation. On the basis of this alliance, we signed the Rambouillet Accords on September 6, 1936, providing for financial co-operation on the part of France in Poland's rearmament program. However, when the growing German menace demanded an emphatic reaffirmation of our alliance as an unmistakable sign of our will to resist—at this critical moment, I regret to say, I found that your Government, and most especially Georges Bonnet, was definitely seeking some legally valid escape clause which might justify France, if she failed to fulfill her obligations. These attempts were in vain, naturally. Unfortunately, news of the maneuver reached Berlin, where the blustering increased. Luckily, your General Staff does not share the views of your Minister of Foreign Affairs. The military chiefs of our two countries have recently engaged in a number of highly important conferences which resulted in a new military alliance which is even more specific and comprehensive than was the old Treaty. All these conversations took place in the greatest secrecy. But the news leaked out to the Germans. And this may very well explain Herr Hitler's relative calm, for the moment. He wants to terrify the others; but he trembles, too, when he thinks the other fellow's stronger than he is."

After dinner, a flood of new guests arrived for the reception. Georges Bonnet was accompanied by Mr. Hore-Belisha, the English Secretary for War, and General Gamelin. They had come directly from a banquet given by the *Association France-Grande Bretagne*. At this banquet, I learned, Mr. Hore-Belisha had made an eloquent speech, reaffirming England's firm attitude and telling of his country's confidence in the Generalissimo of the Allied Armies, whom he had referred to as "*our* Gamelin." The General, unassuming and inscrutable, as usual, had merely smiled a thin little smile, while the guests had cheered him heartily.

The presence of General Gamelin and of Hore-Belisha at the Polish Embassy was, under the circumstances, of considerable political significance which must have been apparent to everyone, including the German Ambassador, Count von Welzcheck.

When the conversation turned to the Franco-Polish military alliance, Paul Reynaud suddenly turned to an officer on the staff of General Georges, and bluntly said:

"Is it true that these military discussions have been made contingent upon renewed diplomatic discussions?"

The officer replied that, on instructions from Premier Daladier, the new military accord had been signed on May 17th by General Smigly-Rydz, head of the Polish Government, and Kapriski, his Minister of War, on behalf of Poland, and by Generals Gamelin and Georges, on behalf of France. "That's all I know about it," he added.

"Well, in that case," said Paul Reynaud, "let me tell you the rest of the story. A few days previously, Monsieur Lucasiewics had requested written assurances from our Government to the effect that the political and military accords would be implemented in the event that the vital interests of Poland were threatened—Danzig being considered as part of these vital interests. These guarantees would make it impossible for Hitler to apply the Sudetenland technic to the Danzig question: namely, to begin by claiming the zone considered to be German, to take this zone by means of dire threats, and thus to pave the way for the annexation of the entire country by breaking the opponent's powers of resistance. . . . The Polish *démarche* did not meet with a clear-cut refusal. No. But the response was not satisfactory. *Monsieur Georges Bonnet, you see, plans to use Danzig as a bargaining point.* What he's really hoping for is another Munich. And he has succeeded, so far, in convincing this noodle of a Daladier that the new accords are not essential and that, furthermore, they bind France unilaterally. Whereupon Gamelin found himself in an awkward situation. He had signed the new military accord at Daladier's request, and had had every reason to believe that the military accord was the sequel to agreements arrived at through diplomatic channels. Then, when the General learned that no such political accord had been concluded, he was obliged to advise his Polish colleagues that his signature as well as General Georges' must, perforce, be considered null and void. All of which was immediately reported to Berlin. For the Nazi Intelligence is well represented in our Army and in the Polish Army, too, of course. . . . And this is the way we're setting out to intimidate Hitler. Nice, isn't it?"

Paul Reynaud turned to me and asked about my recent visit to the United States. He had always been very much interested in America.

I told him that I had found American public opinion furious at the European democracies for having submitted to a Munich. "They don't understand what could have provoked or possibly justified this accord," I said.

"They're perfectly right," Paul Reynaud said, curtly.

"Public opinion in the United States," I continued, "has been drifting toward utter indifference to what goes on in Europe. And we can thank Munich for that. 'If they're so stupid over there,' the Americans say, 'if they don't even want to defend themselves, we'll have to let them destroy each other.' Ninety-five out of a hundred people I spoke to had quite recently become Isolationists. They don't seem to realize that they're just as much involved as we are."

I told Paul Reynaud about the Gallup Poll, mentioning that I had brought back an agreement concluded with the American Institute of Public Opinion, according to which we were going to found a similar institute in France, under the auspices of *Paris-Soir*. The institute was to be sponsored by a number of outstanding personages, and was to be under the direction of a young French scholar, Adolphe Max, who had worked with Dr. George Gallup in New York.

Paul Reynaud lifted his arms heavenward. "That's a marvelous and a frightful instrument, that Gallup Poll," he cried. "It can be of great value in the economic and social fields. But if you begin poking around in the domain of politics with this monstrosity, you'll be shouldering a big responsibility. Supposing, for example, people were asked this question: 'Do you prefer paying taxes or not paying taxes?' Approximately 100 per cent of the answers will indicate an aversion to paying taxes. But now if you ask them another question: 'Do you prefer going to war or not going to war?' Once again, you'll agree, there'll be something like a unanimous vote. Well then, since this is a democracy, and since your Gallup Poll has revealed the astonishing fact that very few, if any, people choose to pay taxes—how, then, can any Government presume to thwart the expressed will of the sovereign people by imposing and collecting taxes? Unfortunately, I fail to see how taxation can be avoided. The question of war is even more serious. If such a referendum were actually taken in France, would one single member of the Parliament dare to vote for a declaration of war? Would he dare to assume the responsibility? I don't think so. If the German people were consulted in this manner, you would get the same reaction as in France and in the United States. But, since there's not the remotest chance of any Gallup Poll being put to a practical test in the totalitarian countries, the net result of your new device would merely be the further weakening of the democratic *régimes*."

Just then Paul Reynaud saw William Bullitt approaching, and beckoned to him.

"Mon cher Ambassadeur," Paul Reynaud said, "I was just telling Pierre Lazareff that the democracies won't win out unless the men they select as their leaders fully appreciate the extent of their powers; but that if these men, lacking self-confidence, feel that they must constantly put democracy itself to a test—we are lost."

Bastille Day was the occasion for an extraordinary display of France's military power. After the brilliant review of the Fourteenth of July, 1939, not one Frenchman in a thousand believed that Hitler would ever dare to challenge an army like ours, with its incomparable leadership, so highly praised even by the captious British. And then, of course, there was the famous Maginot Line. . . . There was, in short, a strong resurgence of optimism. And unanimously, almost—but for a diversity of reasons—the press was unsparing in its efforts to develop this reborn feeling of confidence and security.

However, Jean Prouvost told me that, a few days before the Fourteenth of July, Georges Bonnet had had a talk with the British Ambassador to Berlin who had stopped off briefly in Paris on his way home for a short visit.

"I understand," Jean Prouvost said to me, "that Sir Nevile Henderson told Bonnet that he was convinced that

Hitler wanted war, and that war could be avoided only if Mussolini took the initiative and called a world conference which would, of course, agree on generous awards to the Axis Powers." Jean Prouvost went on to say that Georges Bonnet had been in complete agreement with Henderson, and that he had so informed Daladier, but that Daladier had refused to listen to him.

"Ever since Munich," Jean Prouvost said, "Daladier has firmly believed that Hitler will back down, if we show him that we're not making any more concessions. And he told Bonnet that Hitler was looking for signs of weakness on the part of his opponents, and that he wouldn't make a move until he detected such a sign. Daladier even added: 'I think Sir Nevile Henderson has been maneuvered by the Wilhelmstrasse. The Nazis want this international conference, and they know it can't be successful—from their point of view—unless it is initiated by the Allies.' Georges Bonnet then tendered his resignation to Edouard Daladier, saying that his services could no longer be of value to the Government, since he was in such radical disagreement with the Premier. 'Come, come, Bonnet, buck up,' Daladier grumbled. 'Don't let yourself be the first victim of the war of nerves.' And that was the end of the conversation."

The Government had been showing an essentially firm attitude toward the Nazi threats. For some time, now, Henri de Kérillis, tirelessly, persistently, day after day, had been denouncing the machinations of Otto Abetz and his accomplices.

One of the leading figures in the *Sûreté Nationale's* counter-espionage service, Commissaire Oswald, had told one of our collaborators: "Henri de Kérillis cannot realize the full extent of the service he is rendering his country. We know all about Otto Abetz and his friends. But every time we want to act, we're stopped. *They* say that 'political complications' must be avoided. Our hands are tied. But if Kérillis can do what he's doing without officially creating political complications, he may be driving a wedge, and we may soon be permitted to do something ourselves."

It wasn't long before there was news of the arrest of the notorious banker, Hirsch, whose activities as one of the principal paymasters of the Nazi propaganda machine in France had been called to my attention long ago. Other arrests were made at the same time. They collared Loys Aubin, *Chef des Informations* of *Le Temps*, and Poirier, advertising agent on *Le Figaro*. This Poirier, however, had previously worked for many years on *Le Temps*, too, in the capacity of manager in charge of "relations with foreign Governments." Everybody knew what that meant.

The Baroness von Einem, old friend of Marshal Goering's, who had wormed her way into Parisian society under the expert guidance of Otto Abetz, was to be arrested as head of the conspiracy. But when the police went to her home to arrest her, they were informed that the lady had left France the night before. Who had warned her?

Loys Aubin, a white-haired old newspaperman who had been in harness for many long years—a man who was known as steady, home-loving, and whose only extravagance was an occasional glass of beer at the corner *bistro*—readily confessed that he had accepted millions of francs from the Nazis. But Poirier, on the other hand, steadfastly denied his guilt, despite all the incriminating evidence. He died, shortly afterwards, in prison.

Several days after this round-up, Otto Abetz arrived in Paris from Berlin. He stopped, as usual, at the Hotel d'Iéna, across the way from the former *Comité France-Allemagne* building.

Otto Abetz was sure himself, and felt secure under the protection he enjoyed in France. A dinner had been given in his honor. The host was Horace de Carbuccia, director of the weekly, *Gringoire*. The dinner—given at Carbuccia's apartment on the Avenue Foch—had been attended by a number of men who were more or less prominent in French politics, and who were almost all ex-members of the defunct *Comité France-Allemagne*. Naturally, the Danzig question and the events that were brewing were discussed. And, what was nothing short of insane recklessness, under the circumstances, they also discussed, *in the presence of a foreigner who might very well be an enemy tomorrow, the manner in which they could deal with those in France who opposed giving in to Germany, and most especially with the refractory newspapers and newspapermen.*

Otto Abetz, who had, as usual, partaken freely of the choicest wines of France, left the banquet in excellent spirits and made his way back to his hotel. There, at his very door, he found a *Commissaire* of the *Sûreté Nationale.* He handed Otto Abetz a little envelope, and said: "Monsieur, I have been instructed to give you some unpleasant news. The French Government wishes to spare you the annoyance of being deported. This envelope contains a reservation which you would not have been able to secure as promptly as desired. It is a seat on the plane which leaves for Berlin tomorrow morning. If you should, by any chance, fail to take this plane, you will be arrested tomorrow afternoon. The French Government has also instructed me to advise you that it will be impossible for you, in the future, to return to France."

Otto Abetz took the ticket, thanked the detective politely, stepped into his room and closed the door. . . . Later, it was learned (for all his calls were being closely watched) that he had telephoned the German Ambassador in a rage. Otto Abetz made no secret of his hatred of Count von Welzcheck, who, in turn, did not particularly like Abetz. The phone call awakened the Ambassador. He advised Otto Abetz to take the plane and to report to von Ribbentrop for further instructions. Otto Abetz hung up the receiver. He left France at dawn.

As soon as I heard the news, I wrote an article on Otto Abetz for our weekly, *Match.* He was entirely unknown to the general public—with the exception, of course, of the readers of *L'Epoque* who, thanks to Henri de Kérillis, knew all about this mysterious head of Nazi espionage in France. Before writing my article, I telephoned to Jean Luchaire, the man who had introduced Otto Abetz to France and who was his closest friend. I wanted to get his reaction.

"I was sure," he said, "that it would end this way. But Abetz wouldn't believe me. He wasn't worried, because he felt he wasn't doing anything wrong. I still believe that he's absolutely sincere."

"Sincerely Nazi," I replied.

Over the wire, Luchaire protested loudly—and gratuitously—that he, personally, was a good patriot and opposed to Hitlerism.

That same day, my wife received a letter from Suzanne Abetz, requesting me to intervene on Otto Abetz's behalf. He wanted to be permitted to return to Paris, she wrote, merely in order to clear himself. She added that her husband was suing Henri de Kérillis for libel. I asked my wife not to answer this letter.

My article, which appeared in *Match* on July 20, 1939, ended with the following words:

"In the plane which is taking Otto Abetz back to Berlin, he is dreaming of returning to France, some day soon, as German Ambassador . . ."

I did not imagine, however, that his dream would come true so promptly and under such tragic circumstances.

Chapter Twenty-five

The Last Few Moments of Peace

EDOUARD DALADIER, throughout his terms as Minister and Premier, had retained the post of Mayor of Orange, the little Provençal town which had sent him to Parliament. Toward the end of the month of July, Daladier went to Orange for a few days, to attend the annual festival. It was there that I was granted a brief interview with the Premier.

He was at his desk in the City Hall. He commenced by saying, in a defiant tone: "You know, I'm going to chain down the press. The newspapers are printing too much stupid nonsense, and the times are far too serious to allow this to go on any longer. I have just created a Commissariat of Information, covering the radio, the press and the cinema. If necessary, I'll institute censorship. . . ."

Maintaining his surly manner, Daladier went on: "As I see it, the business of the Information Department is not propaganda. Propaganda is, indeed, an offensive weapon, an instrument of aggression. In a democracy like France, Information should be nothing more than a defensive weapon. . . . I haven't quite decided whom to appoint for this job, Jean Giraudoux or Jules Romains. Which one of the two would you prefer?"

I said, "Both are men of great ability and intellect . . ."

Daladier stopped me. "I've already chosen the man," he said. "Georges Bonnet has been insisting on Jules Romains, so, naturally, I picked Giraudoux."

Then Daladier told me that he hoped the newspapers would co-operate with Jean Giraudoux and the French Government. "The time has come," he said, "for national unity. The destiny of France and of all Europe is in the balance. I believe that war can still be avoided—provided France presents a unified front, and provided the newspapers abandon their controversies and their reckless policies. In any case, I am determined to deal firmly with those who stubbornly refuse to understand all this."

Daladier, as he uttered these words, was trying to look angry. The performance didn't quite come off; it wasn't altogether convincing.

Our conversation was interrupted by the arrival of his friend, Hyppolyte Fabre, the Senator from the Vaucluse, whose son was a member of the Premier's private cabinet.

Daladier said to him, "I was just telling Monsieur Lazareff that peace can perhaps be preserved, provided the newspapermen don't act like fools. As a member of the Senate Military Affairs Committee, what do you think?"

"The Army is really formidable, I tell you," he exclaimed. "Did you see the Review on the Fourteenth of July?"

"How about Italy? And Russia?" I asked.

"Italy! Pffft!!" said Daladier.

"I understand," said Hyppolyte Fabre, "that the other day Marshal Goering told someone: 'As our enemy, Italy will keep two of our divisions busy. But if she's on our side, we'll have to count on throwing in fifteen divisions.' "

After a moment Daladier said: "As for Russia, I can tell you that, despite considerable difficulties, the Anglo-Franco-Russian conversations are soon going to result in an *accord très solide*. From the diplomatic as well as the military viewpoint, everything is all right. And now, if the press does its duty, we won't have anything to fear."

As late as mid-August, Daladier was obliged to summon

the directors of the leading newspapers and plead with them—rather pathetically—to behave themselves.

On his desk, he had the report of the interview which had taken place, on August 11th, between Chancellor Hitler and Monsieur Burckhardt, the High Commissioner of the League of Nations, subsequent to the note sent by Poland to Germany with regard to the Free City of Danzig, where the tempo of Nazi provocations had been steadily increasing.

According to this report, the Führer had put on one of his acts for the benefit of the official from Geneva. For three-quarters of an hour he had engaged in one of his frantic monologues, literally foaming with rage. Then Hitler shouted that he had had more than enough of reading in the democratic press that he, Hitler, was afraid, that he would back down, that he was bluffing, that he was now the only one who was being upset by the war of nerves, and that he was just threatening, but that he didn't dare to translate his threats into action. He had been particularly infuriated by the caricatures of himself published in the French and English newspapers.

"I have created," he screamed, "a war machine, the like of which has never been seen. If they force me to do so, I shall make use of this unbelievably powerful machine, and I shall destroy the world within a few weeks. If my desire to settle the German question peacefully is interpreted as a retreat—then I shall attack like a thunderbolt. The Polish, French and English press must change its tone instantly. If not, I shall change mine. I shall act."

When Monsieur Burckhardt finally escaped from the tornado, he sent a full report to the League of Nations and to the Governments most directly concerned.

And now Edouard Daladier gave the representatives of the French press the gist of this report. Daladier requested the assembled newspapermen to bear the Führer's comments in mind, in order to make the Government's task a little less difficult.

On that same day—and as a sequel to the Ribbentrop-Ciano conference at Salzburg—Hitler received the Italian Minister of Foreign Affairs. And Jules Sauerwein, telephoning from Austria, informed us that Rome had been requested to state whether or not Italy would take an active part in an eventual war with Poland; and that Rome had refused to give a definite reply, invoking a secret escape clause in the Axis pact which stipulated that, if Germany were to be involved in a war within three years of the date of the signing of the pact, Italy was to be permitted to remain neutral.

On August 15, the Day of Assumption, Paris seemed to be a deserted city. At my office I found Nicolas Kossiakov (Yves Delbars), who had for some time been my most dependable source of information on Russian matters.

"I told you so," he exclaimed with childish pride. "The Franco-British delegation to Moscow isn't making much progress. The famous accord, which was to have been signed so promptly, hasn't been signed yet."

And then he added: "It won't be, either. Stalin will sign a pact, all right, but it'll be with the Germans. And before the end of this month."

Two weeks previously, Kossiakov-Delbars had made the same prediction, complete with details and dates. This time he went even further: "The change in Russian policy began," he said, "over three months ago, when Litvinoff was removed from office. Then, through his confidential man, Gregory Astokov, who had already been sent to Berlin secretly a number of times, Stalin entered into negotiations with von Ribbentrop. And in Moscow Stalin repeatedly conferred with the German Ambassador, Von der Schulenburg."

"But what's Stalin's game?" I asked. "How can he possibly ally himself with his worst enemy?"

"Ever since Munich, Stalin has been convinced that, when war appears to be inevitable, the leaders of the democracies will do everything in their power to direct the full weight of the German attack against Russia. Don't forget, the men of Munich are still in power in France and in England. Stalin is very well informed about the activities of Georges Bonnet, for one. How can you possibly expect him to have confidence in a partner like that? Stalin is trying to beat the democracies to the punch. Germany doesn't want a two-front war; she hasn't forgotten what happened last time. And so, while Stalin goes through the motions of negotiating with France and England, he's automatically increasing Hitler's desire for reaching an understanding with Russia. This *entente* will be achieved. And it will be Stalin who will turn the fury of the German attack westward against the democracies. In the meantime, incidentally, Stalin will make many promises to his German ally: promises which he will not keep. On the other hand, he will be taking the maximum of precautionary measures, for he knows very well that, sooner or later, Germany will revert to her original objective—namely, to crush the Soviet Union. But Russia is not, as yet, prepared to defend herself. All her plans were based on the existence of the bastion of Czechoslovakia. Suddenly deprived of those outlying defenses along one flank, Russia's position is defensively weak. And in addition there is the fact that Poland and Rumania refuse to allow Soviet troops to cross their territories, even in the event that Russia becomes their active ally. As for France and England, neither one of them is willing to authorize Russia to seize the Baltic States. . . . How can Stalin help feeling that the Allies consider not Hitler, but Red Russia, to be the real enemy? These are the points on which the Franco-British mission will founder. Furthermore, the attitude of Poland is alarming to the Kremlin. Poland, although definitely pro-German until quite recently, has suddenly assumed an uncompromising attitude with regard to Danzig, *but,* at the same time, is refusing all offers of military aid from Russia."

"In short," I said, "Russia is heading for an accord with Germany at the risk of allowing Germany to expand until she reaches the entire length of Russia's western frontier, and of having this far stronger Germany turn on Russia in the end?"

"That, in Stalin's opinion, is the smaller of the two risks. What he hopes for is to gain enough time to fortify his country, to mobilize his armies and to surround his territory with a belt of buffer States. By striking a series of bargains with Hitler, Stalin hopes to acquire the eastern half of Poland, the Baltic States, part of Finland, perhaps even Bessarabia—and these territories will eventually serve to absorb the first shock of the German attack. Besides, Stalin is gambling on a long war, a war in which all the belligerents will exhaust themselves. Russia—the last one to enter this war—will thus enjoy a tremendous advantage. Not to mention the fact that all these war-weary countries will offer perfect soil for the growth of Communism."

The news came that the Franco-British military delegation—headed by Admiral Plunket and General Doumenc—had had another interview at the Kremlin. The dispatch concluded with the comment: "The negotiations are continuing to proceed favorably."

I showed it to Kossiakov-Delbars.

I said, "This doesn't agree with what you've been telling me."

"Moscow," he replied, "is encouraging the Franco-British delegation in order to exert pressure on Germany. That's all."

Several days later—on August 20th—I met Georges Bonnet and talked the whole matter over with him.

"I believe there's some truth to your informant's story," he said. "He probably goes a bit too far when he envisages a Russo-German accord to be signed by the end of this month, but I'm afraid our negotiations with Moscow are bogging down, all the optimism of Daladier and our diplomats notwithstanding."

Toward 11 P.M. on August 21st, the office called me at my home. Our correspondent, they said, was telephoning from Berlin. They switched the call over to me.

"Von Ribbentrop has left for Moscow," he gasped. "He's going to sign a non-aggression pact!"

"You sure?"

"Absolutely certain. I know it's too late now to get out a special edition, but I wanted you to know right away because I haven't any idea when the news will be announced officially."

I called Jean Prouvost immediately.

"Impossible," he cried. "I don't believe it. Try to get a confirmation from the Quai d'Orsay."

I called Georges Bonnet.

"I haven't heard anything about it," he said. "But . . . just wait a second."

There was a moment of silence. Then Georges Bonnet's voice was changed.

"Havas is flashing the same news. I think it must be true," he said. "If you should get any further information, I'd be grateful to you if you'd let me know."

Shortly after the Havas flash, Reuter confirmed the story: von Ribbentrop had left Berlin for Moscow. . . . There couldn't be any possible room for doubt any more. Kossiakoff-Delbars had been right.

Georges Bonnet had telephoned Daladier as soon as the news had broken. But Daladier had replied: "It's a *canard*, it's idiotic, what you're saying."

In the afternoon of August 22nd, Georges Bonnet and Edouard Daladier engaged in a long and highly unpleasant conversation, as a result of which it was decided to convene, on August 23rd, an extraordinary council of the *Défense Nationale*—a plenary council, including all the heads of the military establishment.

In the hope of finding arguments in support of his own policies, Georges Bonnet had previously (early in August) —and without the knowledge of the Premier—summoned General Gamelin to his office. But the Generalissimo had countered all of the Minister's arguments with a display of calm confidence. He had told Bonnet that the French Army was prepared to meet any defensive test. Gamelin had even told the Minister of Foreign Affairs that, if the conflict really was inevitable, "it would be preferable to have war break out under existing conditions, obliging Germany to fight on an Eastern as well as a Western front."

Paris-Soir obtained a copy of the *procès-verbal*—of the session held at the Ministry of War on August 22nd. This immensely significant document, drawn up during the proceedings by General Decamp, the chief of Daladier's *Cabinet Militaire*, was never published. It reads as follows:

PROCES VERBAL of the Meeting held at the Ministry of

War on August 23 at 18 o'clock (6 P.M.), Monsieur Edouard Daladier presiding.

The meeting is attended by: Messieurs Georges Bonnet, Minister of Foreign Affairs, C. Campinchi, Minister of the Navy, Guy la Chambre, Minister for Aviation; and General Gamelin, Chief of the General Staff of the *Défense Nationale,* Admiral Darlan, Chief of the General Staff of the Navy, General Vuillemin, Chief of the General Staff of the Air Corps, *Contrôleur* General Jacomet, Secretary-General of the *Défense Nationale* and of War, General Colson, Chief of Staff of the Army, General Aube, Inspector-General of the D.A.T. (*Défense Anti-aérienne du Territoire*), General Tétu, Chief of Staff of the Air Corps.

The meeting is called to order at 6:05 P.M.

Daladier, President of the Council of Ministers, announces that three specific questions are to be considered:

1). Can France afford to stand by and watch the disappearance off the map of Europe (sic), of Poland and of Rumania, or of one of these two Powers?
2). What means are at France's disposal to implement her opposition?
3). What measures are to be taken now?

Question One: The Disappearance of Poland and Rumania.

Monsieur Georges Bonnet states that:

One must wait, at the very least, until it becomes evident that Poland will not be supported by the U.S.S.R.;

Rumania will most probably agree to deliver supplies to Germany;

Turkey, no longer backed by the U.S.S.R., will not become involved unless a Balkan State is attacked; in view of the entire situation, therefore, is it better to fulfill our obligations and to enter the war immediately, or to reconsider our stand and to take advantage of the respite thus obtained to strengthen our military position, fully realizing, of course, that France is exposed to being attacked, in turn, within a few months, perhaps?

The answer to the question, as presented, should be based, essentially, on military considerations.

General Gamelin and Admiral Darlan state that it would be desirable to obtain assurances of Italy's absolute neutrality. Monsieur Georges Bonnet replies that steps in this direction might well be taken.

General Gamelin is questioned as to the probable duration of armed resistance offered by Poland and Rumania. He replies that he believes Poland capable of offering "*une résistance honorable,*" which should prevent the main weight of the German attack from turning against us before the coming spring;

and that, by that time, England will be at our side; but that, as far as Rumania is concerned, it is more difficult to have a definite opinion, since the answer to the question depends on the attitude taken by Hungary and Yugoslavia.

In the course of an exchange of views, the following points are brought out:

Although we shall be stronger within a few months, Germany will then be relatively much stronger than today, since she will then have the additional resources of Poland and Rumania at her disposal.

France, therefore, has no choice. She must meet her obligations toward Poland—engagements which were, incidentally, entered into prior to the negotiations with the U.S.S.R.

Question Two: The present state of our resources.

Monsieur Guy la Chambre declares that our aviation is in a far better state than it was in September, 1938. He brings out the following points:

With regard to pursuit planes, we now possess modern machines. These are being turned out in quantity by mass-production methods.

The Franco-British resources in this department approximate those of Germany and Italy combined.

Our bombing planes, however, are not yet being produced in great number. Mass production may be expected by the beginning of 1940.

In the meantime, England may be counted on to execute intensive bombing of Northern Germany.

Effective co-operation between the Air Corps and the Army may be counted upon.

Despite the known strength of the Germans (4,000 first-line planes, 5,000 replacements, 3,000 planes *de co-operation*), the state of our aviation should not influence the Government's decision, as it did in 1938.

General Aube reveals the state of our D.A.T., as representing a cause for grave concern from various points of view: organization, plans for utilization, extent of our resources.

Bombing of the civilian population is admittedly to be feared. Precautions are to be taken to safeguard the nation's morale.

General Gamelin and Admiral Darlan announce that the Army and Navy are in a state of readiness; that, at the beginning of hostilities, little can be done offensively against Germany; but that our armed forces are in a position to act vigorously against Italy, in the event of that Power's entrance into the war.

Point stressed: French General Mobilization would, automatically, relieve the pressure against Poland, by obliging Germany to maintain a number of large units on her Western frontiers.

In conclusion, President Daladier calls attention to the following:

For many years, France has made a concentrated and immense effort to achieve a system of fortifications intended to assure the protection of our frontiers.

Prior to the Spanish War, our High Command considered pursuit aircraft to be the best defense against air-attack. As a result, the development of our D.C.A. (anti-aircraft guns) was relegated to a position of secondary importance.

In view of the present situation, which calls upon France to fight alone in the West for several months, we are fully able to appreciate the security given us by our fortifications.

Question Three: Answers:

Certain preparatory measures have already been taken, including moves to assure the security of our positions Northeast and Southeast, as well as the total preparedness of our D.A.T.

It is imperative to continue moving our effectives into position progressively, in order to facilitate the indicated concentrations of strength in the event of the sudden outbreak of hostilities.

This would lead us to order, successively:

Total preparation of the defensive positions.

General Mobilization.

The meeting is adjourned at 7:30 P.M.

The press, as a whole, continued to keep the public in ignorance of the gravity of the situation. On August 24th, Daladier telephoned to *Paris-Soir* to complain that we were being too "alarmist."

On that same day, there was an extremely stormy meeting of the Cabinet. Paul Reynaud and Georges Mandel insisted upon an immediate declaration of General Mobilization as the only move that might still intimidate Hitler. They accused Georges Bonnet of having telephoned Warsaw—without instructions from the Government and without using the usual diplomatic channels—and of having asked the Poles "not to make any irreparable move in the event that the Reich seized Danzig." Georges Bonnet admitted that he had made this extraordinary *démarche*.

In reply to a question by Albert Lebrun, Edouard Daladier stated that "there was still some hope for an understanding with Russia, the Berlin-Moscow pact notwithstanding."

From this time on, Georges Bonnet was to conduct the course of French diplomacy according to his own personal plans, without consulting anyone—without even consulting Alexis Léger, Secretary-General of Foreign Affairs, or the President of the Council of Ministers. Later he was to publish the evidence of his frantic and highly unusual activities in the French Yellow Book, taking good care, however, to omit certain documents which might compromise even him too seriously at the time. (The Yellow Book appeared during the War.)

"Georges Bonnet makes a mess of everything," Paul Reynaud said to M. Caddet, the London *Times* correspondent, and me. "His very presence in the Government is going to lead us into disaster. He wants to get the entire world to intervene and to beseech Hitler on bended knees to behave himself. Under those conditions, how can the world continue to have the slightest confidence in us? How can we hope to keep our alliances? He has approached, in turn, King Leopold, through the Belgian Ambassador to France, Pol Le Tellier; the Pope, through the medium of the Nuncio; and he has asked the Spanish Ambassador, Felix de Lequerica, to pull strings for him. During the last war, incidentally, de Lequerica was the head of the pro-German movement in Spain. And God knows what else Bonnet has tried. And all these moves, mind you, were made without England's consent. What Georges Bonnet really wants to accomplish—through Mussolini—is another Munich, much worse than the first one. I'm convinced that, with a show of firmness and courage, we could gain precious time, if nothing else. After all, why should Hitler hesitate to attack Poland if he feels that Poland's ally is trembling in her boots at the idea of going to the rescue?"

Caddet, who had consistently been attacking our Minister of Foreign Affairs in his articles in the *Times*, told us what had happened to him that very morning. He had gone to the Quai d'Orsay for some information, and had run squarely into Georges Bonnet.

"I'm surprised, Monsieur Caddet," Georges Bonnet had said, "to find *you* here."

"I don't think people are nearly so much surprised when they see me in this place, Monsieur le Ministre," Caddet had replied, "as when they see *you* here."

Later that same day, Elie-Joseph Bois, following an interview with Georges Bonnet, expressed his opinion in the following stock-exchange terminology: "Georges Bonnet is selling France short."

On the morning of August 31st, the French Ambassador to London, Monsieur Charles Corbin, transmitted a plan for a Franco-British mediation of the differences between Germany and Poland—a plan which had the advantage of obviating intervention by a third party and of permitting the democracies to retain their dignity. Georges Bonnet replied to Charles Corbin that "this procedure was far too complicated and was bound to exacerbate the situation." But when our Ambassador to Rome, François-Poncet, telephoned about an hour later, Georges Bonnet was delighted. According to Count Ciano, Mussolini seemed willing to intervene and to suggest an international conference, provided that Poland would recognize the return of Danzig to the Reich. An hour later, François-Poncet telephoned again. This time he confirmed Mussolini's willingness and even specified that the Duce had set the date of September 5th for this conference.

Almost immediately afterward, Ambassador Corbin announced that Neville Chamberlain had received the same proposition from Mussolini, but that Chamberlain had decided to agree to the conference only on the condition that all the countries concerned, including Germany, first ordered the demobilization of their armies.

Alexis Léger, Secretary-General of the Ministry of Foreign Affairs, showed his common sense when he remarked: "The English are right. This conference cannot take place under any other circumstances. If such negotiations were to be started by a retreat on the part of the Allies and under the threat of German force, the democracies would soon find themselves faced with wholly unacceptable Axis claims. There would be war, anyway, and under especially unfavorable conditions. No, the trap is too obvious."

Georges Bonnet did not share this view. He hunted up Daladier and insisted that a favorable answer be sent to Italy at once. There was no hurry about answering London, not as far as Bonnet was concerned.

Daladier replied that he would convene a Cabinet Meeting for that evening. Georges Bonnet commenced making the rounds of all the Cabinet members whom he knew to be favorably inclined toward his policies—Camille Chautemps, Anatole de Monzie, Queuille, Guy la Chambre, Marchandeau. To each one he said: "We'll have to stand our ground tonight. It's our last chance. If this conference doesn't come off, it means war."

In the meantime, Daladier had had long talks with General Gamelin, with the Polish Ambassador and with Mr. Bullitt, the American Ambassador. He found that all three shared Alexis Léger's extreme mistrust of Mussolini's suggested conference.

Then came the Council of the Ministers.

Georges Bonnet was the first to speak. He read a long paper, recommending the immediate and formal acceptance of the Italian proposal, with the one proviso that Poland be invited to attend the conference at which her fate was to be decided, and with the request that this international conference also serve as the occasion to settle all the differences and disputes with which Europe was beset.

Ministers Anatole de Monzie and Marchandeau expressed their approval of Georges Bonnet's views.

Then Albert Sarraut protested indignantly against "*cette nouvelle démission de la France*" (another abdication on the part of France).

Paul Reynaud, Georges Mandel and César Campinchi most vigorously denounced the perils inherent in another Munich.

Campinchi had barely finished speaking, when Georges Bonnet—without troubling to answer any of the arguments advanced—took the floor to say: "We cannot afford to let this discussion go on forever, because our immediate reply has been requested. Our Ambassador to London, Monsieur Corbin, stressed the importance of coming to a decision without delay."

Then, suddenly, Edouard Daladier looked squarely into Georges Bonnet's eyes and said: "So that's what Corbin told you, is it? I spoke to Corbin, myself, less than an hour ago, and he told me the exact opposite. He told me, in fact, that there wasn't any hurry at all."

Georges Bonnet went deathly pale. Around the green-covered council table there was an appalling silence.

Daladier went on: "I believe that they're trying to trick us. I grant that demanding demobilization is asking a lot. But I believe, above all, that if the German-Polish dispute is to be settled, it can be settled only by direct negotiations."

Then, as Georges Bonnet gave signs of wanting to speak again, Daladier raised his voice. "The English understand this very well," he said. "Chamberlain, just a short while ago, told Corbin: 'It's evident that Italy is trying to get Germany out of an awkward situation, and that Mussolini has been entrusted with the task of promptly getting for Hitler everything he wants—without war.' And that is why the English are in considerably less of a hurry than our Minister of Foreign Affairs says they are."

"I fail to understand," Bonnet said, petulantly, "why anyone should insist on doubting Italy's good will, unless, of course, he wants war at any price. And I repeat that Ambassador Corbin telephoned me at 1 P.M. to stress the importance of a prompt reply. He must have changed his mind after having spoken to members of the British Cabinet, and he must have assumed that the Premier would advise me, since he spoke to him last. In any event, I am convinced that direct conversations between Berlin and Warsaw can accomplish nothing. If we fail to give an immediate reply to Rome, it means bringing on the tragedy."

President Lebrun asked him: "Monsieur Bonnet, you have told us that you spoke to Rome twice on the telephone—at a quarter past noon and again at 1 P.M. In that brief interval, you say, Mussolini decided upon the exact date of the planned conference. How can you explain his having taken this important decision so rapidly?"

"Monsieur le Président, that's just what seems most alarming to me," Georges Bonnet replied. "Rome must have had reason to believe that the moment for the explosion was approaching rapidly, and that therefore it was imperative to act with all possible speed."

"Come, come, Bonnet," said Campinchi. "Do you mean to say you can't see through this little game played by Hitler and Mussolini? One does the threatening and the other suggests terms. The world is terrified and the terms are accepted. Very simple."

Again, Paul Reynaud and Albert Sarraut supported the Minister of the Navy. While they were speaking, Daladier beckoned to an officer in attendance and whispered something into his ear. The officer left the room, came back in a moment and handed the Premier a note.

Paul Reynaud, meanwhile, was saying: "If we go crawling to Rome on our knees, we'll be docile sheep offering our necks to the butcher's knife. For one of two things must happen: either we'll be defeated without a war, or, much worse, we shall have lost our honor without winning the peace. If there's still time left, the only way for us to *éviter la gifle* (literally: to avoid the slap) is to put up our fists instead of turning the other cheek."

Then Daladier held up the note he had just received and proceeded to reinforce Paul Reynaud's figures of speech with simple facts. "I've not only telephoned to Corbin," he said. "I've spoken to Coulondre, our Ambassador in Berlin. He told me, literally: 'Hitler was to have started the war on August 26th. He hesitated. On the 29th, he gave a twenty-four-hour ultimatum. He hasn't budged.' Coulondre says, as he has been saying repeatedly for the past month, that we must stand our ground. . . . We have to do that now."

President Lebrun nodded his approval. Then, turning to Georges Bonnet, he said: "You see, our diplomats agree unanimously. We must resist."

Georges Bonnet suddenly seemed very tired. He saw that the majority of his colleagues were in agreement with the President.

The Council of Ministers was adjourned at 8:30 P.M. Immediately afterward, Albert Sarraut read a brief and simple communiqué to the press: "France will keep her engagements."

We had stayed at the office to get out a special edition for this communiqué. There was some evidence of tension in the air, but much less than the true state of affairs would have warranted. The man in the street was being incredibly optimistic; he seemed to be expecting another miracle, another last-minute escape from war. But, after all, how could he have been aware of the danger when the truth had been systematically kept from him?

I was still at the office when the news broke: the Ambassadors of Great Britain and of France had been abruptly summoned to the Wilhelmstrasse, where von Ribbentrop had read them a long and involved paper to the effect that negotiations between Germany and Poland had been broken off.

A few of us gathered in Jean Prouvost's office. We wanted to try to figure out what Hitler's latest move actually meant.

"Let's call up some of the Ministers to find out what they think," Jean Prouvost suggested.

He telephoned Georges Bonnet.

"It's just as I expected," Bonnet said. "I predicted that this very thing would happen, when I spoke to Daladier after the Council and when I phoned to Corbin just a little while ago. But the English Ministers have all gone to bed and have left orders not to be disturbed. They said that tomorrow would be time enough to give Italy her answer. Tomorrow! Where shall we be tomorrow?"

We finally got hold of Paul Reynaud. He hadn't heard of von Ribbentrop's announcement to the Allied diplomats. After thinking it over for a moment, Reynaud exclaimed: "Just another bluff. Hitler will back down at the last minute."

I stayed in the office and waited nervously in front of the Havas Agency news-ticker. At 4 A.M., the machine began printing the fatal news: German troops had crossed the Polish frontier and the battle was raging.

Chapter Twenty-six

Defeatists and Incompetents

(From my notebook)

SEPTEMBER 2, 1939.

While the German and the Polish armies are locked in battle, we are still debating.

All morning long Georges Bonnet has been telephoning—to London, Rome, Berlin, Warsaw. At noon he dictated a note for Count Ciano to Ambassador François-Poncet, stating that France *unconditionally* accepts Mussolini's proposals—despite the fact that London, in view of the attack on Poland, has refused to answer Italy. London has suggested to the French Government that the Allies jointly give Germany twenty-four hours to withdraw her armies from Polish soil and stop the war. Georges Bonnet has rejected this suggestion.

Paul Reynaud told us all this.

"It's treason," he said. "A firm stand by France and England might still change Hitler's mind. He attacked Poland only because France's hesitant attitude had convinced him that the Democracies would back down and would fall into the trap of the Rome conference, the date of which was set, purposely, for September 5th, permitting Germany to arrive as a mighty conqueror. Furthermore, the move would have made Poland feel that we were with her in any event. And Daladier permits Bonnet to go right ahead, because, as usual, after having arrived at a decision, he immediately sees its flaws and is really delighted when he has to take a step in the opposite direction."

How apt the description of Daladier heard around newspaper offices a few years ago: "Daladier is not the Bull of Vaucluse. He is the cow named Vacillation."

September 3rd:

The Rome Conference farce is still being played. It occasioned a dramatic scene late yesterday afternoon. The Polish Ambassador, Lucasiewics, went to see Georges Bonnet. He stepped up to the Minister of Foreign Affairs and shouted: "There's no time for any more conversation, Monsieur Bonnet. The time has come to fight. And what's your Army doing? What's your Air Force doing? You promised us speedy and powerful assistance. Instead of which you spent your time encouraging Hitler, doing everything in your power to make him feel that he could attack us with impunity because, once again, you would fail to fulfill your obligations. Worse than that, you did everything you could to prevent England from keeping her engagements. The idea of the Rome Conference is absurd. It would be to the advantage of Germany, and of Germany alone. You're now proving to the world that France's promises are worthless."

Georges Bonnet was greenish-pale. "I'll overlook your remarks," he said, "because of your country's misfortunes."

Georges Bonnet rang for an usher and the Ambassador of Poland found himself being dismissed as an intruder.

Anatole de Monzie is thoroughly disgusted with Georges Bonnet. . . . They say Bullitt is furious.

Daladier was wildly acclaimed in the Chamber when he declared:

"We shall keep the promise we have given our ally. The honor of France is at stake. We shall faithfully fulfill our obligations."

Daladier did not mention the Italian proposal; but he indicated that the French Government would spare no effort to achieve a negotiated settlement of the differences, on the condition that the aggressor withdraw his troops from the invaded territory.

Meanwhile, Pierre Laval had come over from the Senate to the Chamber of Deputies, and was whispering and conspiring with Bergery, Jean Mistler (the ex-Minister of the Sixth of February cabinet, now President of the Committee of Foreign Affairs), the Socialist René Brunet, the former Premier Pierre Etienne Flandin, and Marcel Déat.

All of the defeatist politicians and the pro-Nazis and pro-Fascists had plotted on behalf of the Italian proposal. The conspirators were also trying to overthrow the Cabinet, using as an excuse the necessity for a Government *"de large union nationale,"* to be headed by Marshal Pétain and including Laval, Bonnet, Flandin and all the other appeasers.

At the Cabinet Meeting following this session of the Parliament, Georges Bonnet advised his colleagues of the telephone call he had just received from the English Permanent Secretary for Foreign Affairs, Sir Alexis Cadogan, the successor to Sir Robert Vansittart. The British Cabinet firmly held its ground: no conference unless Germany withdrew from Polish territory, and an ultimatum to be presented to Hitler. Chamberlain and Lord Halifax wanted this ultimatum to expire at midnight.

Once again Georges Bonnet pleaded the Nazi cause when he said to Sir Alexis Cadogan: "You cannot sacrifice the last chance of peace for a matter of a few hours."

Georges Bonnet begged his colleagues in the Cabinet not to take any steps before noon on the following day. "By then," he said, "Italy may have found another means of settling matters." The Cabinet agreed to postpone any defiant move until the next day—September 4th, at noon.

Georges Bonnet telephoned to Ciano and boasted of the victory he had won. Chamberlain, meanwhile, was telephoning Daladier to complain of Georges Bonnet's slipperiness.

Jean Zay, the Minister of Education, resigned from the Cabinet to join the Army. Similarly many deputies chose to join their regiments.

Our London correspondent gave me a vivid picture of

the atmosphere pervading England. The House of Commons manifested the greatest anxiety and discontent when they learned that no ultimatum had been presented to Germany within twenty-four hours of the invasion of Poland, despite the definite guarantees Poland had received. Members were expressing their opinion of Monsieur Bonnet in strictly undiplomatic language, and there was a tendency to suspect Mr. Chamberlain and Lord Halifax of being somewhat lukewarm.

Our Ambassador, Corbin, went to 10 Downing Street, where he was received by Chamberlain and Halifax. Without circumlocution, Chamberlain said to our Ambassador: "Public opinion unanimously considers the Italian offer a trap, intended to favor the advance of the German armies into Poland by immobilizing the Allied forces. England is definitely united now, but the country is beginning to be seriously disturbed by the delays due to the vacillating attitude of the French Government. We cannot wait any longer. If necessary, we shall act alone."

Corbin was obliged to listen to similar criticism, even from English statesmen who had always been most friendly toward France. Winston Churchill was one of the most unrestrained. He had even mentioned the possibility of breaking the Franco-British Entente. Corbin had replied that the situation was somewhat different in France, where every man would have to go out and fight, while in England, for the moment at least, the war effort would be mainly industrial.

September 4th

This time it's definite. We're in. We're at war. No wild enthusiasm. There's a job to be done; that's all. As our men leave to join their regiments, they can be heard to say what Daladier said over the radio: "We've got to put an end to this."

The French people have been led into this war blindfolded. They've been lied to and misled, systematically. And here they are, calmly going off to war, just because it's their simple duty. Weapons are being put into their hands. Ringing appeals to patriotism are being made. But these soldiers of France are being informed, in confidential whispers, that "war has been declared, but that doesn't mean that there will be any war." During the past five years, our enemies have done a thorough job of polluting our country.

Civilians have been told, for months now, that "on the very first day of the war, there will be raids on all the big cities . . . and Paris will be destroyed within a few minutes." A number of citizens have left Paris, but not many. Parisians stroll around with their gas-masks slung over their shoulders. Every once in a while, they look up into the sky, but there is no trace of panic. Life goes on.

The atmosphere is extraordinary. It's as though everyone in France had been told a deep secret which serves to assure him that "all this is merely a game which could bring on such an inconceivable disaster that the opponents have agreed, tacitly, to cheat at the game and stop it before anything really catastrophic can happen."

The public is just beginning to hear some vague talk about proposals made by Mussolini. Since the French people have been kept in ignorance of just how France was driven to the brink of the abyss, many Frenchmen and Frenchwomen were inclined to believe that the inevitable could be avoided.

Nor are we making an effort to combat the diabolical propaganda of the Nazis. The censors have permitted the newspapers to publish the fact that an envoy had flown to Paris from Berlin to hand Daladier a personal letter from Hitler, requesting the Premier not to drag his country into the conflict. But the Minister of Information neglected to explain the hypocrisy of this step. The result was that Hitler and Mussolini could pose as the real lovers of peace. And what else could have been expected from Georges Bonnet who believed that the Nazis and the Fascists were always right? And what could have been expected from Edouard Daladier, the man who trembled at the resonant sound of his own voice?

The English ultimatum to Germany was presented yesterday at 9 A.M. It expired at 11 A.M.

On Ciano's advice, Georges Bonnet wanted the French *démarche* postponed until late in the day and to provide for a German answer by Monday, September 4th, at noon. But Daladier was aware of the responsibility he was taking by allowing Georges Bonnet to impose these terms, and the time limit finally set was September 3rd (yesterday) at 5 P.M.

September 12th

Definitely rejected, I went with several colleagues who have been similarly classified to the *Gendarmerie* to volunteer for service in the Army. The Colonel of the *Gendarmerie* of Paris said to me: "You know, all this is quite useless. The General Staff has decided not to consider any of these offers of enlistment."

The recruiting offices were being overwhelmed with applications from foreigners who had long been living in France and who now wanted to do their share in defense of the country. There again, the Colonel said, a number of difficulties had arisen, notably of a diplomatic nature, for orders had been given not to accept Americans, Swiss, etc., as volunteers. With regard to Germans and Austrians, on the other hand, they were given the choice of joining the Foreign Legion or of being interned in concentration camps. The great majority, he said, were choosing the Foreign Legion.

General Mobilization has been effected without a hitch. Less than one-half of one per cent represents the fraction of deserters, objectors, etc. Nevertheless, the entire method of our mobilization seems to be wrong. Thousands of skilled workers have been called to the colors, with the result that production of the most urgently needed defense materials has been slowed down. Furthermore, agricultural districts have been practically stripped of labor, regardless of whether or not the crops have been harvested.

September 15th

Hélène de Portes is convinced that her great moment is at hand. In truth, all of France is looking toward Paul

Reynaud now. Many people see in him the Clemenceau of this war.

The Marquise de Crussol is tirelessly warning Daladier to beware of his dangerous rival, telling the Premier that his Minister of Justice is engaged in dark intrigues against him.

First of all, Hélène de Portes wants to become Madame Paul Reynaud. She wants to oust the daughter of the President of the Order of French Advocates from the enviable position of being Paul Reynaud's legitimate wife. Hélène lives with Reynaud on the Place du Palais Bourbon, opposite the Chamber of Deputies. Jeanne Paul-Reynaud has volunteered as a nurse with the Flying Ambulance Corps. Count Jean de Portes was called to the colors.

But Jeanne Paul-Reynaud refuses to sue for a divorce. Besides, according to French law, remarriage within three years of divorce is forbidden. Hélène wants to have this law changed. Unfortunately, however, this would be within the province of the Minister of Justice, who happens to be Monsieur Paul Reynaud. He could not risk the scandal of introducing a law of which he, himself, would be the outstanding beneficiary.

Hélène de Portes was not to be thwarted. She went to see her adversary, the Marquise de Crussol.

"If you want Reynaud to abandon the idea of becoming Premier," Hélène said, "you must see to it that Daladier gives him an important post, one in which he can really serve his country. The Ministry of Finance, for example. The present Minister, Marchandeau, is a weakling and is said to be a *munichois* to boot. Georges Bonnet has no right to be Minister of Foreign Affairs with the country at war. Let Daladier take Bonnet's portfolio, and let him shift Bonnet to the Ministry of Justice. In that way, the Cabinet will certainly be assured of a longer life."

The Marquise de Crussol took Hélène de Portes to see Daladier who was delighted to find a way of removing Georges Bonnet from the Quai d'Orsay while still keeping him in the Cabinet. Three valid reasons why Daladier did not oust Bonnet completely:

1) Bonnet brought the Cabinet the support of the pacifist Radicals.

2) Bonnet was the man whom Daladier could use some day, in the event that he again wanted to shift his own political line.

3) Recognizing Bonnet as a dangerous enemy, Daladier preferred to keep him on his side.

Thus Georges Bonnet was appointed Minister of Justice.

Without delay, Hélène de Portes went to see her old friend, Odette Bonnet. "You must see to it," Hélène said, "that your husband makes up with Paul Reynaud. He thinks very highly of Georges and he feel that Georges' presence in the Cabinet is indispensable. As a matter of fact, it was really Paul who insisted on keeping Georges. He was most emphatic when he discussed the matter with Daladier. But Daladier insisted on taking the Ministry of Foreign Affairs. Just as soon as Paul Reynaud becomes Premier, he'll take over the Ministry of War and Georges will go back to the Quai d'Orsay. In the meantime, tell Georges to do us a little favor, won't you? Ask him to change the divorce law."

This is how and why Georges Bonnet remained in the Daladier Cabinet.

The divorce law was duly changed by decree. Following divorce, one could now remarry within one year—instead of three. Within one year, therefore, Paul Reynaud would be free to marry resourceful Hélène de Portes.

September 20th

The situation in Poland is very bad.

In France, things are not going any too well.

The other day, the Marquise de Crussol said to some friends: "France, bled white in 1914-1918 and further weakened by a declining birth-rate, cannot now afford to sacrifice another million men. The President of the Council, Daladier, is a humanitarian and will not risk his reputation to win a Pyrrhic victory."

The Marquise has surrounded herself with a group of men who fear responsibility. These are the fashionable defeatists—men like Joseph Caillaux, Jean Mistler, Edouard Pfeiffer.

Following the Russo-German Pact, the Communist newspapers, *L'Humanité* and *Ce Soir* had been suppressed. The Communist organizations had been dissolved; those of their leaders who could be found were arrested. Maurice Thorez, Gabriel Péri and Jacques Duclos had vanished into thin air. Even those who had joined their regiments managed somehow to desert and disappear.

I told the Minister of the Interior, Albert Sarraut, that we were receiving indignant letters from our readers, to the effect that they suspected the Government of having tacitly consented to the escape of these Communists.

Albert Sarraut complained of being interfered with constantly. "What can I do?" he said. "The military are running everything. They've called back into service a bunch of old Generals, and they've given these incompetents some very important posts where these old fogies are making up for lost time and are taking their revenge on the civilian authorities for having forced them into retirement. My own mail is opened by the censor. In the meantime, spies are running wild, propagandists are operating to their hearts' content and Communist leaders are disappearing by evaporation."

October 2nd

We've had a terrible time getting authorization from the High Commission of Information and from the Censorship to publish a series of articles by H. R. Knickerbocker, the American journalist, on the fortunes amassed by the Nazi chiefs and on the ways in which they have attempted to invest their millions outside of Germany. Opera-Mundi, the press agency directed by Paul Winkler, sold us the exclusive French rights for these articles. Altogether, this outfit is doing some splendid anti-Nazi propaganda work, although they are constantly being harassed on the pretext that they are connected with the International News Service and King Features Syndicate, both belonging to the Hearst organization. Hearst is still the *bête noire* of French officialdom.

Knickerbocker's articles did appear finally, and they created such an uproar that Goebbels went on the air and challenged the American newspaperman to prove his statements, offering him 10 per cent of whatever funds he located outside of Germany. Thereupon, the High Commission of Information asked us for the Knickerbocker articles which they had so reluctantly permitted us to publish only a few days previously. They wanted to use this material in pamphlets, to be dropped on Germany by our planes.

October 15th

Nothing is more completely absurd than our High Commission of Information and our Censorship. We're having great trouble in getting out *Paris-Soir* on four or six pages because of the paper shortage. Then we have to contend with the instructions issued by our bewildered Censorship. First we were told to give up publishing cross-word puzzles, on the theory that spies could correspond with each other by means of cross-words. This would naturally imply that the people making up these puzzles for the various newspapers were all spies. At present the authorities are seriously contemplating the advisability of having the cross-word puzzles made up by a special department of the General Staff. We have strict orders, furthermore, not to mention the name of any city, town, etc., in France in connection with any kind of news item. We are always supposed to say: "Somewhere in France." We have also been instructed not to mention any individual names; and, above all, *"ne pas faire de héros"* ("not to build up any heroes"). The German communiqués regularly mention outstanding individual feats. If we hear of any brilliant accomplishment by our men in battle, we are permitted to mention the encounter, but no names—thus depriving the story of all human-interest value.

General Headquarters has taken the stand that "the Army is to be considered as a unit, and there is no necessity for giving publicity to individuals who are merely doing their duty." General Vuillemin (Aviation) is particularly strict in this respect. Yesterday I approached him through one of his friends. I was hoping to persuade the General to reconsider his decision and to permit us to report individual instances of heroism on the part of our flyers.

But the General replied: "I shall continue to oppose any such thing. I feel that the mention of these individual cases would amount to giving the public and our Army undue cause for optimism. These stories might create the impression that our aviation was capable of defending itself against the enemy. Whereas, in fact, we are so weak, numerically, that we shall be simply overwhelmed by the first attack on a really large scale."

The General may be right. But this state of mind in a ranking military leader at the beginning of a war can inspire little confidence.

It has become practically impossible to communicate with foreign countries. Telephone conversations are interrupted; telegrams are mutilated; and what little material does come in from our correspondents is discussed, at great length, by the professors, the old retired diplomats and the decrepit ex-military men who dominate our Censorship. As a rule, we are permitted to publish some 100 colorless words out of an original dispatch of some 1,200 words.

The latest decree is that we are not to mention the name of Lindbergh. The French people are not to be permitted to know that there are some isolationists in America. This ruling was even applied to the mention—in connection with a purely technical discussion of aviation—of the 1927 Lindbergh New York-to-Paris flight. The Censors insisted that his name be deleted from the article. We protested.

"His name is not to be mentioned in the French press. We have our orders, and we shall execute them blindly," they said.

October 20th

Because newspapers cannot send observers to the French front, no one has been informed that the French are prepared to fight. We are being swamped with German photographs—coming through Switzerland and Italy—but it is impossible to get any pictures of French troops in action. The Minister of Information has given us some pictures. One of these showed a motorized column on its way to the front. Lacking anything better, *Paris-Soir* ran this picture. Whereupon we received thousands of letters from soldiers who had recognized this picture as one taken from a manual which had been distributed to the men. The picture had been taken in *1937*, during maneuvers.

October 22nd

Our American colleagues are constantly asking us to do something about the situation. They say that their newspapers are getting nothing but Nazi news and Nazi photographs.

Our friends on *Life* seem to be in a particularly awkward situation. They are not being permitted to do any worthwhile reportage. And when they registered a complaint, they were told: "Your publication is pro-German. You haven't published any pictures yet that didn't come from Berlin."

"We haven't been able to get any others," they had to reply.

Then the Chief of the Censorship, Colonel de Massignac (an old retired Army officer, who, until September, had been at the head of the *Ligue des Jeunesses Patriotes*), glared at them ferociously and said: "If the only available pictures are German—and if *Life* is not pro-German—*Life* will quite simply refrain from publishing pictures. Those are my views on the subject."

I tried to explain to this old fossil that a picture publication is obliged to illustrate its news stories with pictures; and that it would be much better—from the viewpoint of French propaganda—if such pictures were supplied by us instead of by the enemy. But he stubbornly maintained his incomprehensible position.

The editor-in-chief (editress, rather) of a Swedish newspaper, with which we have a working agreement came down from Stockholm and asked me to take her to the

Commission of Information. She wanted pictures giving the French side of the war. Scandinavia, she said, was being flooded with all kinds of German propaganda.

She was received by a Major. She complained about the inadequacy of news from France.

"Madame," the Major replied, "the situation is quite simple. People who are pro-German will not be moved by our propaganda, while those who are pro-French do not require it."

After this magnificent statement of principle, he changed his manner. He looked at the lady quite sternly, and said: "Frankly, I must tell you that your mission cannot fail to arouse our suspicions. We are at war, Madame, and we must receive visitors like you with *beaucoup de réserve*—visitors who see fit to come from a great distance for the avowed purpose of giving us criticism."

The lady got up and replied: "You are quite right, Monsieur. But don't worry. Under your present system, you'll have fewer and fewer visitors."

I went to see Jean Giraudoux to tell him about this deplorable incident for which his Commission was responsible. His desk was piled high with papers. He seemed confused and overwhelmed with work.

"I know," he said, wearily. "We haven't straightened things out yet. The military are hindering us a great deal. The Germans have been spreading their propaganda for years. We are just beginning to develop our Information Service. It may take us years before we get it running smoothly."

"That's fine," I said, "in view of the fact that we're at war now, and that we hope the war will be over within a few years."

Giraudoux's gesture expressed utter helplessness. Then he said pathetically: "We're doing everything we can. Believe me."

Chapter Twenty-seven

Daladier Falls

(From my notebook)

OCTOBER 23, 1939.

I asked an officer of the General Staff why, after having made an advance into German territory during the Polish campaign, we had withdrawn our troops voluntarily.

Things were going badly at General Headquarters, he said. General Gamelin, installed at the Château de Vincennes, was on very bad terms with General Georges, Commander of the Armies of the North and Northeast, with Headquarters at La Ferté. Gamelin wanted to keep General Georges and the General Staff apart. He planned to keep the General Staff half-way between Vincennes and La Ferté, at Esbly. It would be difficult, therefore, for both Generals to maintain contact with the various units of the General Staff.

During the very first days of the war, he said, the younger Staff Officers had been anxious to launch a major assault against the incompleted and notoriously vulnerable Siegfried Line. At the time there were only a few German divisions on the Western front. But Gamelin had rejected the idea, claiming that we lacked the artillery to make the preparations necessary for such an attack. Gamelin was completely devoted to the theory of waging an exclusively defensive war. To date, therefore, our activities have consisted of minor skirmishes with enemy patrols, stealthy surprise attacks on enemy outposts—Indian-style warfare, really—carried on by volunteers on both sides. And, significantly, there were always more, far more volunteers available than could possibly be employed in these restricted operations.

Even at G.H.Q. the rumor persists that there won't be any real war. Colonel Lagarde in command of the *Troisième Bureau* (Operations), and Colonel Gaucher, chief of the *Deuxième Bureau* (Intelligence), had suggested that every Army officer be given a copy of a booklet expounding the lessons learned from the war in Poland. This recommendation had been flatly rejected by General Gamelin.

"France," Gamelin had said, "is not Poland. And Germany will not employ the methods against us that she has employed there. Distribution of such a booklet would only serve to worry people."

October 29th

"Did you hear Stuttgart last night? They put on a dramatization of the old dispute we had with England at the time of the Fashoda incident. And day before yesterday they gave a little radio play based on Napoleon on the Island of Elba. Not bad at all. You must admit, those Nazi swine are pretty clever when it comes to propaganda."

Listening in to Stuttgart has come to be a favorite pastime for many people in France, largely because it's forbidden fruit.

Even though many people say, "It's really disgusting to think that there are French traitors who are willing to do this job for the enemy," yet they listen and absorb the poison. And then somebody will blurt out: "Well, as Stuttgart says, where are the English, anyway?"

Herr Otto Abetz is still functioning efficiently, even from a distance. To deliver French-language broadcasts, Abetz had chosen a man with whom he had long been associated—a man who had been a failure in France, both as a politician and as a journalist—Paul Ferdonnet. Just before the outbreak of the war, he had made a triumphant appearance in his native village, at the wheel of a superb Mercedes and accompanied by a dazzling blonde whom he had married in Berlin. He did not trouble to visit his mother or his daughter. Now his pockets were lined with banknotes. When he returned to Berlin, his job was waiting for him. His French-language broadcasts from the Stuttgart radio station told the people of France that it was Hitler who had been attacked, that Hitler had nothing but the best intentions toward France, that this war had been brought on by the Jews, the capitalists and the British, and that the "English would fight to the last Frenchman," etc., etc. In the meantime, Ferdonnet's English counterpart, the notorious Lord Haw-Haw, told the people of England—in faultless English—that France had dragged Britain into the war.

About mid-September, I transmitted to the *Commissariat de l'Information* a report on the rôle played by Ferdonnet and by his collaborators, Duesberg and Obrecht.

Duesberg, who had long served as Berlin correspondent for the Parisian newspapers, *L'Oeuvre* and *L'Intransigeant*, had originally come to France from Russia at the time of the Bolshevik Revolution. He always claimed to be anti-Nazi.

Obrecht read the texts written by Ferdonnet and Duesberg. This traitor had a voice that was ideally suited to the job. He had served as Adjutant in the French Army during the Occupation of the Rhineland, and had been dishonorably discharged for embezzlement. He had then fled to Germany, where, under the name of Jacques Saint-Germain, he had worked as a movie extra, specializing in portraying French officers—under UFA direction.

These henchmen of Dr. Goebbels were motivated by envy, by desire for revenge and by a yearning to save their necks and to make a little money in the process. They were treated with contempt even by the Germans.

With considerable difficulty, I obtained permission from

the authorities to publish an article exposing the names and the past records of the traitors on the Nazi radio.

I began wondering what had happened to Mouthon who, before the war, had been Ferdonnet's associate on the pro-Nazi Prima Presse Agency.

At the *Cinquième Bureau* I learned that *the Counter-Espionage officer, detailed to look for Mouthon, was none other than Lucien Rebattet, the former Editor-in-Chief of the pro-Nazi publication,* Je Suis Partout—*in short, a former collaborator of Paul Ferdonnet's.*

Finally, thanks to Paul Reynaud's intervention, Mouthon was found and arrested. He had been serving as Captain in the Military Intelligence in a contingent quartered not far from the Maginot Line.

October 30th

I've been cultivating a hobby by collecting pamphlets dropped by the Germans. They're well gotten up, simple to the point of vulgarity. They all harp on the same theme. Some of the propaganda is in the form of picture postcards, showing an English soldier. When held to the light, the card shows a soldier holding a naked woman in his arms. On the back of the card is this caption: "French soldier, where are the English? Where is your wife?" Then there are sheets covered with rather childishly drawn colored pictures showing an English soldier hypocritically pushing a French soldier into a pool of blood and laughing as he watches the Frenchman drown. Then there's a little red booklet containing a collection of anti-French statements allegedly made by outstanding Englishmen. Sources and dates are piously given. One terrifying handbill, bordered in black, read: "Parisians! Prepare your coffins!" And there's a sheet of paper in the shape of an oakleaf, rust-colored. On one side, you read: "The leaves fall in the autumn but grow again in the spring"; and, on the other side: "The French soldiers who died for England will never live again."

The French and the British are also dropping leaflets over Germany. One of these masterpieces was a somewhat bulky booklet of at least fifty pages in very small print quoting the anti-totalitarian passages of the recent Papal Encyclical.

October 31st

Things are certainly not being made easy for our war correspondents. Naturally, the consortium of the big newspapers has taken advantage of the war to regain some of its former dictatorial power. The group succeeded in obtaining the appointment of Monsieur Maillard, General Manager of *Le Matin,* as the sole representative of the press on the High Commission for Information . . . No one seemed to care what line *Le Matin* had been taking these past few years.

As for our foreign colleagues—and especially the Americans—they are only slightly better off now that Robert de Saint-Jean, an outstanding newspaperman, has been in charge of the High Commission's Department for Foreign Correspondents. Incidentally, our American *confrères* are showing a degree of good-will and understanding that is really touching.

Life, however, is not getting on any too well. Major Réa, in command of the press bureau of the Military Intelligence at G.H.Q., has looked upon *Life* and *Time* with suspicion ever since a cable sent by the New York office to the Paris correspondent, asking for some information on the Maginot Line, was intercepted. "Espionage," Major Réa had declared. He had refused to listen to the perfectly logical explanation that *Life* and *Time* would certainly not have sent a dispatch in clear language if they had wanted to go in for espionage. He had also been assured that Mr. Luce and his collaborators were above all suspicion. But the Major had stubbornly maintained his stand; and had further criticized *Life* for having published a photograph of a French soldier sitting on a chair under a tree, with a machine-gun in front of him. This picture had been sent to *Life* by *Paris-Soir,* after having previously appeared in our weekly, *Match,* without evoking the slightest adverse comment. Furthermore, this photograph had naturally been taken with the consent of the military authorities, and had been approved by the censors prior to initial publication. The picture was intended to symbolize the period of waiting at the French front. It was certainly not the fault of our American friends that this photograph was symbolical of something ominous in the eyes of our readers.

Edgar Ansel Mowrer and H. R. Knickerbocker, among others, have done some excellent *reportages* on the front. They told me that they witnessed the famous "war of the placards" from the front lines. Suddenly they saw a large placard in front of the German position. "France for the French," it read. A few minutes later, the Parisians holding this sector retorted by putting up a sign of their own, reading: "Poland for the Poles."

January 1, 1940

Two weeks ago, Paul Reynaud made an excellent speech in which he said: "Chancellor Hitler has constantly gambled on the weakness of the democracies, and up to the present he has always won. The democracies will win, but with sacrifices they have not yet begun to comprehend. If we do not go into this struggle with everything we possess, it will be very easy for us to lose the war. Some people will ask: Shall we now borrow from Germany a régime which is so profoundly repugnant to us? What will be the difference between us, if we do? I reply that the difference between us will not lie in the totality of our war effort, in the unanimous willingness to make sacrifices. The difference will lie solely in the fact that the necessary policies will be determined here by a free Parliament, acting in behalf of a free people. It is possible that this war, begun in a sort of apathy, may come to its conclusion in the midst of a general conflagration. By that time, perhaps, our ideal of liberty may exist only in our hearts; but it will be ready to bloom again after the victory. We shall be victorious. But, in order to conquer the enemy, we shall first have to conquer ourselves."

This speech was only moderately well received by the public, for, unfortunately, the prevailing atmosphere is not favorable to the word "sacrifice."

Daladier, on the other hand, strikes a far more popular

note when, in his radio broadcasts, he repeatedly speaks of "sparing French blood" and of "refraining from costly and doubtful offensives."

At the turn of the year the atmosphere was not what could be called optimistic. However, since the conclusion of the war in Poland, nothing really distressing has happened at the front. The British victory over the *Graf Spee* brought momentary encouragement. The war between Russia and Finland was generally considered to be something "that was not going to be lucky for Hitler."

"We're in a very bad way," Paul Reynaud said to me. "Hitler wants to capitalize on our inactivity. And, once again, we're letting him do what he wants. Daladier is in a worse state of mind than ever. Gamelin is delighted at not having to take any responsibility. And as for Jean Giraudoux, he hasn't the remotest conception of what it's all about. The country's morale is being corroded by Nazi propaganda, against which no antidote is being employed. If things go on this way, we shall wake up one fine day and find ourselves faced with a sudden and violent move on Hitler's part—an offensive which will overwhelm us before we can begin to put up any kind of resistance. What we need is leadership."

It occurred to me that Reynaud was becoming more and more convinced that he was the leader that France so urgently needed.

Daladier seems far more concerned about the activities of his Minister of Finance than he is about Hitler's. The Premier is being subjected to exquisite tortures by the Marquise de Crussol who is constantly telling him that Paul Reynaud is speaking and acting as though he were the coming Premier. Daladier cannot bear to hear that Paul Reynaud has been lunching or dining with important military leaders, such as General Decamp, Daladier's own *Chef du Cabinet Militaire,* or General Giraud, the protagonist of the school of thought favoring an offensive war instead of the strictly defensive, waiting war.

"It isn't my fault," Hélène de Portes said to Jeanne de Crussol, "if Paul Reynaud pursues a policy that is contrary to our agreement. Those men around him, those advisers of his—they're to blame. Why don't you see to it that he gets rid of his *Chef de Cabinet,* Georges Palewski, who detests you and is constantly conspiring with your worst enemies."

She wanted to get rid of her own worst enemy, too. For this associate of Reynaud's had succeeded in counterbalancing the evil influence exerted by the lovely Hélène.

Daladier did not hesitate. He summoned Paul Reynaud and ordered him to ship Palewski off to the front. Hélène de Portes redoubled her pressure, and, finally, Paul Reynaud had to give in. To replace Palewski, Hélène managed to secure the appointment of puppets under her control: the Inspectors of Finances Lecca and Devau.

With Palewski out of the way, the guerrilla war between Daladier and Reynaud broke out anew.

On December 30th, Hélène de Portes said to me, bitterly:

"Daladier knows perfectly well that, in times of war, the Ministry of Finance is the most unpopular of all the Ministries because it has to take money from the civilians and also has to refuse an increase in pay for the military. Daladier hopes, thereby, to make Paul Reynaud so unpopular that he will never be President of the Council. But he'll see."

February 6th

The papers have reported that Daladier had an accident. But the press took good care not to divulge the details. . . . The facts are simply that Daladier fell from his horse. The Premier and the Marquise de Crussol were spending the week-end at the estate of the wealthy politician Raymond Patenôtre, at Rambouillet.

February 15th

A female spy has been arrested in the Champs de Mars *quartier.* She had been the mistress, briefly, of a number of Army officers who lived near or were stationed at the Invalides and at the Ecole Militaire.

While tracking down this spy, the authorities also got hold of several investigators who were working for the

Nazis. This haul also brought to light several documents which were of considerable interest. One of these papers was a questionnaire containing such specific questions as "the political situation in France," "the popularity of Daladier," "Daladier's opponents, secret and known," "Daladier's probable successor," etc. Daladier made excellent use of this questionnaire at the beginning of the secret session of the Chamber of Deputies, convened to discuss the conduct of the war. He pointed to this document as an indication of the fact that Hitler was interested in and afraid of him.

February 18th

Daladier's stock is falling.

The indefatigable pro-Nazis and defeatists are delighted because Daladier refuses to engage in an offensive war against Germany, and because, as far as he dares, he permits himself to be identified with the school of thought holding that no irreparable damage has been done yet, and that the dreaded titanic struggle might quite suddenly be obviated by a nice little conference. At that, the Nazi-lovers are enraged at Daladier because he refuses to attack the Russians in Finland.

On the other hand, the genuine anti-Nazis, anxious to prevent premature peace moves, eager to take the initiative from Hitler and to reawaken public opinion—these men would like to see Daladier and Gamelin send French troops to Finland rather than have our armies continue doing nothing at all.

February 25th

Finland was the one topic discussed at the last meeting of the Supreme Council (Feb. 7th). Gamelin is firmly against making any move in that direction. He is becoming increasingly devoted to the theory of the purely defensive war. Chamberlain doesn't want to take any action in Finland either.

A fortnight ago, Paul Reynaud told me that he considered an expedition to Finland prohibitively dangerous. Now he has suddenly changed his mind. Why?

Perhaps because he feels that this controversy will help him gain valuable allies in his struggle against Daladier.

February 28th

Ever since Marshal Mannerheim has assumed leadership of Finnish resistance against Soviet Russia, he has become a sort of national hero in the democratic countries. The special correspondents in Finland, while giving due credit to the magnificent accomplishments of the Finnish armies, are regularly reporting their concern over the activities of the Nazis in the little Republic.

Under the pressure of public opinion, a small expeditionary corps, composed of French and English volunteers, has been organized. Ships have been selected to move these forces to their destination. Under German pressure, Norway and Sweden are refusing to permit passage of these ships. However, Germany is perfectly willing to let the French and the British fight the Russians in Finland, but what she does not want to see is the movement of important contingents of Allied troops into the Scandinavian zone. These forces might well encourage the Scandinavian countries to resist Nazi plans.

We sent our correspondent, Gaston Bénac, to Norway to look into the situation. From the port of Narvik, he sent us a report to the effect that almost all the freighters in port at this key point on the railroad line were German; that these ships were crowded with troops; and that the freighters, lying off-shore in the harbor, were being supplied surreptitiously at night. He added that most of the stevedores in the port were Germans.

The Censorship has stubbornly refused to let us run this article. We appealed to the Ministry of Foreign Affairs and were told that our correspondent Bénac was misinformed; and France could not afford to risk offending Norway by publishing such an "adventure story."

March 9th

Georges Kessel, our special correspondent to Finland, sent us the following telegram: "Have stenographer stand by for important communication from Amsterdam."

With the Swedish Government serving as intermediary, negotiations have been going on aiming to put an end to the Russo-Finnish War. The Germans are said to favor a compromise peace, for they do not want Russia to occupy all of Finland and thus be at the very borders of Norway and Sweden.

Georges Kessel managed to find out that, while the war was still being bitterly fought, Finnish plenipotentiaries had already left for Moscow. Knowing perfectly well that the censors at Helsinki would refuse to pass such a report, he rented an automobile and drove to Abo. From there he took a plane for Stockholm and telephoned his story to Gaston Bénac in Amsterdam, in order to avoid attracting too much attention. Bénac, in turn, phoned us the story. Exactly an hour after Kessel had put through his call, Sweden temporarily suspended telephone communication with foreign countries.

Our own Censors did not want us to publish Georges Kessel's article. In a black rage, we were preparing to get out the paper minus our scoop. At the last moment, however, the Chief of the Civil Censorship, Monsieur Martinaud-Déplat (Daladier's man) told us that the Premier's office authorized us to publish the article.

The story created a sensation in Paris. No one had expected the war to be settled so soon. Everybody began criticizing Daladier for having failed to act. This criticism was also directed against the English Government.

March 21st

Daladier has fallen—first from his horse, and now from power. At the secret committee meetings of the Senate and of the Chamber of Deputies, Daladier had been urged to carry on the struggle "more energetically." It is noteworthy that the leaders of the defeatist groups were now manifesting the greatest enthusiasm for action. The Premier's inertia was violently attacked in a brilliant but treacherous speech made by Pierre Laval in the Senate. It began with a systematic enumeration of Germany's material advantages and concluded with the remark: "We must fight an all-out war, if we are to fight at all."

Of course, these gentlemen wanted us to act "more energetically" toward the Soviet Union so that we might arrive at an early understanding with Hitler.

But the parliamentarians, who sincerely want to see France adopt a more vigorous attitude toward Germany as well, have allied themselves with the defeatists, suddenly transformed into super-warmongers. As a result, Daladier received only 239 votes in the Chamber, whereas 300 refrained from voting their confidence.

Daladier had barely been overthrown, when a sort of panic swept over the Parliament. Who will take his place? The Radicals are grieving at their loss of power. The defeatists do not feel strong enough to assume the reins of government.

The path seems to be clear for Paul Reynaud—the embodiment of the spirit of initiative and of unflinching resistance to the enemy. And, indeed, he was the man to be summoned by President Lebrun and to be entrusted with the task of forming a new Government. But Paul Reynaud will encounter the gravest difficulties. He will be opposed by every appeaser and Hitler-lover in France, as well as by a solid front of the Daladier-Georges Bonnet Radical group.

Reynaud did not hesitate to confess that he would have preferred to have been called as Clemenceau had been called during the other war—that is to say, as a saviour, after all other political combinations had been tried and found wanting, and at a moment when, with the country in immediate danger, even the most stringent measures would instantly be accepted by everyone.

Now that Hélène de Portes' dream is coming true at last, she is absent from Paris. Paul Reynaud has requested her to stay away for the present.

Chapter Twenty-eight

Before the *Blitzkrieg*

As I CROSSED the threshold of Paul Reynaud's private office a chorus of sighs and groans and exclamations rose behind me. These protests came from people who were in a feverish hurry to arrive at some sort of power. My interview with the new Premier prolonged their agony.

Paul Reynaud, as usual, was sitting bolt upright, his head held high; but he was very pale and his face seemed drawn. He was surrounded by his advisers. Minister Georges Mandel was close beside him.

"What does the press say about me?" Paul Reynaud asked.

"I'm sorry to say that the press is not especially enthusiastic; in fact, it is quite prepared to be hostile," I replied.

I called Paul Reynaud's attention to the fact that at the Ministry of Information the Director of the Civil Censorship, Martinaud-Déplat, was openly working against Daladier's successor. I also expressed my surprise at finding so many shady characters at his door. The country was counting on him to form a small War Cabinet, composed exclusively of men of the very first order.

"I'm doing what I can," Paul Reynaud cut in, "and not what I really want to do. Just because Daladier is attacking me I'm obliged to take parliamentary currents into consideration. I must count on every Minister I select to assure me of a certain number of votes. I must cater to the Radical Party and gain as many votes among as many factions as possible. If I want to act, I must first see to it that I stay in power."

"But how about the war?"

A burst of sardonic laughter came from behind the high starched collar of Monsieur Georges Mandel. "The war?" he exclaimed. "Of all the people who have come into this office today, you, Monsieur Lazareff, are the only one who has even thought of the war."

Paul Reynaud's Government had barely missed being still-born. This Cabinet—a strange and monstrous agglomeration of no fewer than thirty-five men—had been accepted by the Chamber by a majority of precisely one vote. This all-important single vote had been swung over literally at the last moment: the Deputy Deschizeaux was about to put a blue slip into the ballot-box (blue indicating a vote *against* the Government) when the new Minister of Information, L. O. Frossard, seized the Deputy's arm and persuaded him to deposit a white slip (signifying a vote *for* the Government) by promising him an important position in the Propaganda Department.

In spite of manifest lack of unified support, Paul Reynaud decided to try to maintain his Ministry, although with the greatest misgivings.

"The Radicals are deserting me," he said. "Those whom I persuaded to enter the Government are constantly blackmailing me with the threat of resignation—which would, of course, bring on the fall of the Ministry. It would have been natural for me to take on the Ministry of War as well as the Presidency of the Council, as Clemenceau did in 1917. But if Daladier had not been permitted to keep the portfolio of War, the Radicals in the Senate and in the Chamber, instead of merely refraining from voting, would have voted against me, and I shouldn't have had the slightest chance of succeeding. That's why I took on the Ministry of Foreign Affairs."

"But why," I asked, "why does Georges Mandel maintain the Ministry for the Colonies? Why didn't you give him the Department of the Interior? There is a dangerous Nazi Fifth Column which is actively undermining civilian morale and it should be cleaned up."

"Georges Mandel didn't want the Interior. He said that the moment wasn't at hand yet at which he could really do a thorough job of it and uncompromisingly strike at the very roots of defeatism."

"But the whole set-up is dangerous. You, *Monsieur le Président,* want to wage this war aggressively, and yet you have a Minister of War and a Commander-in-Chief of the Armies who are in complete disagreement with your policies. You have a Minister of the Interior who is utterly incapable of preventing Nazi spies and propagandists from corrupting the country. And your Minister of Information is a militant pacifist."

"First of all, I have to establish my position in the Parliament. I shall make some changes in my Cabinet when the Chamberlain Government will have been succeeded in London by a Government headed by Winston Churchill. And this is bound to happen just as soon as the war ceases to be static."

"Unfortunately," I said, "it will be Hitler who will decide the moment for this war to enter into another phase. Léon Blum has said that you have no intention of taking the offensive. Does this truly interpret your fundamental policy?"

Paul Reynaud evaded the question with a gesture. He seemed somewhat irritated. "We shall certainly not undertake any hastily improvised military offensive," he said. "There are many other things to be done: we must prevent the Balkan and Scandinavian neutrals, which are being systematically intimidated by Germany, from giving the Nazis secret but constant and effective help; we must tighten the blockade; we must see to it that America is kept better informed on what is going on in Europe; and we must arrange to have a capable High Command and General Staff. But above all I must do something to unite the people behind me. My hands will then be free."

After a moment, Paul Reynaud asked: "Why is the press so hostile toward me?"

I said, "It's because both the press and the Parliament are being constantly subjected to pressure by those hidden forces which are trying everything to prevent an irreparable break between France and Nazi Germany. It's because you appear to be the only one capable of preventing a *coup d'état* and a subsequent lovely little entente with Hitler. And, now that the Russo-Finnish War has come to an end and the famous anti-Soviet 'crusade' has been postponed for the present, these so-called 'mysterious' and 'unknown' elements in our midst are most particularly afraid that you may see fit to wage the war 'more energetically' not, as they had so warmly recommended, against the U.S.S.R., but against the Third Reich."

I went on: "Permit me to say, *Monsieur le Président,* that you have not surrounded yourself with men who can be of help to you. Jean Prouvost, for one, is deeply disappointed. And now he has turned against you, and we're having the greatest trouble keeping him from attacking you openly. Over at the *Petit Parisien,* Elie-Joseph Bois, is complaining of the cool reception you gave him.

"As for the other newspapers, you never expected to see *Le Matin, Le Journal* or *Le Temps* pleased at your arrival in power. Even if you did denounce Soviet aggression, you and Mandel will be remembered primarily as former partisans of a military accord with the U.S.S.R.

"It's too bad that you agreed to dismiss Georges Palewski. He would have kept you well informed as to the mood of the Senate and of the Chamber, as well as of the press. He volunteered for service with a fighter squadron. He has received a citation in the Order of the Day. He's in town now, on furlough. I brought him along with me. He's waiting outside in the antechamber."

Without a word, Paul Reynaud got up, opened the door, and admitted Palewski. The Premier congratulated his former collaborator on his splendid conduct.

Georges Palewski said, "I can see why you don't ask me to come back and take my place at your side again, but what I cannot understand is why you don't call on

Charles de Gaulle. You always expressed the greatest admiration for his intelligence and character. I should think you could use a military adviser like him now. Or is there some political blackball against him, too?"

"I'm considering de Gaulle," Paul Reynaud replied, becoming even more embarrassed. "But there isn't much use summoning him before I, myself, take over the Ministry of War."

Thereupon, he abruptly shook hands with Palewski and wished him the best of luck. We were alone again.

I said: "I must inform you that I have learned that you are being betrayed at the Ministry of the Interior. For example, they are still giving Daladier, instead of you, the information gathered by means of wire-tapping."

"What do you mean?" Paul Reynaud asked in great surprise.

"The reports on telephone conversations secretly overheard. Since the outbreak of the war, everything said over the telephone by everyone of political importance has been heard by the Inspectors of the *Sûreté Nationale*. Every word has been taken down, either stenographically or on records, and has been delivered to the Premier every morning."

"I never knew about that."

Reynaud changed the subject by announcing that Hélène de Portes was soon to return.

"She'll be of great help to me," he said. "She's such a courageous and intelligent woman."

I left the Quai d'Orsay in a state of terrible apprehension. Paul Reynaud was the hope of so many of us. Were we to be disillusioned again?

Shortly after, I heard that, on Hélène de Portes' advice, Paul Reynaud had chosen for his *Chef du Cabinet Militaire*, a certain Colonel de Villelune. This officer had distinguished himself as a habitué of the *salons* of the extreme Right and by the fact that his defeatist remarks had repeatedly provoked criticism. I also learned that Reynaud had named as Under-Secretary of State and as Secretary *restreint* of the War Cabinet, no less a personage than Paul Baudouin, Director of the National Bank of Indo-

China, a man whose pro-Fascist leanings and whose admiration for the policies of Georges Bonnet were well known.

Paul Reynaud had gone to London and had signed a treaty with the British—a treaty solemnly engaging both countries never to sign a separate peace. He had wanted his first official act to be a move effecting the closest possible *entente* between the Allies. Edouard Daladier, on the other hand, had been faithful to his personal policy of evasiveness and procrastination, and of wanting to keep at least one door of escape open; he had claimed that his "foot was bothering him more and more," and had thus avoided accompanying the Premier to the meeting of the Supreme Council, in the course of which the new Franco-British pact was to be signed.

Despite the objections of the die-hard "pacifists," this treaty had been received with great enthusiasm by a substantial majority of public opinion as well as of the Parliament.

Then Paul Reynaud had achieved his second success when it was announced that mines had been laid along the Norwegian coast and that the sea-route for iron-ore shipments to Germany had been effectively closed. The will to resist Hitler was beginning to be expressed by deeds rather than by mere words.

Furthermore, the country was expecting some early changes in the High Command. Paul Reynaud had conferred with General Gamelin and had summoned General Weygand from Syria for consultations.

Every time Paul Reynaud evidenced firmness and energy, he strengthened his own position. And then, after Hitler had invaded Denmark and Norway, everyone realized that the war had entered a new phase and that it would be impossible to change Governments again. And so Paul Reynaud was definitely in power now and could do as he wanted.

A friend on the General Staff came to see me in Paris and told me he was deeply concerned. "General Headquarters," he said, "is doing everything possible to prevent the sending of even a small expeditionary corps to Norway. They're always afraid of taking any kind of initiative. They want to have as many men as possible locked up in the Maginot Line, all vegetating in the barracks, so as to have the odds all in our favor in the event of an attack against our front. They simply refuse to make the slightest use of their imagination and daring, if any. But even worse than that, there is a manifest unwillingness to obey and properly to execute orders coming from the Government with respect to shipment of volunteers and of matériel to Norway. They are actually permitting themselves to hold back and to cheat on these shipments. The Premier should be told about this."

I requested an interview with Paul Reynaud. When I arrived, I found Hélène de Portes sitting at Paul Reynaud's desk. She was presiding over an assorted gathering of generals, high officers, members of the Parliament, and officials. She was talking in a peremptory tone of voice, giving advice and orders right and left. Every once in a while she would open the door and step into the next room. One could hear her say: "How are you, Paul? Now just relax and take it easy. Don't worry about a thing. We're working."

When she went into Reynaud's room again, the hitherto obsequious "yes-men" showed their true colors.

"Who does this woman think she is?"

Someone mentioned that the antagonism between Daladier and Paul Reynaud had become even more acute as the result of a recent week-end they had spent together, when Hélène de Portes and the Marquise de Crussol had nearly come to blows.

All this talk immediately subsided when Hélène de Portes again took her seat behind the impressive desk.

This was still at the time when the Norwegian campaign was proving successful for the British. A wave of optimism was in the air. But the atmosphere rapidly changed again toward the end of April when the Allied Expeditionary Corps met with its first reverses in Norway.

César Campinchi, who had retained the post of Minister of the Navy, said to me:

"I haven't forgotten the way the report of your special correspondent, Gaston Bénac, was ignored. He was absolutely right. And when you forwarded his report to us, there was still plenty of time for us to prevent the German coup at Narvik from succeeding. But what's the use! You would be amazed if you knew how badly informed the Ministers of the National Defense are, and even the Premier himself. Our military leaders aren't much better off. . . . For example, neither Paul Reynaud nor I know exactly what's going on in Norway. The Admiral of the Fleet, Darlan, is in a towering rage at his General Headquarters at La Malmaison. The English aren't telling him more than a fraction of what they are doing. Perhaps they don't know what's going on themselves."

The inter-office phone between the Ministries rang.

Campinchi picked up the receiver: "Hello . . . Oh! No, I haven't heard anything new. . . . Certainly. I'll call the Admiralty, and I'll call you back just as soon as I can."

I smiled.

"The Countess Hélène de Portes insists on being kept completely informed. She is very active these days. And it seems to me that with regard to Italy, for example, we are conducting ourselves like little boys. Through her intermediary, Paul Baudouin, the Countess is so thoroughly duplicating the efforts of Anatole de Monzie that Mussolini must be getting the impression that each member of our Ministry is going his own sweet way and is willing to outbid the other members for assurances of Italy's neutrality. The Duce must be convinced by now that we're afraid of him. He's taking advantage of this situation to blackmail us—to the greater advantage of his friend Hitler."

Campinchi, a Corsican by birth, and deeply devoted to the cause of democracy, had always disliked the Italians and now hated the Fascists.

Many months ago Anatole de Monzie, Minister of Public Works, in the Cabinets of both Daladier and Reynaud, had been unofficially given the task of improving our relations with Italy.

Anatole de Monzie was the friend of writers, painters

and adventurers. He was a true intellectual. When he was not serving as a Cabinet Minister (but he had been Minister no fewer than twenty times), he lived as a country gentleman on his estate in the South of France. He spent his time editing a new encyclopedia, perusing the classics and attending his private legal practice.

At the Ministry of Public Works, where he had surrounded himself with experienced technicians, he faithfully and industriously did his duty. However, he also managed to transform his office into a sort of rendezvous for literary lights, for clever women, for actors and actresses, and for the most striking, the most bizarre personalities of the day. He had, in turn, flirted wtih Soviet Russia, the Little Entente, Poland, and Hungary. Then suddenly he found himself overwhelmed with a great love for Italy. He had then become obsessed with the idea that he was the man who was going to prevent a war between France and Italy. When, immediately after the outbreak of the war, a number of our younger military leaders recommended an attack on Italy as the only possible way for taking the offensive against Germany, Anatole de Monzie most vigorously opposed this suggestion. He had testified that he not only believed that Italy could be kept neutral, but that he even foresaw the possibility of bringing her into an economic and military entente with the Allies. He had tirelessly labored and struggled toward this end, and had succeeded in having orders placed with Italian industrialists and also in having them supplied with raw materials. His moment of triumph had come early in 1940, when the Fascists delivered Caproni bombers to the Allies.

Anatole de Monzie was constantly sending observers to Italy who were to keep him informed as to the state of mind of the various classes of the population. Never for a moment was Anatole de Monzie's patriotism open to doubt. But he was so violently opposed to war and so firmly in favor of settlement of all differences by negotiation and compromise that he always found himself on the side of the defeatists.

One day I found Anatole de Monzie in a state of terrific anger.

"Really, Lazareff," he said, "your friend Reynaud is a fool."

"I should say that was about the last thing anyone could accuse him of—lack of intelligence."

"Intelligence? But what good is all this intelligence when it is directed solely toward formulating striking slogans and along channels which lead nowhere? For now, if ever, is the time to reject the old proverb: 'All roads lead to Rome.' "

Then, brandishing his pipe as though it were a tomahawk, he exploded: "We were on bad terms. For months and months. On the worst of terms. We didn't even speak to each other any more. And then he kept me on in the Cabinet. Hélène de Portes' advice, of course. She, at least, knows that it would be folly to make one more enemy. Italy . . . Then he, himself, told me that he agreed with me and he had been counting on me to carry on negotiations with Mussolini discreetly. And here he is now thwarting all my plans. Here he is, allowing Baudouin to send envoys to Rome without letting me know. And that isn't all. I understand that Pierre Laval, on the one hand, and the Comte de Paris, the Pretender to the throne of France, on the other, are indirectly acting as intermediaries between our Government and Italy. A fine state of affairs!"

Anatole de Monzie went on: "And it wouldn't be so bad if he did all that because he sincerely wanted to arrive at an understanding with Rome. But he doesn't. Confusion—that's what he wants. And I know that Laval has lost all of his former influence, and that Benito will be furious when he hears of the intrigues the Comte de Paris is carrying on with the Royal Family. At the same time Reynaud is giving a free hand to the Secretary-General of Foreign Affairs, Alexis Léger, who is very nearly as insincere and deceitful as Reynaud, himself—which is saying a great deal—and who is a born Anglophobe."

In his rage, he assailed every one of Reynaud's ideas and policies.

"He would be willing to start another war if it gave him the opportunity for coming out with one of those pet slogans of his."

Anatole de Monzie had never managed to get on well with Edouard Daladier either, during the latter's term as Premier. But now that Daladier was the leader of the Opposition within the Cabinet, de Monzie had had no difficulty in making up with him. He now frequently went to see Daladier at the Ministry of War.

"Poor Dala!" de Monzie exclaimed. "He's very tired. I found him in very bad shape, physically and mentally." He seemed to feel genuinely sorry for Daladier.

"Hitler may launch his offensive tomorrow," I said, "while the members of our own Government are engaged in constant bickering and pulling at cross-purposes. Don't you think this is likely to prove disastrous for France?"

"Disaster! That's the word. This Ministry is headed straight for catastrophe. There's only one man who can save us. Thanks to his prestige—and despite our folly—this man, and this man alone, can make the people of France do what is necessary at this time. That man, of course, is Pétain."

I looked at him in amazement.

"Yes, yes, Marshal Pétain," he insisted. "He honored me with a visit when he was last in Paris. He's still very vigorous and his ideas struck me as being extraordinarily sound. If it should ever be necessary to conclude a peace without victory, the hero of Verdun would be the only one who could make the people of France accept such a solution. He's well aware of it, too, and he's waiting to be called upon. He said to me: 'You'll see, they'll need me toward the middle of May.' "

I was never to forget this startling revelation.

And two days later, Hélène de Portes also brought up the name of Marshal Pétain.

"If Paul reorganizes his Cabinet," she said, "I believe that he will take the Presidency of the Council of Ministers without portfolio, and that he will give the Ministry of War to Pétain."

"But Pétain is our Number One defeatist!" someone exclaimed.

Hélène de Portes reddened with anger. "After all," she said, "one can't very well call Marshal Pétain a defeatist. And if the defeatists want to make use of him against Paul—well, that's just another reason for Paul to take on the Marshal as a trump-card of his own. In any case, there's one man whom Paul must get rid of without any more delay. I mean Alexis Léger, who is a prop for the Russians and an accomplice of Daladier and Gamelin. As Secretary-General of Foreign Affairs, he has direct control over our entire diplomacy. He actually claims to believe that the Nazis and Bolsheviks will end up by coming to blows." She emitted an ironical little laugh. "On the other hand," she said, "he fondly hopes for a break with Italy, and he keeps on saying that Italy as a neutral represents a greater danger to us than if she were frankly allied with Hitler in this war. And the terrible part about it is that he has so much influence over Daladier and Gamelin. Therefore, since Paul cannot get rid of Gamelin for the moment—because Daladier would then show his solidarity by resigning, and that would mean the fall of the entire Cabinet—there's nothing left for Paul to do but to get rid of Alexis Léger, to begin with. But I'm afraid he doesn't dare do that. That's why I'm asking all my friends, who are also Paul's friends, to plead with him to dismiss this man."

Somebody said, "Alexis Léger represents a definite policy, and I must remind you that it was to assure the enforcement of this very policy that Paul Reynaud has been entrusted with his high office. What you have just said is most alarming. The dismissal of Alexis Léger would indicate—not to the public, but to the insiders, to the foreign Chancelleries, to Germany—that Paul Reynaud, now that he is in power, is anxious to pursue the same policy of appeasement which he opposed when practiced by his predecessors."

"No, no. Not at all," Hélène de Portes replied hastily. "The dismissal of Alexis Léger will mean nothing more or less than that we are getting rid of a man who made such flagrantly inadequate preparations for the diplomatic war. Just as the departure of Gamelin will simply mean that we are ousting a man who is incapable of understanding modern strategy. That's all."

There were loud protests. In the eyes of many, Gamelin had not yet lost any of his prestige.

What was Hélène de Portes' real motivation? Why did she so implacably hate this Alexis Léger? Formerly, years ago, when the Countess was nothing more than the provincial little Hélène Rebuffel, trying to get along in the world, she had benefited by the sympathetic advice and help of the Secretary-General of Foreign Affairs. That was surely what she held against him now, for she notoriously resented everyone who had known her in her obscure days.

Despite Hélène de Portes' assiduous care, Paul Reynaud was not making a quick recovery from his recent illness. However, he had decided to convoke the Parliament in order to make a report on the conduct of the Government.

On the evening of May 9th, the celebrated American journalist, Dorothy Thompson, who had been in Paris the past few days, dined at my house. My guests included the Minister of the Navy, César Campinchi, and the distinguished writers, Colette, Henri Bernstein and the brothers Georges and Joseph Kessel. Dorothy Thompson was, as always, full of enthusiasm and radiant vitality. She entertained us with an account—enlivened by vivid impersonations—of her most recent interview with the man whom she liked to call her "intimate enemy," President Roosevelt. She also spoke of Wendell Willkie, whom no one in France had ever heard of. She told us that she was very much afraid that Hitler would launch a sudden offensive, and that Italy would then promptly enter the war against the Allies. Miss Thompson planned to leave for the front as soon as she could, together with our war correspondent, Joseph Kessel. For, as she said, she had a hunch that something very interesting was going to happen there shortly.

Smiling, César Campinchi replied: "Chère Madame, there's nothing to indicate that you might be right. Quite the contrary. A modern offensive demands a long and painstaking preparation which could not possibly have escaped the attention of our reconnaissance planes and of our Intelligence Service. According to the last reports, we haven't been able to observe anything which might be interpreted in such a manner anywhere along the front."

Dorothy Thompson left us at midnight for her radio broadcast to the United States. Campinchi stayed and chatted with us until 3 in the morning.

At 4 A.M., the sirens commenced howling an alarm.

Two hours later Georges Kessel called me on the telephone: "I have just heard a broadcast from New York. The Germans have broken into Holland. This time it looks like the real thing."

Chapter Twenty-nine

The Road to Defeat

(From my notebook)

MAY 14. *Pessimism and Optimism*

Our military expert who signed his articles XXX exclaimed cheerfully: "Well, gentlemen, the Germans have entered Belgium. Hitler has made his fatal blunder."

"Three more fatal blunders like that and he'll be in Paris." It was the celebrated playwright, Henri Bernstein, speaking.

Bernstein from the very beginning of the crisis kept warning us that we were ill-prepared to meet the onslaught. After four days, the Blitzkrieg had shown itself to be far more formidable than even our worst defeatists had ever dared to imagine. Holland, stabbed in the back by a powerfully organized Fifth Column, has been bombed and burned into submission. Belgium, the victim of her misguided King, is putting up gallant but hopeless resistance. Luxembourg has been entirely overrun by the Nazis.

Belgium

On the morning of the attack, Gamelin announced that "the moment he had anticipated since last October had arrived." It was said that he opposed sending a Franco-British Expeditionary Corps to Belgium, but Daladier, Minister of War, and the British Government insisted upon it —despite Paul Reynaud's disapproval.

Everybody seems to be very proud of the speed with which our troops were moved at night, and according to a previously elaborated plan, to bring help to our hard-pressed neighbor. Unfortunately, however, this "previously elaborated, secret plan" was in no way a secret, so far as the Germans were concerned. We had done them the favor of giving a little dress-rehearsal last January.

At about this time the French Government once again requested the Belgian Government to have its General Staff confer directly with ours for the purpose of determining a plan for our common defense. King Leopold refused. Subsequently we sent him several emissaries, both official and unofficial, including, among others, the writer, Jules Romains and the attorney, Henri Torres. Neither of them even succeeded in obtaining an audience with the King.

As explained to us by the Belgian Ambassador to France, Pol Le Tellier, King Leopold had become more and more convinced that the strictest adherence to neutrality was the only way to preserve his country from the horrors of another war, and that involvement in war would mean the end of Belgium. The Ambassador added that the King's idealistic nature moved him to champion the theory of peace at any price.

What Monsieur le Thellier failed to mention was the fact that the young sovereign had fallen more and more under the influence of Henri de Man. This gentleman, the head of the Socialist Party, was a theorist who had been brought up on Germanic principles and who had indeed taught for many years in Germany. He was the originator of *planism* and an intimate friend of Otto Abetz. He claimed to believe only in negotiations and compromises, but now, of course, it was necessary to bow meekly before Germany's might.

Ever since the death of Queen Astrid the Germans had been sending envoys and agents of both sexes to the youthful King and to the Queen Mother (born a Bavarian Princess and sister of William II). But in vain. The King was determined to preserve an attitude of complete independence toward his two big neighbors. He had, in turn, mobilized along the French and German frontiers.

Leopold frequently traveled incognito to Paris, Venice, Salzburg, London and Rome. Although appearing to be a timid man, the King of the Belgians was in truth opinionated, resolute and possessed with a great desire for playing an active role. He had become the leader of a coalition of the remaining monarchs of the Continent, who were anxious to spare their peoples the sufferings of war (and also afraid of losing their thrones), and who were therefore attempting to organize an international movement designed to appease the Nazi ogre by every possible means. The Duke of Windsor and the Prince of Piedmont lent support to Leopold III, as did Queen Wilhelmina of Holland, King Christian of Denmark, the old King Gustav V of Sweden and King Carol of Rumania.

But the French Government knew—and the Germans were surely every bit as well informed—that, despite Leopold's avowed solidarity with the other monarchs, he had, in March, calmly envisaged the expediency of standing idly by and not lifting a finger to help Holland in the event of a Nazi attack—provided, of course, Hitler promised to spare Belgium.

May 15. *The Rout*

Joseph Kessel has returned from the front. He staggered into my office and fell into a chair.

"It's terrible. The Germans are here."

"Here? What do you mean? Where?"

"Not far from Paris. I don't know how I got through. For kilometers on end I didn't see a single French soldier who had kept his arms, who wasn't fleeing in wild panic from the attacks of the dive-bombers, from the waves of tanks. They were terrified, above all, because they felt lost, abandoned, without orders, without leaders. I saw them looking up into the sky for a sign of Allied planes, and along the roads for the tanks, for the reinforcements that never came."

I couldn't believe him. "What's that you're saying?"

"I'm telling you the truth. General Corap's Army, which was to hold the front before Sedan, has been routed. I did see some officers rallying their men, forming islands of resistance. But these men were acting on their own initiative. I'm afraid it's too late. It looks as though all staff work had broken down, as though there were no longer any such thing as a General Command."

Panic at General Headquarters

The first objectives of the German infiltration are: to cut telephone lines, to seize regimental and divisional headquarters, to destroy field radio stations.

The Staffs of General Gamelin and General Georges are in a state of utter bewilderment. These officers, highly trained specialists, were absolutely convinced that the lessons learned in their many years of study at the War College could not possibly be wrong; that the German attack must inevitably come according to the Schlieffen Plan. This Plan, which had been first conceived in 1905, and which had been employed by von Moltke in 1914, called for deploying the entire German Army in a long line against the French Armies and the British Expeditionary Corps. The German Army was to sweep around the strongly fortified French positions at Verdun and Belfort by going through Belgium; and the principal offensive effort was to be made on the northern wing, with the object of effecting a deep penetration and of achieving a decisive result by ultimately enveloping the Allied left wing.

Thus, the great mass of the Allied strength had been concentrated on its left wing, anchored on the Channel. Unfortunately, however, the Germans had not acted according to plan. They had made their thrust between Namur and the northern edges of the Argonne, in the direction of the upper Somme.

The Myth of the Albert Canal

Among the pet theories stubbornly entertained at General Headquarters, the following two were most fondly clung to: 1) that it was impossible to cross the Ardennes without the greatest difficulty; 2) that it would take at least several days to succeed in crossing the Albert Canal, the first line of the Belgian defense. But what has happened? The Ardennes have been crossed without any difficulty at all. And passage across the Albert Canal has been accomplished with the greatest of ease; in fact, practically without meeting any resistance.

Some time ago *Paris-Soir* had revealed that the Albert Canal had been constructed by a German corporation with offices at Essen. The Belgian firm of Monnoyer had farmed out the concession for this job to the German corporation for the tidy sum of 400 million francs. The German engineers had thus been in a position to give the German General Staff a more detailed blue-print of the Belgian section of the Maginot Line than the blue-prints in the possession of the Belgian General Staff itself.

May 16—8 P.M. *Panic*

Where are the Germans? The reports are conflicting. Ministerial and Parliamentary circles are in the grip of an unspeakable panic. The Ministry of Information, whose duty it is to maintain the country's morale, is manifesting the most appalling anxiety and bewilderment.

Throughout the Ministry, everyone is busily packing. Papers and documents are hastily being wrapped into bundles. That's the only work being done there. L. O. Frossard, the Minister, was in a state of semi-collapse at his desk.

"It's terrible to be Minister of Information," he said in a pitiful tone, "and to have nothing but hopeless news to give out."

This morning at 11, Paul Reynaud ordered the evacuation of the files in the Archives of the Chamber and of the Senate. At the same time he prepared a proclamation advising the population of Paris to leave the city. Toward noon the respective Ministers assembled in the Premier's office. Meanwhile, in the courtyard of the Quai d'Orsay, before the eyes of the dumfounded citizenry, guards were setting fire to heaping piles of thousands of documents taken from the cellars and the strong-boxes of the Ministry of Foreign Affairs.

The public is completely ignorant of the fact that the German advance has suddenly assumed such gigantic proportions.

However, various Ministers were still opposing the evacuation of Paris. Daladier declared that even if the Government left, he would stay. A similar statement was made by Anatole de Monzie; and by the President of the Senate, Jeanneney. Anatole de Monzie added that not one train was available for the population, and that less than fifty trucks were at his disposal to evacuate the Archives.

On the other hand, General Hering, the *Gouverneur Militaire* of Paris, was most emphatically in favor of evacuating the city.

No decision had been arrived at when Reynaud called an end to the Cabinet meeting. As the Ministers left the Quai d'Orsay, they saw bonfires burning all over the lawns. Countless documents were going up in flames.

Jean Prouvost went to see Paul Reynaud late this morning. Hélène de Portes had suggested this visit. The Countess, incidentally, is also opposed to the evacuation of the city.

When Jean Prouvost arrived at the Quai d'Orsay, he encountered a delegation composed of former Presidents of the Council of Ministries and of Leftist Members of the Parliament, led by J. Paul-Boncour. They had come to request the immediate release of the anti-Nazi German refugees whom Mandel had had arrested and interned in concentration camps, fearing that some of them might, after all, be Fifth Columnists. Paul Reynaud received the delegation ungraciously and replied that he had far more important things to attend to. It was then that these prominent members of the Parliament first learned that the German armored columns were approaching Paris at a terrifying rate of speed.

The Chamber of Deputies met in the afternoon. In the corridors, many of the Members were asking whether it was true that an order had been signed by the Premier and the *Gouverneur Militaire* instructing the President of the

Chamber, Edouard Herriot, to evacuate the Parliament. And at the very moment Herriot was showing this order to a group of incredulous Deputies, Paul Reynaud, from the rostrum, was declaring with gestures that "he had never even thought of ordering the evacuation of Paris." He solemnly repeated this statement in the course of a radio broadcast that evening. The broadcast was intended to reassure the public, but had precisely the opposite effect. Now the public had good reason to suspect that things must be going very badly indeed.

Most of the Parisian newspapers have begun to move at least a part of their personnel and equipment either to Brittany, to the South or to the *Massif Central.*

May 17. *Pétain Named Vice-President of the Council of Ministers*

Hélène de Portes' predictions have come true. Pétain is Vice-Premier. Daladier is no longer Minister of War. Alexis Léger is no longer Secretary-General of Foreign Affairs. And Gamelin is no longer Commander-in-Chief.

Marshal Pétain had been in Paris some time, apparently in no hurry at all to resume his post as Ambassador to Madrid. Now he promptly accepted Paul Reynaud's proposal—which he had, no doubt, been expecting—despite the fact that Daladier earnestly requested him not to enter the Cabinet at this time, on the grounds that the Marshal's presence was far more urgently needed in Spain under the circumstances.

Reynaud has persuaded Daladier—whom he doesn't quite dare kick out yet—to take over the Ministry of Foreign Affairs. Obviously, Reynaud is merely drifting along, resorting to half-measures. But he has appointed Mandel to the Ministry of the Interior; and of all the Premier's decisions, this one—and the announcement of the dismissal of General Gamelin—made the best impression on public opinion.

On the other hand, the ouster of Alexis Léger has certainly not been well received. The very circumstances of the dismissal of the Secretary-General of Foreign Affairs are particularly alarming because they reveal a new Paul

Reynaud. One cannot help wondering what this man might be planning to do.

Comedy Relief

The time: the night of May 16-17. The place: the office of the *Chef de Cabinet* Lecca, adjoining the Premier's private office, on the ground floor of the Quai d'Orsay.

Together with Marshal Pétain and Edouard Daladier, Paul Reynaud has spent the day at the General Headquarters of General Georges.

Hélène de Portes, smoking cigarette after cigarette, is sitting picturesquely on Lecca's table-desk. She is having all news flashes brought to her as they come in.

At 7:30 P.M. Paul Reynaud enters. He is discouraged, frightened by what his military leaders have told him and by what he himself has heard and seen at the Headquarters of General Georges: rampant defeatism and evidence of the General Staff's utter dissolution. It was in the automobile, on the way back to Paris, that Reynaud persuaded Daladier to accept the Ministry of Foreign Affairs. Reynaud will thus be able to devote himself exclusively to the conduct of the war, together with Marshal Pétain.

On his arrival at the Quai d'Orsay, Paul Reynaud closets himself in his office with Hélène de Portes, Lecca and Devau.

Then Reynaud and Hélène de Portes are left alone in the office. All that is known is that the Countess was trying to persuade him to adopt the defeatist policy of submission.

Shortly after 8:30 P.M., Hélène de Portes, highly excited, enters Lecca's office and says to him: "Kindly draw up a decree at once naming Charles Roux, our Ambassador to the Vatican, to replace Alexis Léger as Secretary-General."

Almost at the very same moment, Georges Mandel, who always knows everything that's going on, arrives and asks to be received by Paul Reynaud.

"Be careful," Mandel says to the Premier. "There's a rumor to the effect that you want to get rid of Alexis Léger. You and he are the very embodiment of the spirit of determined resistance. If you dismiss him now, your move will be interpreted as the first step toward the policies you have hitherto combated."

Immediately after Mandel's exit, Hélène de Portes reenters the scene, triumphantly brandishing the decree.

"Sign this," she says imperiously. "Two days ago, when you telephoned Charles Roux at the Vatican, he told you he was perfectly willing."

But Reynaud, remembering Mandel's warning, hesitates.

Hélène de Portes gets impatient, angry. She says, "Even at a time like this, you're constantly reconsidering your decisions. And look at the way you used to criticize Daladier."

Thereupon, the Countess walks out on Reynaud. She doesn't trouble to close the door as she stalks into Lecca's office and takes her seat again on top of the broad desk.

Paul Reynaud says, "I'll think it over."

Hélène de Portes says stubbornly, "It's really shameful to be so lacking in will-power."

She raises her voice as she goes on to make her point: "It's imperative for you to have control over everything. In view of what's happening, no one must be able to oppose your decisions."

The lady obviously knows what she's doing. She knows that Paul Reynaud is very tired. Giving up the struggle, Paul Reynaud finally signs the decree at 11:45 P.M.

The document is rushed by automobile to Albert Lebrun. The decree must be countersigned while Paul Reynaud is still Minister of Foreign Affairs—that is to say, before midnight.

The President of the Republic is asleep and must be awakened at once. Albert Lebrun manages to open one eye, and then asks whether Alexis Léger has been advised and is in agreement with this move. Assured that he has, Albert Lebrun signs the decree and promptly goes back to sleep with a clear conscience.

The following morning Alexis Léger read in the *Journal Officiel* that he is no longer Secretary-General of Foreign Affairs. Monsieur Charles Roux has been appointed to take his place.

At 10:00 A.M., he has himself announced at Paul Reynaud's office. The Premier disguises his embarrassment by assuming an attitude of cordiality and excellent spirits.

"I was just going to call you to tell you some good news," Paul Reynaud says.

"What good news?" Alexis Léger asks coldly.

"You're going to leave to perform a miracle, which is the only thing in the world that can save us. You're the only man who can possibly perform this miracle. The United States must be induced to take a definite stand before the Battle of Flanders comes to an end. You are the only man who can accomplish this mission."

"No, *Monsieur le Président.*"

"Why?"

"How can you expect a man to perform a miracle when you have just discredited him? Day before yesterday you said in the Chamber that 'some incredible mistakes have been made—mistakes which will be punished.' Everybody understood that you were aiming at the military leaders, and perhaps you really were. But now I find myself to be the first one affected, and everybody will think that I am the first one being punished for those mistakes."

"Come, come, Léger."

"Furthermore, my name means something in England. I'm very well known on the Continent. But in the United States I'm scarcely known at all. You should send a well-known figure, Herriot, for example. Everybody in America remembers the stand he took in favor of paying the War Debts."

"No, I don't want to send a politician. I want to send a diplomat."

Alexis Léger is unable to contain himself any longer. *"Monsieur le Président,"* he says, "if you had really thought for a moment that I might perform a service to my country by going to Washington, you would not have done what you have done. You would have discussed the matter with me. The Chancelleries have already interpreted this morning's decree as a demotion, as a disgrace. The press has drawn the same conclusions. Have you seen

Stéphane Lauzanne's article in *Le Matin*? You, of all people, have sacrificed me to satisfy the whim of the adversaries of our policy. . . ."

Paul Reynaud is ill at ease. He stammers: "I guess I've made a mistake, Léger. I'll summon the press. I'll make up for everything."

"No, Paul Reynaud. Haven't we always been in complete agreement as to the general lines of French foreign policy?"

"Yes, we have."

"Did we ever disagree on any questions of administrative nature?"

"No. Never. I always felt that I could close my eyes and sign any of the documents you had drawn up. Three days ago I wanted to address a public appeal to President Roosevelt. But I didn't. And do you know why? Because someone said to me: "Léger doesn't think you should make such a move now. He feels it would be tactless; that it would embarrass the President.' "

"Well, then," Léger says at last. "What's wrong? What has come between us?"

"What do you mean?"

"I mean, quite simply, that your closest confidants have been consistently trying to turn you against me for some time."

"That's true," Paul Reynaud replied, unhesitatingly. "And do you know how much weight that sort of thing has had with me? None, none at all."

"Well, then . . . ?"

"Well, sincerely, I believed that you were the only man who could possibly save us by performing this miracle in America."

Léger throws all restraint to the winds as he raises his voice and says:

"Stop it, Reynaud. Why do you have to go to pieces like this, why do you have to distort and debase yourself in this hour of dreadful danger? You stood for everything that was fine, sincere and courageous. And what has become of you, Reynaud? I'll tell you what you are today. You're a hypocrite, a liar, and you're yellow. Reynaud, you're a coward."

Alexis Léger turns on his heel and leaves the room.

May 20. *Gamelin*

General Maurin dropped in at *Paris-Soir* this morning.

Everybody rushed up to him. "Is it true?" they asked. "Is it true that Gamelin has committed suicide?"

The rumor has been going around to the effect that the ex-Commander-in-Chief killed himself after having "admitted his mistakes" in a letter addressed to the man who has just been named as his successor—General Weygand.

But General Maurin laughed heartily.

"Gamelin? He's home and in the best of health. I just saw him a short while ago. He was attending to the roses in his garden. He told me he was preparing a report in defense of his strategical theories. He's just as cool and calm as ever."

Strange man, this Gamelin. Some months ago—during the Norwegian campaign—my wife wanted to publish a picture story about General Gamelin on the Children's Page of *Paris-Soir*. Naturally, we had to submit the story to the Censors. They held it a long time, and finally returned it to us with corrections and marginal notes *all in General Gamelin's own hand*. The officer who brought me the corrected manuscript stressed this point most particularly. The General had taken pains to mention the precise number of buttons on the jacket of his uniform, the manner in which he wore his stripes and epaulets in 1912, and the dimensions and cut of his mustache as of 1918!

Some interpreted this incident proved a genius for detail, a perfectly balanced, methodical mind, as well as proof of our leader's complete sangfroid in the face of the present situation. Others, however, saw in it evidence of appalling superficiality, and of a small, mean, egocentric character, capable only of concerning itself with petty and trivial matters.

Mandel put it this way: "Gamelin has the makings of

an outstanding Prefect. But what we need right now is a good Captain."

I remember what was said of Gamelin one day back in 1936 at Marshal Pétain's.

"It's difficult to appraise him," said the old General Adelbert de Chambrun. "The only thing we really know about him is that he never won any battles."

"Don't say that," exclaimed a tall Major. "He wins battles every day—on the blackboard."

I leaned toward my dinner partner and whispered: "Who is this man, this officer who has a sense of humor?"

"He's a military writer. The Marshal thinks very highly of him. His name is Charles de Gaulle."

May 27. *Weygand*

I've just received a *pneumatique* from Madame la Générale Weygand.

We were preparing a special issue of our weekly, *Match,* on the new Commander-in-Chief. Madame Weygand had been of great help to us, furnishing us with numerous photographs and anecdotes.

Her letter reads as follows:

Cher Monsieur:

I saw my husband for a few moments yesterday, and told him of your plans. He asked me to beg of you not to publish this special number. He feels that it is preferable not to undertake anything in the tragic days we are now living through, in view of the fact that nothing in the present situation can permit us to hope that France will be able to extricate herself from her present predicament for which she alone is responsible. If we submitted to twenty years of spinelessness, six years of *Front Populaire,* etc., we shall perhaps be able to bear the present disgrace.

I read this letter over and over again. I am suddenly filled with a great apprehension. I know that Madame Weygand, an ardent patriot of Polish origin, is in complete harmony and agreement with her husband. I know that on return from his tour of the front, Weygand went to see his wife before calling on the Premier. Suddenly, and for the first time now, I feel that the situation is hopeless.

Weygand's return from Syria had caused a wave of confidence to sweep over France. This former companion of Foch, this man who had affixed his signature to the Armistice of November 11, 1918, but who was still youthful and aggressive despite his age, had, immediately on his return, thrilled and inspired the Army and the civilian population by his display of unhesitating and vigorous initiative. He had promptly gone to the front by plane, flying over the enemy lines. The pilot who had flown him on this dangerous expedition subsequently told us of how, shortly beyond Arras, the plane had been surrounded by bursts of German anti-aircraft fire.

The pilot had shouted to his passenger, "The shells are bursting all around us!"

"So I see," Weygand had replied calmly. "They have to burst somewhere, don't they?"

We had some trouble in obtaining permission to publish in *Paris-Soir* the story of this trip, in the course of which Weygand conferred with the French, British and Belgian leaders of the Army of the North, now completely cut off from the main body of the French forces. The Minister of Information secretly opposed publication of the story.

The Censorship and Propaganda Departments have been in a state of panic ever since May 16th. During these past few days everything possible should have been done to allay fears caused by the advance of the Germans and by the streams of refugees flowing in from Belgium and our invaded regions. But the Ministry of Information has seen fit to issue only one general order: "Above all, prepare the public for the worst."

May 28. *Weygand Speaks*

This morning, over the radio, the people of France heard Paul Reynaud's peremptory voice announce that they had been betrayed by King Leopold III.

The Council of Ministers met last night at 10 o'clock. Weygand attended the meeting. I have just received a report of the proceedings.

To begin with, the Premier made the incredible statement that he had not received any information concerning the circumstances under which the Belgian Army and its sovereign had surrendered. To all questions, Paul Reynaud regularly replied: "I don't know anything more about it than you do. All I can say is that our General Staff received no advice of the impending capitulation."

Neither Pétain nor Weygand said a word. This seemed to confirm Reynaud's statement.

Then Italy was discussed. Edouard Daladier stated that he had considered sending the Vatican the outline of a plan according to which the Pope was to serve as mediator between Italy and France and which would offer Mussolini Djibouti, the Tchad, and the joint dominion over Tunisia. Lord Halifax was said to favor direct conversations with Mussolini, but he was quite unwilling to specify the concessions.

Anatole de Monzie declared that he was opposed to Daladier's project and in favor of Halifax's.

Reynaud gave the floor to General Weygand. Weygand presented a completely pessimistic picture of the situation at the front. He said that the counter-offensive in the North, which had been undertaken as the only possible way to extricate the forces encircled in that area, had failed utterly, and that the numerical strength of the enemy made the outlook extremely grave. Weygand added that he had found the Army in such a state of disorganization and the General Staff so abysmally ignorant of the requirements of modern warfare, that he felt it would be futile even to attempt to carry out the plans he had envisaged.

Meanwhile, Paul Reynaud had noticed that the Minister for the Blockade, Georges Bonnet, was taking notes. "Tear up those papers!" Paul Reynaud suddenly cried. "Tear them up."

There was a moment of silence.

Then the voice of the Minister of Finance, Lucien Lamoureux, was heard, muttering: "If that's the way matters stand, I think we'd better ask for an armistice at once."

Then the President of the Republic, Albert Lebrun—referring to a passage in Weygand's statement—said with considerable surprise: "The British have only two divisions on our front, and their fleet has not been concentrated in the Mediterranean—have I heard correctly?"

No one answered him. And the President gave vent to his feelings in a sweeping and fatalistic gesture.

The meeting broke up shortly after midnight.

May 30. *Direct Overtures to Italy*

Anatole de Monzie has won out. Together with the Vice-Premier, Camille Chautemps and Edouard Daladier, he has drawn up a note which will be transmitted directly to the Duce. The project of sending a dispatch to the Vatican has been abandoned.

Paul Reynaud, Pétain and Weygand and the British have agreed on the language of the note.

The Italian Ambassador, Guariglia, has complained that the note does not define sufficiently concrete proposals. However, according to the text, there is a specific promise of "concessions, in conformity with Italy's views, of territories now within the French Empire," as well as the unequivocal declaration "that France will accept measures which will permit Italy *d'assurer sa liberté maritime*" (to enjoy the freedom of the seas). Furthermore, Anatole de Monzie and the Minister of State, Ybarnegaray, have authorized the Ambassador to add, in their name, "that the envisaged territorial concessions were Djibouti, the Tchad, as well as an agreement with regard to Tunisia."

June 1. *The Result of an Automobile Accident*

My friend, the officer on the General Staff, gave me the following résumé of the situation:

"First of all, we are now paying for our short-sightedness. Then, too, we are the victims of a whole series of bad 'breaks.' Among these unfortunate 'breaks,' I include the fact that the Germans captured General Giraud. During the last war, Giraud was captured twice, but he managed to escape both times. This series of misfortunes also includes the death, in an accident, of General Billotte, who was in command of our Armies in Flanders. I've heard what Weygand has had to say at General Headquarters.

The death of Billotte caused him to consider further resistance hopeless, and moved him to adopt an anti-British line."

My friend went on to explain in some detail:

"After Gamelin had, to all practical purposes, ceased functioning as Commander-in-Chief, and before Weygand had succeeded in joining the Army of Flanders—during this interval, the situation of the Allied troops was becoming more critical hourly. General Ironside, head of the British General Staff, felt that, in the absence of an effective Commander-in-Chief of the Allied forces, it was imperative that he, Ironside, take immediate steps. He flew from England to Flanders, and there conferred with Lord Gort, General Billotte and the King of the Belgians. The decision was reached to launch a counter-offensive with the objective of breaking through the German lines and thus joining the main body of the French Army. The British were to attack at dawn on May 26th. They were to be supported by the French and the Belgians. Ironside returned to London. The following day Weygand arrived in Flanders. He, too, had elaborated a plan for breaking through the infernal ring of steel. Meanwhile, however, General Billotte had been killed, not by enemy action, but in a stupid, commonplace automobile accident caused by skidding. As a result of Billotte's death, Weygand was not informed of the plan decided upon by Ironside; nor had Ironside been advised of the imminent arrival of Weygand at the front. And so, when Weygand asked the British to put his plan into operation, he learned to his amazement that the British were already engaged in an attack which had been launched several hours previously in the northeast sector. This move ended in a complete failure. The French had never received the order to take part in this offensive, for Billotte's two Staff officers, who were to have transmitted the necessary orders, had also been killed in this automobile accident. The British finally retreated, after having suffered severe losses. The Weygand plan had become impracticable. The flanks of the Belgian Army were now even more exposed than before. In the general confusion, the only remaining course was to attempt evacuation of the troops."

June 1. *Weygand and the British*

Could the King of the Belgians have avoided surrendering himself?

Again the Staff officer provided an answer: "As early as May 12th, both France and England began making earnest efforts to persuade Leopold III to give up his place at the head of the Belgian Army and, together with the members of his Government, seek refuge in France, there to continue as Sovereign and Chief of State—precisely as his father had done in 1914. But Leopold refused, insisting that he wanted to share the fate of his soldiers and of his people. And because of this he is now being accused of treason. Future historians will be inclined to deal more leniently with him.

"Weygand unjustly blames the British for the loss of the Battle of Flanders. He had placed all his hopes on that maneuver. He had counted on re-establishing the entire situation. He will not forgive the English so soon."

I remembered Madame Weygand's sudden outburst: "I only hope they won't recall my husband now and *rob him of his glory*."

The Staff officer went on:

"Weygand is as straight as they come. But he's high strung; cold and impassive as he may appear to be, he is capable of incredibly violent bursts of temper. He never had any real affection for the English, but he admired them. He particularly liked their code of 'fair play' and their devotion to the old traditions. Furthermore, he always believed that the one great menace to France was Germany, and that, therefore, the alliance with Britain was an absolutely indispensable part of our national defense. And then what happened? First, the British opposed the realization of his fondest dream: the establishment of a real, dynamic Eastern front. I've heard the way he raves and rants against them now. There's something about his impotent fury that reminds you of a sadly betrayed lover."

June 2. *Toward a Compromise?*

The outlook is no better. During the most recent interview between Paul Reynaud and Winston Churchill in London, the French Premier envisaged the possibility of being obliged to ask for an armistice—for France, at any rate.

Here's the head of our Government—a man whose name had become the very symbol of fearless resistance to the enemy—now pursuing a course of compromise.

Paul Reynaud went to see Daladier the other day, and said to him: "We can't afford to snarl at each other any longer. We must agree either to make terms with the enemy or to call upon our last ounce of strength and defend our country to the bitter end."

Daladier rose. He clenched his fist—his favorite, "strong-man" gesture—and crashed it heavily onto the table, producing a display of resoluteness and iron determination. Then, Daladier bellowed: "Well, in that case, let us make terms with the enemy."

June 2. *Paul Reynaud and the United States*

Everybody has been advising Reynaud against his idea of telephoning President Roosevelt with a request for a thousand airplanes. Such a call would be entirely useless because he simply hasn't got the planes. All these appeals to the United States can be interpreted only as an attempt on the part of Reynaud to take out insurance against any drastic decisions he may make in the future. He will then be able to say: "America was unable to help us in time, and we were therefore obliged to give up the struggle."

What a great change has come over this man within the past few months!

Henry R. Luce, the owner and director of *Life, Time* and *Fortune*, and his wife, the playwright Clare Boothe, have given Reynaud a perfectly clear and accurate account of the present state of public opinion in America; they also gave him their opinion as to the help the United States might be willing to contribute in the future.

Paul Reynaud also listened to, and surely understood, what Eve Curie had to say.

She has just returned from her lecture tour in the United States. She didn't sugar-coat the pill, either. No one knows it, but she has donated to the national defense every penny that she earned lecturing in the United States. Furthermore, she is sending the United States *reportages* on the courage and heroism of the French Army—articles which we are publishing in *Paris-Soir*.

The defeat is becoming more disastrous day by day.

Paul Reynaud has consulted the best informed experts on the American question—Professor André Siegfried, Robert de Saint-Jean, and, by cable, Raoul de Roussy de Sales, and of course our Ambassador to Washington, René de Saint-Quentin.

These men have told him the unvarnished truth about the situation. Why doesn't he listen to them?

The American newspapermen in France are amazed and actually angry at Paul Reynaud's absurd conduct in the face of the state of public opinion in the United States.

Correspondents like Phillip, Elliott, Janet Flanner, Vincent Sheean, Waverly Root, Edmund Taylor, Edgar Ansel Mowrer and H. R. Knickerbocker have given the American public a vivid and honest picture of the way the people of France were feeling and reacting. Similarly, Raoul de Roussy de Sales (Jacques Fransalès) has been endeavoring to interpret America to the French public. The American journalists are being compelled to view this war through the distorting lenses imposed by our General Staff, our Ministry of Information and our Censorship. And as for Raoul de Roussy de Sales' communications, we are barely permitted to publish one-tenth of the material he sends in to us.

I tried to discuss this point with Paul Reynaud. He evaded the question. He is deliberately giving the people of France false hopes by letting them believe in the possibility of prompt and effective help from America, help *for the days to come*! He stubbornly refuses to allow the people to be informed of the gravity of the situation.

June 3. *Paris Bombed*

I've just been to see the *quartiers* of Paris that were bombed today, the first time since the beginning of the war that the capital has been hit.

The United States Ambassador barely missed being hit by a fragment from an aerial bomb.

Wherever they struck—at the Citroën plant (where only the offices were burned), in sections of Passy and Auteuil (where a number of apartment houses were totally, and some partly, destroyed), and in the suburbs to the west and northwest (where the casualties were far more numerous than in the city proper)—the bombs made people clench their fists and say: "The swine! Berlin must be bombed! Berlin! Tomorrow!"

June 5. *First Steps against the Fifth Column*

At last! Some pro-Nazi Frenchmen have been arrested today: Charles Lecca, Director of the publication, *Je Suis Partout,* and his collaborator, Alain Laubreaux; the notorious Adrien Thierry de Ludre, chief of the Führer's "Social Brigade," and his two henchmen, Baron Robert de Fabre-Luce and Count Serpeitle de Gobineau, habitués of the *salons* of the Wilhelmstrasse and of the Congress of Nuremberg.

At the same time, Charles Julien Masson, industrialist and Reserve Captain of the Army of the Air, was condemned to death, together with two of his accomplices. Masson confessed to having supplied the Nazis with information which enabled them to bomb a number of our airdromes with great precision.

The order to arrest our most arrogant pro-Nazis was Georges Mandel's first display of power as Minister of the Interior.

Mandel

Monsieur Mandel is one of the strangest figures in French political life. He's short, rather stout, clean-shaven, with a cold, penetrating look in his gray eyes. His real name is Rothschild, but he is not in any way related to the famous bankers. He comes from a well-to-do, middle-class Jewish family in Paris. He entered politics by a side door. Well recommended, he managed to get a job on *L'Aurore,* the newspaper directed by Clemenceau. This was in 1905. One day he was asked to do a short article. Monsieur Clemenceau didn't think much of it. He summoned the young man to his office and said: "A sentence consists of a subject, a verb and an object. If you should ever care to venture beyond that, you'd better consult me first."

That was Mandel's first contact with the man who was to shape his entire career. The young journalist knew how to make himself very useful to the statesman. He was soon appointed assistant *Chef du Cabinet.* He was well on the road to a political career. He was never to leave Clemenceau's side. He became his confidant, his disciple. Mandel made himself indispensable to Clemenceau. He knew everything, he remembered everything.

By the time the first World War broke out, Georges Mandel had twice run for Deputy and had been defeated both times. He was declared unfit for military service because of his weak constitution.

When Clemenceau was called upon to form a Cabinet, Mandel—well prepared for this contingency—produced a paper on which he had drawn up the complete roster of a tentative Cabinet. Clemenceau then appointed Mandel *directeur de cabinet* (approximately: Secretary-General to the Premier). As head of the Government, Clemenceau devoted himself exclusively to the war effort, and left everything else entirely in Mandel's hands. "See Mandel about this," he would say. "See Mandel."

While the war lasted, Mandel's power was enormous. After the victory, riding the wave of Clemenceau's popularity, Georges Mandel, the Tiger's closest collaborator, was finally elected Deputy from the Gironde.

For a while, Monsieur Mandel remained silently in the background. But the very first time he got up to speak, he made the Chamber seethe. He had received such a bad reception that some of the Deputies were convinced that their new colleague would never again dare to speak in the Chamber. But they didn't know him. He was every bit as sarcastic and even more aggressive than he had been the first time.

A Socialist Deputy, who had been singled out for attack, slapped Mandel's face. When order in the Chamber was restored, Mandel calmly proceeded with his speech, in the course of which he referred with utter contempt to the incident. His third speech was given a respectful hearing.

Later, Mandel became Postmaster General in a Cabinet headed by Flandin. He proved himself to be very strict with his personnel. Mandel kept reminding the satisfied customers of what he was doing by publishing a daily communiqué detailing the names of the postal employees who had been reprimanded or punished as the result of complaints registered by the public. He became very popular—but not among his subordinates. They staged a violent demonstration against him the day he left the Ministry.

Thereafter, Mandel was almost always in the Government. As Minister for the Colonies, he did a great deal toward making the French people conscious of their Empire.

Nothing much was ever known about his private life, except that he lived in a sumptuous suite at the Ritz, that he couldn't work in a room unless it was overheated and that he never really seemed to be happy unless he was at his ministerial desk, surrounded by mountains of dossiers, notes and newspapers. Quite late in his career, he was often seen in the company of a very charming and lovely actress of the Comédie Française. In the dark days of misfortune, she was to prove herself his devoted companion; and it was only then that it became known that she had had a daughter by him, and that she herself was bringing up this child.

Mandel always warned against the Nazi menace and declared that war with Germany was inevitable. Although violently against Communism, he was one of the strongest advocates of the military alliance with the U.S.S.R. As he put it, he was eager to enter into an accord "with anyone at all," so long as it was directed against Hitler.

He was called "a war-mongering, pro-Russian Jew," particularly by those same Rightist elements which had previously showered him with praise because of his efforts to restore the Government's authority in domestic affairs, notably with regard to Labor.

He would say: "After suffering disaster on disaster, we'll end up by winning the war."

He was convinced that he would be selected to direct the destinies of France. He never quite trusted Paul Reynaud.

Chapter Thirty

On the Brink of the Abyss

(From my notebook)

JUNE 6. *Jean Prouvost's Mission*

Jean Prouvost returned last night from a secret mission to London. Because he and Lord Beaverbrook were very close friends, Paul Reynaud had sent him to London in order to explore the possibilities of a joint Franco-British request for an armistice and a negotiated peace. Although now one of Winston Churchill's principal collaborators, had not Beaverbrook been, for years, the leader of appeasement and of isolationism in England? That must have been Paul Reynaud's line of reasoning. Jean Prouvost had also been requested to visit Churchill, who, after all, had long been his collaborator in the field of journalism.

But neither Churchill nor Beaverbrook had been in the least inclined to discuss his proposals. They had told Prouvost, in effect: "No armistice, no negotiated peace. The Battle of France is only one battle in the World War. And the war will go on, even if this one battle should be lost: Furthermore, since the outlook for this battle is indeed almost hopeless, we shall not throw any more of our troops into it. We will, on the contrary, husband our resources for the next battle, which will be the Battle of Britain. Our French allies should fight a delaying action as long as possible—so that we may be given time to make our preparations—and the French should then withdraw to strong positions in their Colonies, abandoning their home territory, but only to await the day when the ultimate Allied victory will see the last German driven from the soil of France."

Jean Prouvost was extremely sceptical about England's ability to put up much resistance, England having practically no army and no arms. After his report to Reynaud, Jean Prouvost was appointed Minister of Information.

The Ministry has been transformed. Daladier is out. Paul Reynaud takes over Foreign Affairs, with Paul Baudouin as Under-Secretary of State in this Ministry. General Charles de Gaulle, who just recently covered himself with glory at the front when he led a brilliant counterattack against enemy tanks, has been named Secretary of State in the War Ministry. Two of the most outspoken appeasers in the Cabinet—Anatole de Monzie and Lucien Lamoureux—have given up their portfolios. But so has Albert Sarraut, who was one of the strongest supporters of the policy of an all-out war effort. The Secretary-General of the Ministry of Finance, Yves Bouthillier, moves up and becomes Minister.

June 6. *At the Ministry of Misinformation*

The Nazis have thought up something new. They are publishing a newspaper by the name of *Paris-Soir*—an amusing parody of our paper. Copies have been dropped from planes and shipped in through neutral countries. These give ample evidence that the Nazis do not relish the campaigns we have been conducting. They were particularly enraged when we published a series of articles entitled "What Hitler Told Me," by Hermann Rauschning. The Führer's former collaborator and ex-President of the Danzig Senate revealed, on the basis of direct quotations from conversations between himself and Hitler, the full extent of the Austrian house-painter's diabolical plans for achieving world domination.

Nonetheless, there are some officials at the Ministry of Information who were obviously annoyed at us for having published this material. One of these gentlemen, a Colonel, expressed his views in the following manner: "All that stuff you're writing about Germany and about Hitler! The only people you're really helping are the Reds."

And the Germans are within 80 kilometers of Paris!

I met Paul Winkler at the Ministry of Information. He was considerably surprised, to put it mildly, at this manifestation of the official attitude.

Paul Winkler directs the biggest press agency on the European continent, *Opera-Mundi,* which has handled a great number of important documents on Nazi Germany, including Lajos' book on Germany's industrial strength (this book was *verboten* in the author's own country, Hungary), H. R. Knickerbocker's articles on the corruption in the highest circles of the Third Reich, the articles and books by Otto Strasser, chief of the German Black Front, etc., etc.

One of Paul Winkler's important contributions was the creation of *Presse et Publicité,* a journal in which he conducted a splendid campaign designed to bring about some sadly needed housecleaning in press and advertising circles. The campaign might very well have produced some results, had not publication of this weekly been suspended, due to the war.

Winkler also published *Confidences,* a popular weekly, with a circulation of almost one and one-half million, as well as the leading juvenile publications. Furthermore, he had planned to launch a new magazine, conceived along highly original lines, and to be called *Mon Journal.* But Jean Prouvost brought pressure to bear on Winkler to dissuade him from going ahead with this new enterprise. Winkler had to endure from Prouvost the very indignities that he had suffered at the hands of the consortium of "big" newspapers.

Winkler had been offered the post of Director of *Excelsior,* and there had been some talk of his ultimately succeeding to the same post on *Le Petit Parisien.*

Winkler said to me: "As you know, I'm not especially fond of Jean Prouvost, but I'm delighted that they've named him Minister of Information. He's an extremely competent man, and I'm sure he'll manage to put some life into this outfit. From now on we'll be able to get to work and feel that we're really accomplishing something. In this kind of war, Propaganda and Information are weapons, just as tanks and planes are. Unfortunately, our leaders haven't shown that they had so much faith in tanks and planes, either. But the only thing this so-called Ministry of Information has done is to break morale and inspire defeatism. It's a mighty good thing they've decided to make this change."

Jean Prouvost is absolutely aghast at the number of useless functionaries cluttering up the Ministry.

"The wheels aren't turning," he said. "I'll have to begin by cleaning out the whole place. We'll have to start all over again from scratch. The only thing that worries me, under the circumstances, is whether it isn't too late?"

From the beginning of the war, Jean Prouvost has fluctuated between moods of the highest enthusiasm and the deepest despair. He now seems to have committed himself irrevocably to the all-out defense line.

He said to me today: "Everyone must be made to understand that if the Germans set up their Nazi dictatorship here, the civilization of the entire world will be imperiled and the private life of everyone will be made unbearable. As far as I'm concerned, I'll give up the newspaper business if the Germans win this war. I'll never take orders from them, either directly or indirectly."

Then, after a moment, he went on: "The situation is very grave, far worse than anyone can even imagine. But in the end the Germans must lose."

I told him about the conversation I had had with Paul Winkler—of whom, incidentally, he has a very high opinion—and I mentioned that Winkler had already moved his personnel to the provinces.

Jean Prouvost instantly flared up. "We're not going to do anything like that," he cried. "*Paris-Soir* must continue to be published in Paris—just as long as possible. I'm convinced that if the Germans take Paris it means the war is over."

June 6. *Charles de Gaulle and Military Strategy*

De Gaulle has been named Secretary of State for War! What sweet revenge!

The son of a professor at the *Institut Catholique,* Charles de Gaulle commenced his military career as lieutenant in an infantry regiment under the command of Colonel Henri-Philippe Pétain. He fought in the War of 1914-18, and was wounded three times. He received the last—and most severe—of his wounds before Verdun, where he was picked up by a German patrol. As prisoner of war, he made five attempts to escape, but was caught each time and severely punished.

Then, after the peace treaties had been signed, he served as one of Weygand's principal lieutenants in the Polish campaign against the Bolsheviks. He had, by this time, commenced to make a name for himself as a strategist and a military writer. Both Pétain and Weygand thought very highly of him. He was soon named Professor of Military History at Saint-Cyr and then passed the highest competitive tests at the *Ecole de Guerre.* While Pétain was Commander-in-Chief of the French Armies (1927), Charles de Gaulle served as his aide-de-camp. Subsequently, de Gaulle was attached to the Army of the Rhine and the Army of the Near East. He went to Iraq, Persia, Egypt.

But it was in 1932 that the significant phase of his career really began. After having been appointed *Secrétaire-Général de la Défense Nationale,* he published his first book, *Au Fil de L'Épée* (*At the Edge of the Sword*), eloquently dedicated to Marshal Pétain.

His *Vers L'Armée de Métier* (*Toward a Professional Army*) appeared in 1934, and was completely ignored by the general public. In military circles, however, the book had the effect of a bombshell. It expounded theories which were in diametric opposition to those entertained by the men at the head of the French military establishment. De Gaulle vigorously attacked the concept of a purely defensive war. He predicted German rearmament and insisted that France must provide herself with an army of expert professionals, equipped with great numbers of tanks and supported by a powerful air corps.

The top men in the military hierarchy were living on the best of terms with the politicians, and were resting tranquilly, as Paul Reynaud has put it, "on the soft pillow of the Maginot Line."

And here was this Charles de Gaulle permitting himself to criticize these high-ranking gentlemen for their laziness in accepting such an easy solution! He wanted to give a series of lectures on the subject at the Sorbonne. But the gentlemen in command of the situation decreed otherwise. There were no lectures on the subject.

Paul Reynaud had read *Vers L'Armée de Métier*. He had found the book not only interesting, but entirely convincing. He arranged to meet the young officer, and then decided to call Parliament's attention to the theories which were being systematically suppressed.

On March 31, 1936, Paul Reynaud, in the Chamber of Deputies, presented a proposal for a law, in two articles, based on the concept of Charles de Gaulle.

Article One provided for ". . . a corps to be recruited, in principle, of men contracting to serve for a given term."

According to Article Two ". . . this corps is to consist of ten divisions *de ligne* (roughly, shock troops), one light division, general reserves and auxiliary services."

In defining the reasons for establishing such a corps, it was further specified that ". . . these units were to be constituted essentially of modern tanks and of motorized infantry and artillery."

The proposal was rejected.

During the debate, however, Paul Reynaud was moved to say: "If you are to pursue an interventionist policy in Europe, you must put yourselves into a position to back up this policy. If you are unwilling to do this, you must abandon hopes of being able to intervene effectively."

A Minister rose from the Government bench to deliver a reply to this revolutionary, to inform him—and the Chamber—that the views expressed by Deputy Paul Reynaud did not correspond with those of the General Staff, which was, after all, better qualified than the Deputy to judge military matters. And the Minister went on to add: "How can anyone believe that we're even dreaming of undertaking an offensive, when we are spending billions to establish our line of fortifications?"

The name of this Minister was Pierre Laval.

Events have proved that Charles de Gaulle and Paul Reynaud were enormously right. For one thing, such a professional army would have permitted us to move swiftly —without having to contemplate a cumbersome and costly General Mobilization. It would have enabled us also to prevent Hitler from remilitarizing the Rhineland, for it now seems highly probable that he would not have persisted in that move in the face of so much as a display of determined resistance.

One cannot help recalling the prophetic words pronounced by Paul Reynaud in 1936, when he paraphrased Charles de Gaulle's book in the following language:

"We must create a body of shock troops—a shock army —capable of striking with lightning speed and equipped with devastating fire-power. Modern tanks—land cruisers —can move at the rate of 40 kilometers per hour over favorable terrain. The *corps de manoeuvre specialisé*, creation of which was suggested in my counter-proposal of March 31, 1935, would have 100 per cent greater fire-power than that of the *entire French Army of 1914*.

"There is still some talk, in certain quarters, of the *levée en masse* (levy of all available man-power). This sort of thing was all very well when we had the man-power. At the time of our Revolutionary Wars, the population of France was equal to that of all the German States and of England combined. But in a modern army, as in modern industry, the man must know how to serve his machine. In the next war, the internal-combustion engine will be the outstanding new feature.

"We must not hesitate. We must decide to play the game for all it's worth. The strength of an air corps depends upon the number and quality of its planes. The strength of an army will, in the future, depend, not on its numerical strength in men, but on the number and power of its engines of war. Blind adherence to a strategic plan which keeps our forces tied up within our frontiers makes it impossible for us to fulfill our international engagements. In other words, it must automatically prevent us from doing our share—from helping others—according to the principle of collective security from which we, in turn, count on deriving such great benefits in the dangerous days that lie ahead.

"Our lines to the northeast are very strong, unquestionably. But we cannot permit ourselves to consider them as absolutely impregnable. Let us not forget that, during the last war, Russian, Belgian and French fortresses were taken without having been destroyed. They fell because the morale of their garrisons had cracked under the strain and suffering of siege. *It seems likely that the German Army, preceded by powerful motorized spearheads, will break through Holland and into Belgium. There, we must ardently hope, the Albert Canal, running from Antwerp to Liege, will be sufficiently well fortified and manned to check the attack. If the Germans break through there, their main attack will be in the direction of our 350 kilometer northern frontier.* [Note: The so-called Maginot Line Extension, never to be confused with the Maginot Line proper.]

"Fundamental considerations of National Defense make it imperative, therefore, that we have at our command an army of shock troops—a force which will be able, for one thing, to go to the aid of the Belgian Army, as well as to deal effectively with enemy forces attempting sudden invasion of our territory."

But Charles de Gaulle and Paul Reynaud were speaking to deliberately deaf ears. To have listened to these warnings would have meant new tasks to be undertaken, new responsibilities to be assumed, and that was precisely what French civilian and military leaders wanted to avoid—the military perhaps even more than the civilian.

The name of Charles de Gaulle was far better known in Germany than in his own country. General Guderian, the creator of the Third Reich's mechanized forces, did not hesitate to proclaim his indebtedness to Charles de Gaulle's book. Some time ago Philippe Barrès told me that the first time he had ever heard mention of the name of de Gaulle was at the National Socialist Congress at Nuremberg.

Charles de Gaulle made the mistake of keeping the chiefs of our Army awake when they met at the round table for the periodical conferences of the Supreme War Council—meetings which were held only out of deference for tradition. Since this irritatingly alert young man was so very fond of tanks, the venerable gentlemen got rid of him by shipping him off to Metz, more or less in disgrace. There he was placed in command of a regiment, and subsequently of a brigade, of tanks.

Ever since the beginning of the Blitzkrieg, however, more and more people had begun to realize that it might have been better if they had listened to him more attentively. At any rate, on May 15, 1940, he was put in command of the Fourth Armored Division. He gave a brilliant account of himself, operating in constant liaison with the British First Armored Division and the Fifty-first Division of the British Expeditionary Corps. Although he received a citation in the Order of the Day and was raised to the rank of General on the battlefield by Weygand, Charles de Gaulle was not called upon to take part in the direction of the war effort. Why not? Because he was deliberately excluded by a clique which had been strengthened by the sudden and unexpected support of Hélène de Portes. The presence of such a strong personality might tend to weaken her own influence with the Premier.

But today, at last, Paul Reynaud overrode all this obstruction. He recalled his old friend and adviser, and placed him in a position he should have held long ago.

Paris-Soir is running an article on Charles de Gaulle in order to acquaint the public with this man. Outside of military circles, his name is still almost totally unknown.

General Maurin, twice Minister of War, stormed into my office. He was in a terrible rage.

"It's madness," he shouted, "to give all this publicity to a guttersnipe like de Gaulle. And it's even worse for them to make an Under-Secretary of War out of this—this de Gaulle. Did you ask me why? Well, because a young man who has just been given his first star is going to be in a position to command veterans, old Generals with *five* stars. It's intolerable, I tell you. I've just seen General Colson, chief of the Supreme General Staff. He's already threatening to resign. If one wants to fight a war, the first thing one must do is respect the hierarchy."

June 7. *The Maginot Line*

Everybody is now asking: "Why didn't the Maginot Line extend all the way to the coast?"

Strangely enough, practically no one knew about this gap. The most fantastic explanations have now been advanced.

To get at the truth of the matter, I've had some research done. Here's what I've discovered:

Following Belgium's Declaration of Neutrality in October, 1936, preparations were made to extend the Maginot Line all the way to the coast of the North Sea. It is now being claimed that the Belgians opposed this undertaking, and that they even went so far as to say that they would consider such a move to be an "unfriendly gesture." This is utterly false. On the contrary, the Belgian Ambassador to Paris, Baron Gueffier d'Hestroy, stated, in 1933, and the President of the Council, van Zeeland, among others, subsequently declared that they would look upon this project as *an additional guarantee of Belgium's security.*

Moreover, this vital section of the Maginot Line was not constructed for the simple reason that our General Staff decided that "it would be a useless and inefficacious measure," to quote the words of the Supreme War Council's reply in response to an inquiry. (Specifically, the Ministry of War transmitted this answer to the Senate Military Affairs Committee in reply to a written inquiry by the Committee's chairman, Monsieur Daniel Vincent.)

Speaking from the rostrum of the Chamber on March 1, 1937, Edouard Daladier stated that the line of fortifications would be extended as far as Dunkerque, *despite strong opposition from various quarters.* Speaking before the Chamber of Deputies on another occasion (December 22, 1939), Daladier revealed: "High-ranking military authorities had for many years opposed the project of fortifying the region along our northern frontiers, on the grounds that the construction of such defense was unfeasible there because of the nature of the terrain, which gave cause to fear infiltration of water, and also because of the agglomeration of large industrial establishments which practically covered the entire surface of that region." Daladier added, however: "Nevertheless, completion of the fortifications in the Vosges and along the northern frontier had been ordered—fortifications on which work had been proceeding ever since 1933."

The truth of the matter is that, when the war broke out, work had just barely been commenced on this northern extension of the Maginot Line—known as the Daniel Vincent Line—which was to be far more similar to the Siegfried Line than to the Maginot Line proper. For the new section was to consist of light fortifications, built in depth.

During the first eight months of the war, tremendous and concerted efforts were made to strengthen and multiply the defenses of the powerful Maginot Line proper—while work on the pathetically inadequate Daniel Vincent Line was entrusted to non-specialized *soldats travailleurs* (soldiers with pick and shovel). The results, unfortunately, are well known.

June 8. *Aviation*

There's more and more talk of evacuating Paris. The Battle of the Somme is practically over. German tanks are said to be pushing ahead in all directions. But now the French troops are trying to make a stand.

Joseph Kessel and Eve Curie have returned from the front. They are furious, filled with despair—and with admiration. Our air force, they say, is putting up a magnificent fight in the face of overwhelming, hopeless odds.

They ran into Antoine de Saint-Exupéry, the great aviator and distinguished writer, who, by his own request, is serving as a night reconnaissance pilot, and who has refused innumerable offers to take a post behind the front. Saint-Exupéry is the prototype of the French officers belonging to this elite corps. In his instance the tragedy is even greater than that of the others, for with his imagination, with his keen analytical mentality, he must be spending every instant of his dangerous existence in full awareness of the utter futility of his sacrifice.

Who are the guilty ones? Who is responsible for the deplorable state of our aviation? I've spoken to at least twenty technicians, and they all say the same thing:

"They haven't any right to blame the manufacturers and the workers any more. Ever since the beginning of the war, the plants producing motors and bodies have always delivered *more motors and more bodies than the orders called for*. It is true that, formerly, selfishness and jealous intrigues on the part of the manufacturers, on the one hand, and the paralyzing effect of labor troubles in 1937, on the other, did, undoubtedly, delay certain deliveries and above all tend to create pessimism as to the aviation industry's ability to achieve adequate production. The nationalization of the factories in the aviation industry—as conceived and put into practice by Pierre Cot, and which allowed the heads of the factories to receive the profits, while relieving them of all responsibility, and destroying the spirit of initiative and of competition—did, to a certain extent, dampen our technicians' enthusiasm for further research. But these are only incidental causes of the present state of our military aviation."

In 1934, a plan was adopted by Parliament and immediately put into practice, according to which our Army was to receive 1,000 first-line planes and 200 planes in first reserve, but by May-June, 1936, only 637 units had been delivered. In August, 1936, and in accordance with the new plan adopted in view of the first reports on the German rearmament effort, 1,500 first-line and 1,000 reserve planes were to be ordered, with delivery before the end of 1939.

Toward the end of the year 1936, however, Air Minister Pierre Cot demanded an increase in this Plan II. He made his request before the Permanent Committee on National Defense, calling the Committee's attention to the new figures he had received, figures revealing an enormous increase in German aircraft production. Pierre Cot's new plan called for an appreciable increase in our entire anti-aircraft defenses, as well as for an order for 2,600 first line and 1,500 reserve planes. This project was duly studied by the Supreme General Staff of the Army, headed by the Minister of the National Defense, Edouard Daladier, Marshal Pétain, General Gamelin, Air General Vuillemin, and the Admiral of the Fleet, Darlan. The project was unanimously rejected by these high authorities, who went on record with the declaration: ". . . *There was no need for enlarging or modifying the plan for the expansion of our aviation.*"

In 1937, Georges Bonnet, the Minister of Finance, reduced by more than a billion francs the Air Budget planned for 1938. He did so despite vigorous protests by Pierre Cot, who warned the Army and the Cabinet that, if they persistently refused to look the situation in the face now, they would be in for a cruel awakening later.

It was not until the spring of 1938 that the Supreme General Staff finally woke up and decided upon a new program, which, incidentally, was practically identical with the plan proposed by Pierre Cot in 1936.

Pierre Cot was succeeded by Guy la Chambre. And this gentleman's management of the Air Ministry soon evoked —well, let me say, considerable surprise. I have a photostatic copy of an extraordinary letter, dated April 28, 1939 —one month after the German invasion and occupation of all of Czechoslovakia. The letter reads as follows:

AIR MINISTRY

To: *Monsieur l'Administrateur-Délégué des Usincs Gnome-et-Rhone*

Monsieur l'Administrateur-Délégué:

My letter Number 13202 of December 5, 1936, advised you that I had given the Walter Company of Prague an order for 200 Gnome-et-Rhone motors 14 M, and I requested you to supply this company with all data concerning this type of motor as promptly as possible. The Walter Company now informs me, in its letter of April 18th, that you have suspended all deliveries of documents and information since the recent events in March, and asks me to instruct you to resume delivery of these papers which are essential to the manufacture of the motors within the given time.

I have the honor to inform you that the events of last March have not, as yet, caused me to cancel the contract awarded to the Walter Company; and I beg of you, therefore, to satisfy the requests for these necessary documents until further notice.

Veuillez agréer, Monsieur l'Administrateur-Délégué, etc., etc.

Signed: For the Minister and by his Order,
The Technical and Industrial Director.

In other words, the Air Minister was formally ordering our biggest motor manufacturer to send the Germans secret documents concerning the manufacture of the motors used in our military aircraft.

At the outbreak of the war, France had precisely sixteen modern bombers capable of 400 kilometers per hour (Lioré 45) and 400 modern fighter planes incapable of reaching 400 kilometers per hour (Morane 406, Devoitine 510). And there were a few Curtiss P 36's—speed over 400 kilometers per hour.

The Devoitine 52, with a Hispano-Suiza motor, and capable of 550 to 600 kms. per hour—and considered to be an excellent machine—was just beginning to be produced by the plant in Toulouse. The majority of French airplanes have been built by extremely slow and very costly methods. The construction of the Lioré 45, for example, unquestionably our best bombing plane, required no fewer than 45,000 work-hours.

During the past month (May, 1940), we produced at the rate of 1,800 planes per month. We had 350 Lioré 45 and 80 Amyot 340. Potez, the most modern plant in France, turned out 400 Potez 63's (reconnaissance plane) monthly—but this factory, situated at Meaulte in the Somme, had been completely destroyed on May 12th.

The factories producing motors had also made great progress. Gnome-et-Rhone was producing at the rate of 920 motors per month, as compared with 400 last September. Hispano-Suiza had stepped up to a rate of 500 motors per month, as compared with about 200 in September.

Almost all the aircraft factories were exposed to bombing by the Germans, the majority of the plants being located in the neighborhood of Paris. The Air Minister had steadfastly refused permission to build aircraft factories in the Colonies, in Indo-China, for example, or in Morocco.

What Guy la Chambre is to be criticized for most of all is that he relied altogether too much on American production—at a time when this production was practically nonexistent. It is now only too clear that he should have taken care of the immediate requirements by stimulating French production by every possible means, including creation of an aircraft industry outside of France but within the French Empire—in addition to which he should have continued, of course, to order as many planes as possible in America.

When the war began, Guy la Chambre had awarded contracts to the amount of 85 million dollars to one American firm—United Aircraft. (This sum equals the entire 1938 budget for French aviation.)

In the Chamber of Deputies, Guy la Chambre was questioned several times as to the state of our aviation. Each time he gave figures and data which seemed reassuring enough. It was later discovered, however, that Guy la Chambre had deliberately given misleading figures. He had, for reasons of his own, included among "available" aircraft all planes that were *on order* at the time, and some of these machines were to be delivered by an American company which was still erecting the plant in which the planes were to be built.

According to the most reliable sources of information, we probably had some 2,000 planes at the beginning of the Blitzkrieg. The Germans had 14,000 to 15,000. But of our 2,000 planes, only a little over 1,000 were combat planes immediately available for service in France proper. Of the German planes, some 8,000 were available for first-line duty.

Armament

"I need heavy artillery," Gamelin said over and over again. "Heavy artillery and still more heavy artillery."

To the bitter end, he could think of nothing but a

strictly defensive war and the protection of the Maginot Line.

Raoul Dautry, a highly intelligent official and a first-class organizer, had given proof of his executive ability in the French State Railways, and had recently, in the Armament Ministry, brought about prodigious results, but too late. His appointment had not come until just before the war. Besides, he had to cope with too many difficulties.

For example: When he wanted to build new factories for the manufacture of tanks, Daladier, having consulted the General Staff, told him: "Not too many tanks. We want heavy artillery and munitions and still more munitions. But as to tanks, *Gamelin isn't very fond of them.*"

And then, when Dautry wanted to devote the facilities of the factories making uniforms to the manufacture of parachutes, he was told by the General Staff: "Parachutes are a Russian invention. They're intended to create a big impression, but they'll never be of any value at all. It's true that Pierre Cot created a corps of French parachute troops, but that was only to please the Russians whom he admires so much. This parachute business makes very good reading, but of what possible use can it be in actual warfare?"

After the Germans had overwhelmed Poland, Dautry wanted to build amphibian tanks. French engineers had perfected plans for such tanks which were far superior to the German product. But the spokesman for the General Staff said to Dautry: "We don't need any tanks *de cinéma.*"

In short, the Armament Minister was obliged to produce, as well and as promptly as possible, only those types of armaments which were ordered by our military leaders. We have a great supply of long-distance cannon and of large-caliber shells. The trouble is that we haven't been able to make use of any of them yet. Shall we ever have a chance to use them?

Chapter Thirty-one

The Collapse

PARIS fell yesterday. Six hundred of us from *Paris-Soir* and the other Jean Prouvost publications are in Clermont-Ferrand. Here Pierre Laval is king. We appeal to him to help us find accommodations.

"What a foul mess!" Pierre Laval mutters. "What a bunch of swine!"

After an hour on the telephone, arrangements are made, more or less, for accommodations for our people.

Pierre Laval asks me to stay in his office. He wants to tell me about the plans he had for avoiding or for at least limiting the extent of this war.

"Throughout this entire conflict, I have never ceased maintaining contact with Mussolini," he says, "and with Franco. They were neutrals, weren't they? What I tried for many years to accomplish was the creation of an effective opposition to Germany's might by the formation of a confederation of the great Mediterranean States. My dream has now been drowned in blood."

He goes on to tell me of his resentment of England. "She has always thwarted my plans for controlling the Mediterranean," he says. And as for America, "The Americans don't know anything about anything."

The news coming in is vague and sketchy. Our truck-drivers have been our best source of information concerning the position of the German armies.

There is a rumor that our troops are holding a line along the Loire, and that the situation is not quite hopeless.

And Pierre Laval tells us, in all seriousness, that he plans to write his memoirs. He does not want to justify his policies, but to show how he could have saved France.

Hervé Mille, editor-in-chief of *Match*, and Hubert Giron, Art Director of *Marie Claire*, and I went to Lyon in search of a press for our magazines. We soon managed to come to terms with plants that were in a position to print our weeklies and succeeded in finding rooms for our editors and personnel. When we returned to Clermont-Ferrand, a man in a mud-covered uniform jumped onto the running-board of our car. It was Joseph Kessel.

"Come right away. I want to speak to you. It's important. Hurry," he said.

A moment later, we were alone in the back room of a café.

"It's all over," Joseph Kessel said.

"What?"

"Listen to me. Don't interrupt. Don't ask any questions. General Headquarters has retired—or fled—to Briare, not far from Saint-Etienne. At least half of the officers of the General Staff are missing. They had either been captured or taken prisoner or lost along the roads. Everywhere our armies were prevented from advancing to the front by the endless streams of refugees which blocked all the roads. The bombings grew worse and worse.

"Paul Reynaud was at the front. Together with the Commander-in-Chief, he tried to find the exact line of our troops. Charles de Gaulle has finally convinced our Ministers and ranking officers that his tank technique should have been applied from the very beginning.

"Meanwhile the Council of Ministers devoted their discussion almost entirely to the Italian question. Paul Reynaud recounted the successive failures of all attempts initiated by his Government to arrive at an understanding with Italy. Finally, on June 9th, Ciano told our Ambassador François-Poncet: 'Even if you offered us all of Tunisia now, that wouldn't be enough. The die is cast. Italy will enter the war.'

"At this time the Germans were advancing toward Paris from all sides. The attack they had launched on June 5th had progressed so rapidly that Paris was already more or less encircled. Weygand, back from the front, and Charles de Gaulle, just returned from London, reported to the War Committee on the situation.

" 'The English,' de Gaulle said, 'declare that they cannot send us their total force of combat planes, as requested by us, because many of these units are imperatively needed for the defense of their island. But they will send us troops if and when these forces can be adequately supported by French artillery.'

"Weygand did not attempt to conceal his grave anxiety. 'Preparations have been made for embarking two French divisions and one British division from Le Havre . . . At the beginning of the battle, the Germans had eighty divisions in reserve, while we had a total of sixty-five divisions, first-line and reserve. I have been obliged to order a general retreat.'

"De Gaulle was of the opinion that the Government should leave for Brittany and should make its headquarters in a district that could be defended with relative ease (known in the military places as the Breton Redoubt). Under the protection of the Army the Cabinet could there continue to function, at least nominally, as the Government and if the situation became untenable the Ministers could embark from the Breton Peninsula, either for Africa or for England.

"Weygand and de Gaulle disagreed bitterly. By 5 P.M. the Government had decided to leave for Tours. All the Ministers were to be ready by 9 o'clock at the latest. At General Headquarters, you could tell that there was very little fighting spirit left, and that the situation was considered as absolutely beyond repair. So I went on to Tours. I wanted to witness the final act of the tragedy . . . The Ministries were running around in circles. Quite a few of the Ministers, caught in the jam along the roads, hadn't even arrived yet. And only bad news came streaming in. Worse than ever.

"On June 11th, at 7:30 P.M., the Ministers convened at the Château de Cangey. I drove there with Weygand.

"Later, I was given the details of this historic meeting of the Cabinet. To begin with, there had been considerable delay. However, at last, everybody had arrived, with the exception of L. O. Frossard. The meeting was called to order and the usual formalities were dispensed with.

"Reynaud immediately gave the floor to Weygand. The Commander-in-Chief painted the picture in very dark colors. 'After Dunkirk,' he said, 'I had in all fifty-five French and two English divisions left with which to face 140 German divisions. But it is not fitting for a General or for a nation to admit defeat, and I therefore decided to wage another battle.' Weygand then went on to describe this battle in minute detail. In conclusion he said: 'And that, Messieurs, is how we lost the second battle, which I had named, in order to stress its importance, the "Battle of France." Of the three divisions that had been driven back to the coast of the English Channel, the two British divisions reembarked and the French division was forced to capitulate. Paris can no longer be defended. Our Army has been cut up into fragments. We shall continue to offer resistance if the Council of Ministers orders me to do so. But I tell you, Messieurs, unequivocally, that we must ask for an armistice. We have lost the war.'

"Now the dreaded words had been spoken by the Generalissimo of the Allied Armies. Weygand broke a long moment of silence: 'The only possible reason for continuing the struggle would be for the honor of our arms and our flag. But as Commander-in-Chief and as a Frenchman, I must also be concerned about the maintenance of order in the country. It is my opinion that everything must be done to avoid the danger of anarchy which so often follows in the wake of military defeat. Messieurs, much as it pains me, as a soldier, to speak in this manner, I repeat: it is imperative that we request an armistice.'

"All eyes turned toward Pétain. He had been constantly

nodding agreement with Weygand's statements, but he refrained from committing himself.

"And Weygand went on again: 'What are the causes of this defeat? Behind the ramparts of the Maginot Line the country went to sleep. Our soldiers fought bravely. But what was lacking was materiel. Today, in the face of thousands of German airplanes, we have some 350 to 400 left. We never did have anything that might properly be called an air force; and those who told you the contrary lied.'

"Then Pétain got up and said: 'We must speedily ask the victors to state their terms, so that hostilities can be stopped before our armies suffer complete defeat. We shall thus be able to throw the weight of our remaining intact forces into the negotiations.'

"At this point Weygand offered to withdraw, on the grounds that he was not properly a member of the Council of Ministers. He was requested to remain.

"Then Campinchi and Yvon Delbos protested against the conclusions arrived at by the Generalissimo. We should not lay down our arms, they said. We should try to hold the lines along the Loire, along the Garonne, in the Breton Redoubt. We should withdraw from France, if necessary, and continue resistance from positions in the Empire. We should employ our Navy, still intact. We should not, under any conditions, consider the war lost just because we had lost the Battle of France. If we did, we should be betraying the sacred covenant binding us with Britain; and we should be delivering that country up to an enemy who has demonstrated his contempt for treaties and solemn agreements, and who has announced his desire to crush and enslave France.

"Georges Monnet, the Socialist, declared himself to be in agreement with Campinchi and Yvon Delbos. But the other Socialist, Février, supported Weygand's and Pétain's views. Raoul Dautry, the Minister for Armaments, came out strongly in favor of continuing the struggle. He added, however, that he realized that it would be difficult to improvise a war industry in North Africa. Although belonging to the same party as Campinchi and Yvon Delbos, the Radicals, Chichery and Queuille, supported the opposite viewpoint, declaring that they considered it wiser to abandon the struggle.

"It was late evening now. The salon had grown quite dark. An usher came in to attend to the lights. He seemed to be holding up the proceedings for an eternity.

"Finally the President of the Republic lost his temper. 'Get out!' he shouted. 'Get out!'

"The Government of France had to continue its deliberations by the dim light from one candelabra in that vast room.

"Then Jean Prouvost got up. 'I prefer an armistice, at which we can discuss terms,' he said, 'to the continuation of a hopeless struggle and to the inevitable capitulation of our Army. As far as I'm concerned, I've made up my mind. I'm never going to be an *émigré*. After your departure, France will very soon get tired of its Government-in-Exile. France will turn to a new and perfectly legal Government at home, which will of course be in open opposition to you. There will be invasions, or attempts at invasion. There will be bloodshed. The country will be exposed to the horrors of civil war . . . We have been under foreign influence too long. Let us seek *une solution nationale*.' "

This was the first official attack on England.

I interrupted Joseph Kessel. "Are you sure he said just that?"

"Jean Prouvost told me so, himself," Joseph Kessel replied. "But let me tell you the whole story.

"Yvon Delbos protested. 'The remarks made by the Minister of Information are substantially irrelevant and are not to be taken into consideration,' he said. 'We must continue to fight, wherever possible and with any and all means at our command.'

"It was up to Paul Reynaud now to announce his conclusions. He declared that he was in favor of leaving for the Breton Redoubt. But, he said, before making his final decision, he was going to see Winston Churchill; and he informed his colleagues that he was to meet the English Prime Minister the following day at Nantes, at 5 P.M.

"Then Camille Chautemps proposed that Churchill be

invited to attend the Council of Ministers, so that he might learn the exact truth about the situation in France.

"The Council accepted this suggestion. And Reynaud undertook to inform Winston Churchill to that effect by telephone.

"At 11 P.M. the Ministers left the Château de Cangey. I joined Campinchi. He was thoroughly disgusted, but he was by no means depressed.

" 'There are traitors in our midst,' he said to me. 'These people want to take advantage of a military set-back to further a political scheme at which they have been plotting and conspiring for years.'

"The following afternoon I saw Georges Mandel for a few minutes. He had refrained from intervening the previous evening, wanting to save everything he had for the day of the final decision. He told me that Winston Churchill, together with Lord Halifax and Lord Beaverbrook, had arrived in Tours. Churchill had refused to appear at the session of the French Council of Ministers since he did not want to place himself in a position which might well render him incapable of making his decisions with all possible sangfroid in this grave emergency. But he saw Paul Reynaud, Georges Mandel and Paul Baudouin. The British Prime Minister was profoundly grieved by the misfortunes which had overcome France, but he declared that he could not release France from her solemn engagement not to sign a separate armistice. Then he and Reynaud agreed on sending one last appeal to President Roosevelt. They also agreed to confer again, following the receipt of Roosevelt's reply.

"Paul Reynaud spent the rest of the evening drawing up the text of his appeal to the United States, in which he begged them to send 'clouds of planes.' The British Ministers had already left for London.

"Late that evening, while Paul Reynaud was broadcasting his radio message to America, German planes bombed Tours. They hit the Château de Cangey, headquarters of Albert Lebrun. He was there at the time, but escaped injury.

"Meanwhile, the Germans had been advancing with

such speed that even Tours seemed threatened. The Cabinet decided, therefore, to leave at once and to make for Bordeaux.

"And that's the whole story," Joseph Kessel said. "Incidentally, Jean Prouvost asked me to tell you that he's expecting you—you and Hervé Mille—to show up in Bordeaux as soon as possible. It seems that Paul Reynaud wants to see you, too."

I hurried over to *Le Moniteur* and met Pierre Laval at the entrance to the building.

"What's happened?" he asked me.

I told him.

His face seemed to become even greener than usual. "Are you—are you sure?" He seemed to have trouble opening his fleshy lips. "Are you absolutely sure?"

He took my arm and dragged me into one of the offices.

Pierre Laval soon managed to put through a telephone call. I was standing beside his desk, and heard every word he said: "So it's true? . . . That's terrible. I told you so, didn't I? . . . You think I should come? All right. I'll leave right away . . . Yes, I'll hurry.

"You were right," he said to me. "I ought to go down there. Senator Albert Buisson will drive me to Bordeaux. I hope to see you there, Lazareff. I'll be stopping at Adrien Marquet's house."

We hurriedly arranged to leave. We formed a little caravan. Pierre Laval's car went on ahead.

Because of the countless obstacles along the road, we didn't get to Bordeaux until shortly before midnight. There was a total blackout. Clermont-Ferrand was a deserted city compared with Bordeaux.

The Cabinet had been conferring since 10:30 P.M., after having held a session lasting from 3 to 7:30 that afternoon. I went over to the Hotel Splendide, where Paul Reynaud and most of the Ministers were stopping.

In the teeming lobby of the Splendide, I met Charles de Gaulle's right-hand man. He told me how and why the General had suddenly left for London the previous day. In conference with Paul Reynaud, de Gaulle had insistently urged that the Government adopt his plan calling for withdrawal to strong positions in Brittany—the Breton Redoubt. Reynaud had asked him to elaborate this plan down to the most minute details, and then to present it to him at his office. Charles de Gaulle agreed to do so. When he returned to Reynaud's office—with the plan fully drawn up—Hélène de Portes appeared on the scene. She rushed up to Paul Reynaud, and exclaimed: "Oh, Paul, Paul. I simply *must* tell you something strictly confidential." Charles de Gaulle made a move toward the door, but Paul Reynaud gestured for him to stay. De Gaulle could not hear what they were saying, but he gathered that they were in disagreement about something. Suddenly Paul Reynaud turned and said to de Gaulle quite simply: "As far as the Breton Redoubt is concerned, I've definitely given up that idea. The Government is going to Bordeaux." Then, without another word, Paul Reynaud left the room.

Charles de Gaulle drew his own conclusions. He immediately decided to leave for London, resolved to do everything in his power to prevent the signing of an armistice under conditions which he considered dishonorable.

At 12:30 A.M. I managed to find Jean Prouvost at the Hotel Montré. He began by giving me a summary of what had taken place that day. Substantially it was as follows:

All morning and all afternoon, London and Bordeaux were in constant contact. Telephoning from London, Churchill told Reynaud that all England was filled with profound sympathy for France in her great misfortune. Then the British Prime Minister declared that, come what may, England pledged herself not to lay down her arms until France regained her liberty, her integrity and her sovereign rights. Churchill stated, furthermore, that England would undertake to indemnify France for a share of the war damage. But those were not the words Paul Reynaud wanted to hear. He again urgently and insistently requested release from the engagement concerning a separate armistice. Winston Churchill then replied that he was prepared to grant him this authorization, on the one condition that the entire French fleet enter British ports and remain there for the duration of the armistice negotiations.

Charles de Gaulle then telephoned from London, begging the French Government not to make any decisions before 5 P.M., at which time England was to "make a proposal of the very greatest importance."

The Cabinet proceeded with its conference. The discussion centered around President Roosevelt's reply to Paul Reynaud's appeal. The note was most friendly and sympathetic, but was unanimously considered unsatisfactory because it contained no mention of specific and immediate action, referring only to the possibility of a decision ultimately to be taken by the Congress. In this connection, a number of Ministers recalled the attitude of the United States Senate in 1918, when ratification of the Treaty of Versailles was rejected.

Meanwhile, the military leaders had been conferring uninterruptedly. General Vuillemin, chief of the Air Force, wholeheartedly supported the stand taken by Pétain and Weygand. But Admiral Darlan, on the other hand, had emphatically declared himself in favor of continuing the struggle from the French Empire and of immediately sending our entire navy to our North African ports.

At 5 P.M. Sir Ronald Campbell delivered to Paul Reynaud the text of the famous English proposals mentioned by Charles de Gaulle. The terms called for: immediate creation of a complete union of France and Great Britain, every citizen of France to become a British citizen and, reciprocally, every British citizen to become a citizen of France; one army in common, under a unified command; one common financial and economic system; and legislation suitable for the needs of both countries. The establishment of this union would, according to the note, constitute a "moral and material bloc of unequalled strength," and would simultaneously serve as the nucleus for the future United States of Europe.

The Ministers who had already decided on surrender vehemently rejected the proposal. Jean Prouvost frankly admitted that he had denounced the entire proposition as an allegedly generous move intended to reduce France to the status of a Dominion within the British Empire. A majority of the French Ministers voted to reject Churchill's proposals.

Then Weygand insistently demanded that the Government decide, without further delay, to ask for an armistice.

His voice, usually calm and self-assured, was quavering. "I urge you, in order to preserve our country from the greatest of all misfortunes, to ask the enemy to state his conditions while we still have forces at our command which can serve as a bargaining point in the negotiations, so that the conditions imposed upon us will not be too severe."

Everyone knew that Weygand was referring to his *bête noire,* revolution and civil war.

Raoul Dautry, the Minister for Armaments, made a stirring plea: "Be careful, Messieurs. Our choice lies—and don't forget it—between an Anglo-Saxon and a Germanic civilization."

Camille Chautemps had been unable to make up his mind. He had been wavering and dodging between the two viewpoints that were dividing the Cabinet. But then, after a number of lengthy and strictly private conversations with Marshal Pétain, Monsieur Chautemps suddenly and most resolutely took his stand; and then he, in turn, in the course of a series of secret conversations, succeeded in convincing a number of hitherto unconvinced Ministers by suggesting the following move: with Switzerland acting as intermediary, we were to ask Germany—before entering into direct negotiation—what the armistice terms were likely to be, *in principle.*

When the Council of Ministers again took a vote on the question, there was a 13 to 11 majority for an armistice.

"Thereupon," Jean Prouvost said to me, "Paul Reynaud immediately tendered his resignation. Pétain and Albert Lebrun retired to the adjoining room. And there Pétain formed the new Ministry—the Cabinet which was to ask for an armistice. I'm not to be a member. Pétain had already drawn up the roster—he had the paper in his pocket—and I know there isn't going to be any such thing as a Ministry of Information."

Jean Prouvost was already giving an indication of the attitude he was to assume in the days to come, when he told us that the Germans couldn't afford to treat France too badly, after all. In his opinion, the war would be over within two weeks or so because the English would have to give up the struggle, too.

Tired and disheartened and disgusted, above all, we left Jean Prouvost and went to the offices of the Ministry of the Interior. There we heard that Pétain was consulting the future members of his Government. The most amazing lists of the new Ministry were being passed around. Every one of these tentative lists was made up exclusively of names of the most notorious defeatists and pro-Nazis.

Shortly thereafter, the definitive roster of the first Pétain Government was announced. It included, notably, the names of General Weygand (as Minister of the Défense Nationale), Paul Baudouin (Foreign Affairs), Admiral Darlan (Navy and Commerce).

Marshal Pétain had requested the Spanish Ambassador, Lequerica, to transmit, through the Spanish Government, a request for an armistice to Hitler; a similar request, with regard to Italy, had been addressed to the Vatican.

An English colleague told me that Winston Churchill had just boarded a train in London on his way to Bordeaux at Paul Reynaud's invitation, when he was handed a dispatch informing him of the formation of the new French Cabinet. Naturally, he got off the train at once, and returned to 10 Downing Street. He then immediately sent a wire to Marshal Pétain, reminding the new Premier of the solemn engagement entered into by France.

As for General Charles de Gaulle, he had just arrived in Bordeaux by plane from London. He was bringing Paul Reynaud all the details concerning the proposed Franco-British Union. When Reynaud had told him what had happened, Charles de Gaulle refrained from making any comment. He merely saluted, turned on his heel and took the same plane back to England.

Meanwhile, the Germans were advancing irresistibly.

We heard that the Maginot Line had been flanked; that the city of Tours had been partly destroyed by an intensive bombing raid. Yet no one seemed capable of realizing the true extent of the tragedy.

I saw Hélène de Portes—in flat-heeled shoes, her face ghastly without makeup, her hat at a slovenly angle—coming down the main staircase of the Hotel Splendide on the arm of Paul Reynaud. I was talking to Philippe Barrès. She came up to us, and asked us to take her to the Ministry of Foreign Affairs.

As soon as we were out of the hotel, she commenced speaking; and she kept up her monologue all the way.

"You know, Paul Reynaud made a mistake, resigning that way," she said. "Of course, he had to step down to let the Marshal attend to the Armistice. But he'll be back in power soon. I know he will. Everything's been arranged. This is only an *entr'acte,* of course. But, still, I think things could have been handled differently. I want you to know that if he is out for a while, why, nothing better could have happened for him. For us, I mean. We'll be able to live the quiet and peaceful life for a while, the two of us. We're going to be married. But one must think of France, naturally. Oh, my, what a terrible state of affairs! After all, one mustn't give up hope for the future. . . ."

At the entrance to the building on the Rue Vital-Charles, where the Ministry of Foreign Affairs was installed, the guard refused to let Hélène de Portes enter.

"But I've been coming here every day," she screamed. "Don't you know who I am? I want to see Monsieur Baudouin at once."

She was really shouting. An officer came up and told her, politely but very firmly, that visitors were not being admitted. She was in a rage.

"They're kicking me out," she exclaimed. "The swine. I really *must* see Baudouin. It's about an appointment for Paul Reynaud as Ambassador to Washington. I sent my children there early in May. We simply must go there and join them. Besides, there'll be some important work for us to do in Washington . . ."

We escorted Hélène de Portes back to the hotel.

Then, a few moments later, on the street, I heard someone calling my name. I recognized Madame la Maréchale Pétain.

Madame Pétain said, "You see what a nice pickle we're in? But I just left the Marshal a moment ago, and I can tell you that he hasn't lost confidence. He takes the long view, and feels certain that this country isn't lost, that it can't possibly be. I've just come on from Biarritz, where I direct a hospital, and I'm going back just as soon as I've seen the Marshal comfortably installed here. But tell me, what are you going to do?"

I replied that I was trying to make arrangements with our colleagues on *La Petite Gironde* to enable us to publish an edition of *Paris-Soir* in Bordeaux because the Germans were advancing on Clermont-Ferrand, and we didn't want to risk failing to appear for so much as one day.

"So you aren't planning to leave France?" Madame Pétain asked, in considerable surprise.

The idea hadn't even occurred to me.

"Well, I'm very much afraid people like you will be exposed to a great deal of unpleasantness. But, you know, there's going to be terrible anti-Semitism here. Even in those parts of the country which the Germans won't occupy." And Madame la Maréchale sincerely and very kindly told me not to hesitate to call upon her if ever she could be of service to me.

Then I ran into Henri Bernstein. He told me that Pierre Laval had been looking for me.

Because I was hungry for news, I looked up the ex-Premier and arranged for dinner at the *Chapon Fin*. There were four of us at the table that evening: Pierre Laval, Senator Albert Buisson, Hervé Mille and myself.

Pierre Laval seemed particularly anxious to explain just why he had refused to become a member of this Cabinet.

"Immediately after my arrival here," he said, "I saw the Spanish Ambassador and drew up the protocol of the request for an armistice. I had already undertaken to perform this service for my country—even before I had had occasion to see the Marshal—for the many conversations I had previously had with the present head of the Government had thoroughly convinced me that he would promptly call on me and ask me to act as his principal collaborator. Pétain offered me the Ministry of Justice. I replied that I should be unwilling to accept anything less than the Ministry of Foreign Affairs. The Marshal seemed embarrassed. 'That portfolio has been promised to Baudouin,' he said, 'but I'll see what I can.'

"Well, he summoned Baudouin. He's an opportunist and a frantic climber. I never liked the man. Besides, he always managed to fumble, to complicate matters, every time he was sent to deal with the Italians. Naturally, he was very cool toward me. He listened to what the Marshal had to say. He didn't seem pleased, but when the Marshal had finished, Baudouin said: 'I shall do whatever you ask of me, Monsieur le Maréchal, if you feel that it is in the best interests of our country. I agree to relinquish the portfolio of the Ministry of Foreign Affairs and to accept the post of Minister of State.' Then, as he left the room, he just barely nodded to me.

"Continuing my private conversation with the Marshal, I expanded my views concerning our foreign policy, and I gave him my opinion as to how he could best have himself named Chief of State and acquire full constitutional power. I assured the Marshal that I should be able to induce the thoroughly frightened Parliament to commit suicide, so to speak, legally. I was dwelling on this point, when General Weygand was announced. I don't know the General very well, but I immediately suspected that Baudouin must have asked him to interrupt my conversation with the Marshal. At any rate, Weygand came in, took the Marshal aside, and spoke to him at the other end of the room. I couldn't hear a word of what he was saying. All I know is that, suddenly, Pétain turned and said to me: 'Pierre Laval, General Weygand informs me that your nomination to the Ministry of Foreign Affairs would be interpreted as an affront to Great Britain; and that, therefore, neither he, Weygand, nor Baudouin would agree to enter the Cabinet under those conditions. In short, you must content yourself with the Ministry of Justice.'

"After Weygand had left, the Marshal insistently urged me to enter the Cabinet—for the present, at least—by the side door. I refused categorically. As I was leaving, I told the Marshal that I was going home, but that I knew he would call on me before long.

"Then, a few minutes later, Adrien Marquet—who was also to have been included in the Cabinet—tendered his resignation, too, as soon as he heard of the stand I had taken.

"And this morning, at the *Hôtel de Ville*, I saw Sir Ronald Campbell, and went right up to him: 'Well, Monsieur l'Ambassadeur,' I said, 'it seems that Great Britain has blackballed me.'

"Sir Ronald unhesitatingly replied: 'I assure you that you're entirely mistaken. We haven't blackballed anyone. Besides, we haven't any such intention, or, for that matter, the power to do so if we wanted to.'

"I'm sure Sir Ronald Campbell was telling the truth. And it's perfectly simple to see what's at the bottom of the whole story. Weygand is afraid that when Pétain is named Chief of State, he'll appoint *me* head of the Government—which is the job Weygand wants. And that's all there's to it. Baudouin is just gambling on Weygand's coming out on top."

That was Pierre Laval's story. And it certainly revealed how the same old political intrigues were being played at a time like this.

A few moments later Pierre Laval saw H. R. Knickerbocker, the American correspondent, and beckoned for him to join us. Since Pierre Laval's knowledge of the English language is precisely zero, and Knickerbocker's knowledge of French is not much better, Hervé Mille and the ex-Deputy Lillaz, who had joined us, served as interpreters.

Pierre Laval said: "You must make it clear to the Americans that we had no other choice, that we were obliged to ask for an armistice."

Knickerbocker replied: "I consider that it was France's duty to continue the struggle. The war will last five years, possibly ten. But Germany will be defeated. France's surrender will make the worst possible impression in my country."

"Tell him," Pierre Laval said to Hervé Mille, "that five years from now, or ten years from now, there won't be anything left of France." Then he added as an aside: "I'll certainly never see eye-to-eye with these Anglo-Saxons."

After Knickerbocker had left our table, I told Pierre Laval angrily that I thought the American was right.

Pierre Laval replied. "You don't understand this at all. France has a chance of getting out of this mess fairly well *now*. What they should have done, though, is this: they should have named me chief of the French Armistice Delegation. It's a tough job, but a good old Auvergnat like me has a couple of good tricks in his bag. It would have given me a lot of pleasure to put one over on this Hitler."

Shortly after leaving the *Chapon Fin,* I heard that Georges Mandel had been arrested.

General Buhrer, who was in command of the Colonial troops, had been arrested at the same time as Mandel. Both arrests, it became known, had been the result of an anonymous letter accusing the two men of having made preparations for an insurrection. The stupidity of this charge was so obvious that the Minister and the General were released that very evening. And Pétain summoned Mandel to offer his apologies.

Mandel demanded a written apology. Pétain scribbled a brief note. Unsatisfactory, Mandel said. And then and there dictated to the Marshal—and the Marshal wrote—an adequate letter of apology.

Overnight, Jean Prouvost had completely changed his tone and his general attitude. And this amazing metamorphosis was due to the fact that everybody believed that the Germans would choose to make the armistice impossible, and that therefore the war would continue to be fought, probably from bases in the Empire. The Germans were still advancing all along the line. And now Jean

Prouvost announced that he had no intention of falling into the hands of the dirty Boches.

He said to me: "Hurry up and make arrangements to have *Paris-Soir* published here in Bordeaux. Then leave for Lisbon. I'll meet you there just as soon as I can, and we'll continue to publish *Paris-Soir*—in Africa, if necessary, or even in the United States."

He even went so far as to apply for passports and visas for himself and his family.

The Pétain Cabinet, which had convened for its first session on June 17th, met for the second time on June 18th at 11 A.M., immediately following Marshal Pétain's radio broadcast announcing that an armistice had been requested. Weygand informed the Ministers that an enormous pocket had been opened south of Rheims, and that the entire front was under such strong enemy pressure that our armies were rapidly dissolving into isolated fragments, some of which were still offering heroic resistance, but which were now facing almost certain annihilation. And the General added: "We made a great mistake to hesitate so long before requesting an armistice."

During this session of the Council of Ministers, word was received from Mr. Biddle, acting as United States Ambassador in the absence of Mr. Bullitt who had remained at his post in Paris. Mr. Biddle transmitted a message from President Roosevelt, expressing concern lest the French Navy be delivered to Germany. Thereupon, the Council unanimously decided not to hand over the fleet.

In the absence of a German reply, the Cabinet discussed the possibility of moving the seat of the Government to North Africa.

Following a joint meeting of the Houses of Parliament (held in a public school), the Presidents of the Senate and of the Chamber declared to the Council that ". . . neither the Ministry nor the Parliament could properly and freely function in Bordeaux under enemy pressure."

To leave or not to leave? This was a question which everyone in Bordeaux had to answer. The German tide had swept over three-quarters of France; and was still advancing.

On Wednesday morning, the Spanish Ambassador informed our Government that the Government of the Reich had declared its willingness to receive our plenipotentiaries, who would be given the terms on which the Germans would consent to cease hostilities. The German message specified that the French plenipotentiaries were to be equipped with the authority to accept or refuse the conditions, without having to return to Bordeaux for consultations. That was the gist of the official message. Secretly, however, Hitler had let it be known that he did not wish to see the name of General Weygand among the plenipotentiaries.

The Council of Ministers, therefore, chose General Huntziger to head the delegation—the army under his command had been the one that had offered the strongest and the most effective resistance to the invader—and the Government furthermore addressed an appeal to Hitler, through the Spanish Ambassador, to halt the advance of his troops on Bordeaux, for the duration of the negotiations.

Marshal Pétain had promised that our fleet would not be surrendered to the Germans. Paul Reynaud told me that he had suggested that the fleet be sent to the United States. He had been appalled by the change in attitude he had observed in Admiral Darlan. As Reynaud had put it: "Within the past forty-eight hours he has managed to switch over completely from a firm resistance-at-all-costs stand to a sort of craving for making use of the fleet as a trump card in the armistice negotiations, which forebodes no good."

Toward midnight the sirens began to scream an air-raid alarm. I heard the thud of explosions. The all-clear didn't sound until eight in the morning. We were told that the casualty lists were very high.

At 8:30 A.M. the Ministers convened again. They now decided that, since the Germans had not halted their advance, the Government must move on to Perpignan. The steamer *Massilia* had been made available to transport those members of the Parliament who wanted to leave for Africa at once. Among others, Daladier, Mandel and Campinchi had already signified their intention to take advantage of these facilities.

Meanwhile, from the port of Bordeaux, all available shipping was leaving for England, crowded to the gunwales with British contingents that were being withdrawn, as well as with numerous refugees, who, for one reason or another, would be in especially grave danger in the event of capture by the Nazis. German planes were unceasingly bombing these ships; one had been sunk and several others hit.

The Portuguese Government had invited us—my wife and myself—to attend the festival commemorating Portugal's foundation as an independent nation. This previous invitation now made it easy for us to get our passports and necessary visas.

During my last conversation with Jean Prouvost, he very severely criticized those who, in their panic, were prepared to "give anything and everything to Germany, and who were forgetting all about France." He again asked me to be sure to keep in touch with him, to tell him where I'd be stopping in Lisbon because "we'll surely get together again before long."

Arriving at Saint-Jean de Luz that evening, I was greeted by some friends with the remark: "Do you know that your boss is in the Cabinet again? We've just heard the announcement over the radio. Marshal Pétain has named him High Commissioner for Information."

We proceeded to Hendaye.

We had successfully crossed all the police lines, when, at the entrance to the bridge which separates France from Spain, we were told to return to the Military Bureau where our passports had already been stamped. There a Captain informed us that we needed an *ordre de mission.*

Very fortunately, a friend of mine was returning to Bordeaux. I asked him to notify Jean Prouvost of my predicament.

Then we took a room at a hotel in Hendaye, and settled

down to wait for instructions from the High Commissioner. Several hours passed. While we were at dinner, I was called to the phone. It was the special *Commissaire* at the frontier, informing me that the famous *ordre de mission* concerning my case had been received, and that I could now leave at my pleasure.

We crossed the frontier the following morning.

Several hours later, at San Sebastian, I learned that Jean Prouvost had broadcast a bitterly anti-British speech and that *Paris-Soir* had been the first newspaper in France to launch an anti-Semitic campaign.

Chapter Thirty-two

Deadline

IN WHAT I saw of Northern Spain, the scars of the Civil War had not yet begun to heal. Conditions had deteriorated during the two years of so-called peace under Franco.

As soon as we got over the line into Portugal, our standing as official guests of the Government, and the solicitude shown by the Director of Propaganda, Antonio Ferro, the writer, made it possible for us to reach Lisbon without delay.

On the way, we stopped at Guerra, a town high in the mountains. There, to my great surprise, I heard a voice speaking in French from a loud-speaker.

"France has lost a battle, but France has not lost the war. The men who happened to be at the head of our Government may have surrendered. These men, permitting themselves to be carried away by their panic, have forgotten the meaning of the word 'honor' and may have consigned the country into slavery. But, in truth, this means very little. This means nothing, because this war is a world war. And the immense and incalculable forces of freedom in this world have not, as yet, commenced to make themselves felt. The day will come when the strength of free men will crush the enemy. And it is imperative that

France take a part in this battle; that France be present at the victory. Then, having done her share, she will again be free and as great as ever before. That is my goal, my only purpose. That is why I call upon you, upon all Frenchmen, wherever you may be, to unite and to join me in this struggle. Our country is in mortal danger. We must save her. *Vive la France*."

All of Portugal, at that time, was hooked up with the BBC. These comforting words had been broadcast from London. They told us that General Charles de Gaulle was working for the preservation of the true spirit of France.

In Lisbon I waited for news from Jean Prouvost, in vain. I was determined to stay in Portugal long enough to organize a network of informants on the Continent and to perfect methods for transmitting messages, despite the vigilance of the Nazi Censorship. When I heard about the Armistice conditions, I made up my mind to leave.

We arrived, at last, in Canada and stayed there six weeks. During that time the Vichy Government belatedly announced that I had been deprived of my citizenship—belatedly, I say, because the German newspapers had already made this announcement two months previously. I also learned that my property had been confiscated. The furnishings of my Paris apartment represented the sum total of my earthly possessions.

Late in November we settled in the United States, where we were most cordially and hospitably received, and where my wife and I were able to resume our work as journalists.

A year has passed now since the curtain fell on what I consider to be only the first act of the tragedy. Since then I have observed that Americans are puzzled by what has been happening in France. The American public was being misinformed concerning the attitude and the conduct of the French people. During all this time, I was uninterruptedly receiving reports on what was actually going on in the two zones into which the victors had arbitrarily divided France. I knew that the French people were constantly defying the invader.

The history of France—from the signing of the Armistice to the day these words are being written (August, 1941)—may well be divided into four periods.

First Period: The Pétain Plot

Under the impact of the crushing defeat, France was stunned and silent.

On Tuesday June 25th at midnight, hostilities officially came to an end on all fronts.

Since Bordeaux was located within the zone to be occupied by the enemy, the Government withdrew to Vichy, with the object of creating at least the illusion of sovereignty and independence.

As Pierre Laval had accurately predicted, he was soon called upon to fill the post of Vice-President of the Council of Ministers.

The French people in the Occupied Zone, who had expected the Germans to act like Huns and Vandals, were disconcerted to find that the Nazi troops were behaving like well-mannered, courteous human beings. "Correct," was the word. Otto Abetz had been chosen to represent the Führer in Paris at this stage of the game. For all that Hitler wanted of France now was docile co-operation and Nazification. That was all, for the present.

And the Führer's plans were admirably well served by the fact that the Government, which had forced itself upon the country, had succeeded in maintaining at least the semblance of legality. This feat had been accomplished largely by Messrs. Pierre Laval and Camille Chautemps, who had persuaded the duly elected representatives of the people to surrender all their powers to the recently constituted Government. The French Republic was thus assassinated by the stroke of a pen.

Gradually the people began to grasp the magnitude of the disaster. They began to feel an urgent need for something—for someone—they could believe in. The aged Marshal Pétain appeared to be the man, the one man.

I had heard the Marshal dwell on his pet theories more

than once. First and foremost, he would declare, it was imperative, in view of the declining birth-rate, that France be spared any further blood-letting. The Marshal never attempted to conceal his fundamental aversion for the democratic regime. He considered Fascism to be "revolutionary and, in some respects, almost as dangerous as Communism." His utopia was a sort of authoritarian republic, built around the Army, and ideologically based on: 1) education in the humanities; 2) corporatism; 3) accent on religion and on the family.

As early as 1936, the ex-anarchist Gustave Hervé, who had suddenly transformed himself into an ultra-reactionary writer and who was the founder of the "socialist national" movement, published a book entitled *C'est Pétain Qu'il Nous Faut* ("We Need Pétain"). In this book, the author expressed a yearning for "an authoritarian Republic . . . which would be a sort of Bonapartism adapted to the needs of the day, just as the Fascist regime is an Italian form of Bonapartism, and as Hitlerism is Bonapartism in the German fashion."

The readers of *C'est Pétain Qu'il Nous Faut* were, in effect, given the innermost thoughts of their revered Marshal. In any event, Gustave Hervé's book now brings additional proof that the present Chief of the French State had long hoped and painstakingly planned to assume power.

Following the election of the *Front Populaire*, Gustave Hervé wrote:

> We must create a Pétain Front. For we know the name, the glorious and beloved name of this man, the heaven-sent man who has come—as he has always come—to the salvation of France in her darkest hour. Who is this man? Pétain, the hero of Verdun. Is he too old? Field Marshal von Hindenburg was an old man, too, in 1925—he was 78—when Germany, too, stood at the crossroads. The election of the aged Field Marshal saved Germany from further anguish. Then, when the Hitlerian wave became irresistible, Hindenburg wisely avoided civil war by naming Hitler to be his Chancellor. Now, surely, no one will deny that Hitler put Germany on her feet again. He was a grand old man, Hindenburg, who died as President of the Reich at the age of 84, and who laid the foundation for the resurrection of his Fatherland. With such an example be-

fore us, how can we hold Pétain's age against him? Pétain, so hale and hearty, physically and mentally.

Gustave Hervé also wrote the following:

> When it comes to speaking to militaristic Germany and to working toward a complete reconciliation between the two countries . . . no man in France is so well fitted for the task as the great soldier of Verdun.

Hervé pointed out that, in the event Pétain was no longer available, Weygand would have to be chosen to play his role. ". . . Weygand, who is ten years younger, and whose name will be as popular and almost as illustrious . . ."

Marshal Pétain waited patiently, but he did not wait in passive idleness. For years he was in constant contact with all those figures in French political life, who, like himself, firmly believed that France must withdraw into herself, must be willing to make all compromises and concessions in view of her relative decrease in population. For years, Pétain had been in the closest political partnership with Pierre Laval, whose appointment to the Ministry of Foreign Affairs in 1934 was largely due to the Marshal's wire-pulling. The name of Pétain was indirectly involved—yes, indirectly, for the Marshal was always prudent, not to say defeatist, in every undertaking—but he was definitely implicated in the various abortive conspiracies against the Republic—in the bloody Sixth of February, as well as in the *Cagoulard* plot. The Marshal's closest collaborator is Henri du Moulin de la Barthète, one of the ring leaders of the attempted insurrection of the Sixth of February. Furthermore, immediately following Pétain's arrival in power, he chose no less than four *Cagoulard* chieftains to serve as his associates in the Government—Eugène Deloncle, Henri Martin, Dr. Méténier (the Marshal's physician) and Colonel Loustaneau-Lacan.

In Vichy today, there is a rumor to the effect that the Germans made certain promises to the Marshal while he was in Madrid; that they assured him that they would gladly adopt a generous attitude toward France, in the event that he, Pétain, became head of the French Government. Most cautiously, *pianissimo,* it is also being whispered these days that the venerable Marshal has begun to feel disappointed; because the Germans are not living up to their solemn promises.

In March, 1940, Pétain had told Anatole de Monzie: "I'll be called upon to head the Government some time about the month of May." If this was nothing more than a haphazard prediction, it was a good one.

Here's another astonishingly accurate prediction made by the clairvoyant Marshal Pétain. Admiral Darlan, when interviewed by Henri Béraud for the publication *Gringoire,* revealed that on May 5th—five days *before* the outbreak of the Blitzkrieg and the day before the Marshal's entry into the Reynaud Ministry—Pétain had mentioned the likelihood of an imminent *coup d'état,* and had asked the Admiral to join the conspiracy.

The country had to know disastrous defeat before the Marshal could assume power; he was convinced that it was indispensable for the welfare of France that he take over the helm. Did he not have good reason to believe that he—and he alone—would be granted generous terms by Hitler? In his feeble hands, the Marshal's bâton—which forty million people were prepared to consider as a magic wand—was to serve both as a sceptre and as a rod for meting out chastisement.

From June 17 to December 13, 1940, Pétain's popularity in France declined steadily. At first, the people had seen him as the returning hero, still radiant with the glory of Verdun. At first, the people had hailed him as the farsighted humanitarian, who, by signing the Armistice, had saved the country from a bloody defeat. Furthermore, Pétain was given full credit for having named Weygand pro-Consul of North Africa, and for having steadfastly refused to surrender the fleet to the Nazis, thus maintaining possession of a powerful instrument of counter-blackmail to eventual Nazi blackmail. And, finally, there was the widespread and persistent belief that the Marshal was an extraordinarily skilful statesman and diplomat, because he was adroitly playing both sides of the game. As the people saw it, Pétain was not definitely committing himself so long as the outcome of the war was not definitely certain. If and when Germany appeared to be the certain winner, Pierre Laval was at hand to throw in enough of our resources—at the very last minute, and on the winning side, of course—so that it might be said that France had contributed to the Axis victory. But if, somehow, England should ultimately win the war—why, in that event Pétain would be in a position to say that he had given the Germans nothing but honeyed words. And in those early days of the Pétain regime some people were actually suggesting that Charles de Gaulle had, in fact, been sent to England by the Marshal, himself—with the object of taking out additional insurance for France against the remote possibility of a British Victory . . . In times like these, there was something to be said for the devices of a Machiavelli or a Talleyrand.

But the people soon began to wonder. What was the Marshal doing? Why all these arrests? These severe sentences? Why were de Gaullists—good Frenchmen—being executed? Why was Pierre Laval so manifestly eager to submit to Berlin's dictates? Slowly the myth was fading. Then this reversal of opinion was accelerated by certain highly injudicious utterances on the part of the Marshal. In the now famous article published on September 15, 1940 in the *Revue des Deux Mondes,* Pétain had not hesitated to write that ". . . the most ancient and hallowed traditions of France were today authentically reproduced by National Socialism." Nor did Pétain blush to state, in an interview given to the Parisian pro-Nazi weekly, *La Gerbe,* that ". . . he was envisaging the exploitation of the riches of our colonial Empire in partnership with Germany."

French public opinion commenced to stiffen. The French, a fiercely proud people, now felt ashamed and somehow guilty, when they contemplated the admirable resistance being put up by the gallant people of England. The French now soon forgot their bitter resentment that had flared up following the British attack on French naval units at Mers-el-Kebir—that painful incident which the pro-Nazis had exploited so assiduously. And, besides, it had become increasingly clear that the so-called *Révolution Nationale,* far from bringing back the "good old days" of before the war, was in fact saddling the people with unbearable restrictions. The people were awakening to the realization that democracy, which they had blamed for all their suffering and renounced in a swift moment of anger, was the only form of government for them.

In the Occupied Zone, relations with the invader were becoming increasingly tense. The initial display of elaborate courtesy on the part of the invader—all his "correctness"—had been designed, purely and simply, to facilitate the task of looting the French people of all their possessions. It was also designed to convert the most individualistic and independent people on earth to the totalitarian way of thinking. What it meant to live under German domination had soon been brought home to every citizen, personally, by the infernal system of the two Zones. There was scarcely a family that didn't have at least one member who was a prisoner in German hands.

These essentially mental tortures of the early days of the German occupation were soon aggravated by physical suffering. Food was getting scarcer, day by day. Every word in every magazine and newspaper, every word that came over the radio—although in French—spoke the language of the Nazis.

The Berlin propaganda, accusing Britain of wanting to starve France by means of the blockade, was not too convincing to the French who were seeing the Germans make off with whatever they wanted in the way of food, clothing and fuel.

When, following the Hitler-Pétain interview at Montoire (for which the groundwork had carefully been laid in a series of Hitler-Laval-Abetz conferences), the Marshal came out for the famous "collaboration" policy, even his most loyal admirers understood that he was nothing more than a blind instrument in the hands of the wily Auvergnat politician, Laval.

But then, on December 13th, the summary dismissal of Laval marked the beginning of a sharp recovery in Pétain's prestige. The "grand-old-man, hero-of-Verdun" myth was hastily restored.

Second Period—Laval versus Pétain

It will be years, perhaps, before the whole truth concerning Laval's ouster is known. But certain significant facts have already come to light. It is known that Laval wanted Pétain to confine himself strictly to his role of Chief of State; to be a Hindenburg, while Laval was to be the real and active head of the Government. Later on, of course, Laval was to play the part of Hitler to Pétain's Hindenburg, taking over both offices at the old Marshal's death—as was indeed provided for in Article 2 of the *Acte Constitutionnel* which Laval had prescribed. Laval wasn't the only one who wanted to be heir apparent. Moreover, Laval was already acting, or trying to act, as though he were Number One. He knew very well that he was detested, that he could not for a minute count on the Army, the Navy or the forces in the Empire. The Army, now dominated by General Huntziger, had become nothing more than an instrument in the hands of the military clique. And Darlan had not only kept his firm grip on the Navy (all the key positions were filled by his henchmen), but he had also succeeded in placing his cronies in commanding positions in the Colonies. As for Weygand, he hated Laval more violently than ever. In addition, Weygand wanted to play his own game. As master, in effect, of the Empire, he had already protested to Vichy against the seizure of the Navy in what he considered to be his territory.

Weygand had succeeded in dominating the North African situation. They were proud in Morocco, Algeria and Tunisia, to have retained a sort of autonomy under such a renowned leader, and they were doubly proud of being able to play the role of a constant menace to the invader of France proper.

Various powerful groups had one thing in common: they all mistrusted Pierre Laval. There was one group headed by Weygand and his friend, Paul Baudouin. There was the Darlan group. And there was a third group, consisting of Marcel Peyrouton, the Minister of the Interior, Pierre Etienne Flandin and Raphael Alibert, the Minister of Justice. They were all against Pierre Laval because they knew that if he ever became top man they would all be out. And so they joined forces, with the single objective of getting rid of the Vice-President of the Council. They were able to convince Pétain that Pierre Laval had made certain agreements with the Germans in Paris without having previously discussed or even mentioned these matters in Vichy; that he had gone over the head of the Chief of State; and that he was planning to have Hitler insist that he, Laval, become absolute head of the French Government. At the urgent advice of his personal cabinet—and sensing, no doubt, that here was an opportunity for regaining some of his lost prestige—Marshal Pétain decided to act.

What role did the Germans play in this tragi-comedy? Obviously, they could have forced Laval on the French people if they had really wanted to. But what good would that have done them? The only power Laval would have had, under those circumstances, would have been the power with which the Nazis, themselves, invested him. Otto Abetz, therefore, suggested a far more subtle game. While Pierre Etienne Flandin was timidly installing himself as Minister of Foreign Affairs, and while Pétain was trying to govern by himself, or at least with the assistance of his Cabinet and with the renewed support of the people, the Germans calmly set up Pierre Laval in Paris, to serve as a sort of counter-balance to Vichy.

The Germans had induced most of the newspapers to return and resume publication in Paris. The Parisian press, slavishly obeying orders from the Kommandatur, now unanimously launched a violent campaign against Vichy. Singing in perfect harmony, these so-called newspapers chorused their denunciation of Vichy as the center of reaction and the men of Vichy as "the gang with the strong-box, the sword and the holy-water sprinkler." Marshal Pétain was exempted from personal vilification. But he was warned to take "national and socialistic" measures; and to surround himself with "*collaborationistes* who were determined to govern the country in a truly revolutionary manner, and who were anxious to have France treated not as a vanquished nation, but as a partner in the New European Order."

Marcel Déat, who had long been an accomplice of the Nazis, Eugène Deloncle, the chief of the *Cagoulards*, and Jean Fontenoy, the pro-Fascist journalist, founded a political party, called "Rassemblement Populaire National," which was to unite all the partisans of "collaboration." The famous "*Rassemblement*" barely managed to sign up some ten thousand members.

When winter set in, the spirit of resistance became stronger. The exceptionally cold weather, together with the acute fuel shortage, added immeasurably to the sufferings of the poor people. Following Laval's ouster from Vichy, the Nazis retaliated with repressive measures, notably with regard to traffic between the two Zones. Because transportation of foodstuffs was interrupted, the food situation became even more grave. More and more people risked hearing the BBC and broadcasts from America. They rejected the Nazi interpretation of the tragic Dakar incident. They listened to Charles de Gaulle and did their best to execute his orders.

The first acts of sabotage were being committed—and brutally punished. This was the time of the first overt and spontaneous rebellions. The British parachutists were surreptitiously landing on French soil, and were being given aid and comfort by the people. And every night, from points all along the coast, Frenchmen were secretly casting off in small boats—headed for England.

Meanwhile, the Armistice Commission at Wiesbaden was becoming increasingly exacting in its demands on the French. If Vichy didn't change its tune, a Government would be set up in Paris which would be recognized by Germany as the legitimate Government of France. In addition the entire Non-Occupied Zone would be invaded —and promptly.

Admiral Darlan, who had succeeded Pierre Laval as the roving contact man between Berlin, Paris and Vichy, soon managed to appease the Germans. He soon convinced them that he was a far more effective ally than his predecessor ever had been, inasmuch as he had the Navy and the Colonies firmly in hand.

This ambitious sailor had spent almost his entire naval career on terra firma, in the offices of the Ministries. On February 25, 1941, he finally succeeded in getting himself named Vice-President of the Council and thus became heir-apparent to the aged Marshal Pétain.

The Flandin-Baudouin-Peyrouton-Alibert clique was thrown overboard to placate the Nazis—and also to please Laval, whom Darlan never failed to consult in Paris.

Third Period: Darlan in Power

As soon as Admiral Darlan was firmly in the saddle, the Nazis resumed the negotiations which had been interrupted by Laval's abrupt departure from Vichy. Generously offering to sign a separate peace with France, on the condition that the two countries entered into a complete political and military alliance, it only meant that France would have to hand over her Navy and relinquish the use of her bases in the Colonies.

They had to proceed with caution, however. For one thing, French hostility to the Nazis was increasing. Then, too, Pétain was inclined to be stubborn and had to be handled with care. They still needed him.

On economic matters only were agreements reached. It was very simple. Every important business enterprise in France, including l'Agence Officielle d'Informations (ex-Agence Havas) and the Messageries Hachette, came under German financial control. Factories were reopened, but only to fill orders for the Nazis. Unless they chose to stay at home and starve to death, thousands of French workers were forced to go to Germany and work in German factories.

Prefects and Governors were swept out of office and replaced by Darlan's henchmen. New men entered the Government, men whom the Nazis had reason to trust, notably Jacques Benoist-Mechin, Paul Marion and Pierre Pucheu.

Jacques Benoist-Mechin had worked with me on *Paris-Soir*. He was once secretary to William Randolph Hearst. Then, attracted by Germany's display of strength, he became official writer for the *Reichswehr* in 1937. On the basis of documents supplied by the Nazi authorities, he wrote *A History of the German Army*. The Germans considered it such excellent Nazi propaganda that they had the book translated into many foreign languages, and distributed throughout the world. This young man was named Secretary of State for the Premier's office, from which point of vantage he directed the Vichy end of the negotiations for a separate Franco-German peace.

The Vichy Propaganda Department was entrusted to Paul Marion, formerly an ardent Communist, ex-Director of the Bolshevik School at Bobigny, founder of the *Jeunesses Communistes* (Communist Youth), who had been delegated to represent the French Communist Party in Moscow, and who had subsequently been expelled from Russia. On his return to France, he joined Marcel Déat and then became the right-hand man of the pro-Fascist agitator Jacques Doriot. In this capacity Paul Marion directed a violent campaign of anti-Semitism in Doriot's newspapers.

The Ministry of the Interior was given to Pierre Pucheu, a young industrialist, puppet of the *Comité des Forges.*

The surrender of Indo-China to Japan, the admission of German forces into Syria, the subsequent hostilities between the Syrian garrison and the British aided by the Free French, and Darlan's anti-British pronouncements—all these developments inflamed French public opinion. The public was additionally alarmed by a series of warnings addressed by the United States to the people of France; by the increasingly pro-British attitude on the part of the United States; by the heaping up of coercive and restrictive measures decreed by the Vichy Government; and by the now widespread persecution of foreigners and Jews.

The big trusts, which the Marshal had promised to strangle, were now more firmly entrenched than ever.

The poor were getting less and less to eat; but food was available at fancy prices in the forbidden Black Market. Nazi oppression was unbearable in the Occupied Zone. Their game was becoming apparent. If Germany was not applying the same ruthless methods to France that she had applied and was still applying to Poland and to Czechoslovakia—if the Nazis were not, as yet, systematically eradicating the French race from the face of the earth—it was partly because they needed living Frenchmen as laborers. It was also because they could achieve murderous results by destroying the health of 1,800,000 prisoners of war. For if a part, at least, of this vast army of Frenchmen might be expected to survive the deprivations and tortures of the Nazi prison camps, they would be broken men forever.

Fourth Period: Effective Resistance

The people took heart when they learned that the Nazis had declared war on the U.S.S.R. They found encouragement in the changed attitude of the United States toward Germany.

The ranks of those who steadfastly opposed and resisted "collaboration" were now reinforced by the still-intact forces of the Communist Party. Hitherto, resistance to the Nazis had been sporadic, haphazard. But now underground groups were being formed everywhere, and Hitler hurriedly sent his wiliest Gestapo agents to Paris to cope with the situation.

General Weygand, summoned to Vichy, firmly refused to fight the de Gaullists who were holding the Free French colonies in Africa. Whereupon Darlan was put in supreme command of all French forces, and Weygand was thus placed directly under the Admiral's orders.

Later the Germans demanded Weygand's resignation. They insisted upon giving the command of the French African troops to those generals, formerly kept prisoners in Germany, who had pledged themselves to collaborate with the conquerors. Meanwhile, in the occupied zone, German officers and soldiers were murdered, ammunition dumps were blown up, cases of sabotage were increasing and the Gestapo had to be constantly on watch.

The collaborationists: Pierre Laval, Marcel Déat, Jean Fontenoy, Yves Paringaux (aide of Minister of the Interior Pierre Pucheu) were victims of assaults. The British and de Gaullists were making more and more incursions. Terrorist measures were used to stop this wave of revolt. But arrests, executions of innocent hostages, mass deportation of notables were only stiffening French resistance. The full-hearted collaboration as planned at Montoire had become impossible in reality, because collaboration cannot be enforced upon forty million people stubbornly hostile to a policy of submission.

A newspaperman of the *Giornale d'Italia,* made this statement on September 17, 1941: *"There remains but one feeling, strong, unshakable, incorrigible in the hearts of the French people—the hatred of the Germans; hence their desire of revenge against the nation which has conquered them."*

The reversals of the Germans in Russia and the entrance into war of the United States, increased Hitler's difficulties in France at the very time when "collaboration" was becoming to them most urgent. Hitler, because of the tremendous losses in men before Moscow and Rostov, had to withdraw from France half of the occupying forces—about 500,000 men. In order to re-establish his position by an attack on Africa and the Orient, Hitler urgently needed the help of the French Fleet and the French Empire.

The dream of Pétain came to a sudden end with the United States' entry into war. It is known that the old soldier had still been hoping to play the role of mediator for the Axis powers, the same role the United States would have played for the Allies. He would then have sat around the table at the Conference of Peace as the leader of a great nation, justifying himself before History. Events wrecked his hopes. A German victory appeared more and more doubtful, and the French people at home, in the colonies, in the Army and Navy showed themselves resolutely opposed to becoming enemies of the Anglo-Saxon world. Pétain began to realize that only the United States could invite him to the Peace Conference as the representative of France. When the first Japanese bombs crashed over Pearl Harbor, the effective resistance of defeated France received a tremendous impetus.

Daladier, Reynaud, Léon Blum, Georges Mandel and Gamelin are in prison. They were to have been tried long ago. Yet no one dared bring them to trial. Not that the gentlemen of Vichy are squeamish. But they have been told by every judge who examined the documents in the case that it would be impossible to proceed with the trials without incriminating the man, who, from the end of the last war to the outbreak of the present war, organized and gave to France the Army as *he* wanted it to be, the man, who, in turn, was Generalissimo, Inspector-General of the Armies, *Chef de la Défense du Territoire,* Inspector-General of Aviation, Vice-President of the Supreme War Council, Minister of War, and then Permanent Member of the Inner War Council—Marshal Pétain.

This does not, however, minimize the guilt of the members of the entire pre-War regime. These men are to be blamed for their weakness and blindness, for their unwillingness or inability to recognize and face the true situation.

What matters for the future is that 99 per cent of all Frenchmen—at home or overseas—are united in their determination to destroy Nazism and to liberate their country. France was undermined and betrayed from within. The French people were systematically misled by a venal and treasonous press. France fell. The world was shocked by her fall, but it will be amazed by the suddenness of her resurrection.

Index